A New India

A New India

Selected Writings 2014–19

Arun Jaitley

Foreword by
Prime Minister Narendra Modi

JUGGERNAUT BOOKS
C-I-128, First Floor, Sangam Vihar, Near Holi Chowk,
New Delhi 110080, India

First published in hardback by Juggernaut Books 2020
Published in paperback by Juggernaut Books 2022

10 9 8 7 6 5 4 3 2 1

P-ISBN: 9789393986207
E-ISBN: 9789353450786

Typeset in Adobe Caslon Pro by R. Ajith Kumar, Noida

Printed at Thomson Press India Ltd

Contents

प्रधान मंत्री
Prime Minister

Foreword

Arun Jaitley was a truly multi-faceted personality. A friend to many, excellent legal mind, effective minister, consummate communicator – one can go on. However, there is one side of Mr Jaitley that stands out as extremely important because there have been very few like him. As a public intellectual with immense grasp on policy issues, he brought a unique quality of felicity to public discourse that is very important for a vibrant democracy.

Few are the people who have a natural interest in complex policy issues. Fewer still are those who can grasp them and understand them. Among these, those who can reduce complex issues and explain them in a simple manner are rarest of the rare. Arun Jaitley, in this aspect, was one of his kind.

Whether he was speaking from the Opposition benches or from the Treasury side, Mr Jaitley was heard by everyone in rapt attention. People knew that he would always bring in a unique point of view to the issue being debated. When such precision and intellectual depth allied with the internet via the medium of blogs, Mr Jaitley's brilliant analyses reached an even greater number of people and enriched public discourse.

When he began to blog in September 2013, even while the medium was a new one, Mr Jaitley's enormous powers of persuasion made the transition seamlessly from soaring speeches to searing blogs. Unsparing of the UPA's misgovernance, he wrote about the ruling coalition's leadership crisis, their economic mismanagement and corruption. As the elections of 2014 approached, his writing became so prolific that sometimes there was more than one blog on a single day!

Of particular interest to those who are seeing the revocation of Article 370 dominate the discourse would be a blog from November 2013 by Mr Jaitley titled 'The Anti-Daughter Position in Jammu and Kashmir'. He had spoken about the prevalent status quo in Jammu and Kashmir that discriminated against women and also written unequivocally that 'it must be accepted by one and all that such discriminatory provisions which also compromise the right to live with dignity have no place in Indian law.'

An emotional moment for the party and myself personally, is that, now looking back, Mr Jaitley' s final blog in August 2019, too, was on the same issue. '*The popular belief that the promise BJP made on Article 370 is an unachievable slogan has been proved wrong*', he wrote powerfully, barely a couple of weeks before his passing.

For any youth looking to imbibe the importance of understanding public policy, Arun Jaitley' s blog is a goldmine. The sheer range of issues he elaborated upon, through his blogs, is expansive.

Be it his first blog after the 2014 election victory which said that it was time to take on challenges now that the celebration was over, or his explanations of the policy nuances of structural reforms such as the GST, there was something valuable in every blog. As a minister in the Union Government, Mr Jailtey was always one of the most reliable voices to pierce through the fog and make important points on the outlook of the government.

His blog on the significance of the decisions taken by the government on Triple Talaq, views on the Budgets, excellent insights into the impact of poverty-alleviation schemes or unique views later on how agriculture, health and rural development could do well with a GST Council like structure, Mr Jaitley always brought an incisive eye that could grasp the finer aspects while also not losing sight of the larger picture.

Arun Jaitley's series of blogs called 'Agenda 2019', on the issues that the elections of 2019 would be fought on, was prescient in its analysis. It also set the tone for the election season in many ways, with Mr Jaitley articulating the government's work in a way that few could.

I hope that a large number of people, especially youngsters, read this collection of his blogs. It will not only make them reflect upon the genius that Arun Jaitley was but also arm them with informative insights on public policy.

Personally speaking, reading Arun Jaitley's blog makes me nostalgic about the loss of not only a friend but also a brilliant mind that always put its intellect in the service of the nation.

New Delhi
19 November 2019

(Narendra Modi)

Part One

How Narendra Modi Is Changing India's Destiny

1

A New Man, a New Style

From top to bottom, Narendra Modi has ushered in a new way of governing the country, sweeping away the old coteries and power brokers who used to swarm the corridors of power. The hallmarks of his style are clarity and decisiveness. The prime minister's soaring vision has placed the country at an inflection point for growth and prosperity for all. His detractors are struggling to keep up with the scorching pace of change. Policies once deemed impossible are now seen as feasible, thanks to 'Modi hai toh mumkin hai'.

My Reflections on the NDA Government After Four Years in Power

Posted on 26 May 2018

The NDA government led by Prime Minister Narendra Modi has completed four years in office. Today it enters its fifth year in office.

The change

The preceding ten years of the UPA rule had unquestionably witnessed the most corrupt government since Independence. Prime Minister Narendra Modi created transparent systems through legislative and institutional changes which have given this country a scam-free governance.

Unlike the UPA, the prime minister is the natural leader of both his party and the nation. We have witnessed a journey from indecisiveness to clarity and decisiveness. India has transformed from being a part of the 'fragile five' to the 'bright spot' on the global economic scene. A regime of policy paralysis has been transformed into one of decisions and actions. India, which was on the verge of becoming a 'basket case', has today been transformed into the fastest-growing major economy in the world and is likely to hold that position in the years to come.

The country's mood from despair has transformed into hope and aspirations. Good governance and good economics have been blended with good politics. The result of this has been that the BJP is more confident, its geographical base has become much bigger, its social base has expanded and its winnability has hugely increased.

The Congress is in desperation without the perks of office. From being the dominant party of Indian politics, it is moving towards the 'fringe', its political positions are not of a mainstream party, but those usually adopted by 'fringe' organisations. Fringe organisations can never hope to come into power. Its best hope lies in becoming a supporter of regional political parties. State-level regional political parties have realised that the marginalised Congress can at best be either a junior partner or a marginal supporter. Karnataka had witnessed a telling example of this.

A regional political party whose base at best is confined to a few districts was able to extract a chief ministership of the Congress to which the Congress meekly surrendered. It had even lost its bargaining capacity. It is today putting on a brave face in Karnataka where the losers are masquerading as winners.

Scam-free governance

Prime Minister Modi has institutionalised a system where discretions have been eliminated. Discretions lead to abuse of power because they can be misused. Allocations of contracts, natural resources, spectrum and other government largesse, which were being distributed through discretions, are now allocated through a market mechanism. Laws have been changed. Leaders of the industry are no longer seen repeatedly visiting the South Block, the North Block or the Udyog Bhawan. Environmental clearance files don't pile up. Foreign Investment Promotion Board (FIPB) has been abolished.

For cleaning up the economy, India has to transform from a tax non-compliant society to a tax-compliant society. The enactment and implementation of the Goods and Services Tax (GST), the impact of demonetisation, effective tax compliance are all steps against black money, steps which are formalising the Indian economy. The Insolvency and Bankruptcy Code (IBC) has changed the lender–creditor relationship. The creditors no longer have to chase the debtors. If you cannot pay your creditors, you have to exit through a statutory mechanism.

The social sector priority

For the first time in history, the poor and the marginalised are holding bank accounts as part of the world's largest financial inclusion programme. The MUDRA Yojana has made cheaper credit available to the weak and the marginalised. The biggest beneficiaries of this have been women, SC/ST, minorities and other weaker sections. Rural roads with a hugely increased expenditure are a success story. Policies aimed at connecting every village with roads and electricity, affordable rural housing, toilets and gas connections in all homes are intended to change the quality of life in villages.

The Crop Insurance Scheme and the government's decision that farmers must get 50 per cent above cost are steps intended to eliminate agricultural distress. The UPA government had sanctioned Rs 40,000 crore under MGNREGA but with budget cuts spent only Rs 29,000 crore. Today that expenditure has been doubled. Under the Food Security Programme, the expenditure has been increased to Rs 1,70,000 crore to ensure cheaper food grain availability to the eligible. On the healthcare front, the destiny of India's poor will change when 40 per cent families at the bottom of the ladder will get a treatment up to Rs 5 lakh for hospitalisation which will come from the government scheme.

Economic management

Under the UPA government, India had fallen off the global radar. In its initial years when the world economy was booming, India grew on the strength of global tailwinds. When the global situation became challenging, the UPA's decisiveness and performance collapsed. The last two years of the UPA witnessed substantially lower growth rates. From the very first year of the NDA, India is the world's fastest-growing major economy with the highest GDP growth rates. This is also the global projection for the next few years.

The Current Account Deficit (CAD) saw an unprecedented 6.7 per cent deficit in the year 2012–13. The NDA has consistently maintained a CAD of under 2 per cent on an annualised basis. The poor economic management was visible when under the UPA fiscal deficits remained alarmingly high. The government was spending more and earning less. We witnessed fiscal deficits of 5.8 per cent, 4.8 per cent and 4.4 per cent in the UPA's last three years. Having inherited the mess, the NDA, year after year, has brought it down to 3.5 per cent and shall, this year, try and deliver a 3.3 per cent fiscal deficit.

The UPA's economic management was such that even when fiscal deficits were high, expenditure cuts of over Rs 1 lakh crore were done in order to make the fiscal deficit optically look slightly better. Cut in expenditure means cut in growth. During the NDA years, revised estimates of expenditure were always higher than budget estimates. The UPA in its last years provided India an inflation figure up to 9 per cent and at one stage it even crossed into double digits.

The NDA has tried to contain inflation and, on most occasions, remained within the target of 3 to 4 per cent. The poor economic management of the UPA resulted in the high cost of borrowing for the Centre and the state governments. The bond yields had touched an incredible 9.12 per cent in April 2014. We have on average, been able to contain it between 6 to 7 per cent with a low of 6.3 per cent on one occasion and rarely in the 7 per cent range (and that) only when global factors impacted either the currency or the crude prices.

The infrastructure expenditure has increased by 134 per cent from the last year of the UPA to the current year. The Congress president must remember that taxes don't go into the pocket of the government. They go back to the people for better infrastructure, better social sector expenditure and poverty reduction programmes. The social sector expenditure has seen a substantial increase from both the central and the state governments.

The road sector programmes have witnessed a 189 per cent increase between the last year of the UPA and the fourth year of the present government. Resources are transferred to the states with 42 per cent devolution of taxes, Finance Commission grants and assistance through the CSS schemes. Notwithstanding the perpetual grumbling, the last year of the UPA witnessed Rs 5,15,302 crore being transferred to the states. This year the proposed transfer is 145 per cent higher and will be Rs 12,62,935 crore. This is over and above what the states earn from the GST where they have been constitutionally protected with a 14 per cent annual increase. The states independently levy their own taxes.

Institutional changes thus being enacted and implemented are putting the Indian economy on a far stronger wicket.

The fifth-year debate

As we enter the fifth year of the government, the NDA's priorities are clear. This will be our year of consolidation of the policies and programmes which we have implemented. In our prime minister, we have a strong leader with a mass appeal. His capacity to change India's destiny is globally recognised. His insistence on integrity, his indefatigable capacity to work, his clarity of policy and direction, his boldness in taking steps in larger national interest give the NDA a natural political advantage. Clarity and credibility are hallmarks of the NDA government.

The last few days have witnessed a discussion about a 'fictional alternative'. A group of disparate political parties are promising to come together. Some of their leaders are temperamental; the others occasionally change ideological positions. With many of them, such as TMC, DMK, TDP, BSP and the JD (S), the BJP has had an opportunity to share power. They frequently change political positions. They have supported the BJP, claiming that it is for the larger national interest and then turned turtle and opposed it in the name of secularism.

These are ideologically flexible political groups. Stable politics is far from their political track record. Some amongst this disparate group have an extremely dubious track record of governance. Some leaders are mavericks and others include those who are either convicted or charged with serious allegations of corruption. There are many whose political support base is confined either to a few districts or to a particular caste. To rule a large country like India through coalitions is possible but the nucleus of the coalition has to be stable. It must have a large size, an ideologically defined position and a vested interest in honest governance.

A federal front is a failed idea. It was experimented under Shri Charan Singh, Shri Chandrasekhar and by the United Front government between 1996 and 1998. Such a front with its contradictions, sooner or later, loses its balance and equilibrium. Remembering 1996–98 as perhaps one of the worst periods of governance, the aspirational India which today occupies the high table in the world shall never accept an idea which has repeatedly failed.

History teaches us this lesson. Aspirational societies with vibrant democracies do not invite anarchy. A strong nation and the requirements of good governance abhor anarchy. The political agenda for the debate this year will appropriately be 'Prime Minister Modi versus an anarchist combination'. The 2014 election conclusively established that in the New India chemistry will score over arithmetic when it comes to deciding the country's destiny.

The Congress Gave Slogans to Rural India – Prime Minister Modi Gave Resources

Posted on 13 July 2018

Recently released World Bank data reveals that India has now become the sixth largest economy, relegating France to the seventh position. Obviously, on account of disparity in the size of the population, there would be a very significant difference in the per capita of the two countries. If we keep growing at the rate which is being projected, it is likely that next year we will be the fifth largest economy, ahead of Great Britain. This is in consonance with the rest of the narrative. Having been the fastest-growing economy for the last four years, we can look at the next decade as one of economic expansion. We have already seen a significant move up in India's ranking in ease of doing business and as a preferred investment destination. Today we stand to be tested in the midst of a global challenge thrown on account of the international crude oil prices and the trade war.

Obviously, we have started witnessing many of the advantages of a fast-growing economy. More consumption, more production, more industries, expanding service sector, greater urbanisation, many more jobs, more economic activity and certainly more revenue. However, ever since Prime Minister Narendra Modi took over, the government's own yardstick for performance has become stiffer. How quickly we are able to deplete poverty levels of a section of our people poses a major challenge. How are we able to translate the advantages of this faster growth to rural India which has always been less advantaged? How are we able to bring a significant section of our people into the neo-middle class so that their aspirations can also be met?

The government's approach

The government's approach in this regard is one of clarity. We will not follow the Congress party model of the 1970s and 1980s. That model essentially involved populist slogans rather than sound policy and actual expenditure for the welfare of the poor. The 1971 'Garibi Hatao' model was one of redistribution of poverty rather than the generation of wealth and resources. The result of this misguided approach was that the lives of the poor did not move up significantly. On the contrary, the present prime minister is a man of many words and many more actions. He announces stiff targets and programmes which at first sight appear to be difficult, if not impossible. He follows it up with the actual implementation and delivers on the promise. It is, therefore, important to analyse the actual delivery in rural India.

Specific programmes

In the current year, the total amount to be spent for livelihood and infrastructure in rural areas, from the Budget, extra-Budget and non-budgetary resources, is Rs 14.34 lakh crore. The social sector expenditure which also benefits the rural areas is in addition to this. Agricultural credit to be disbursed is Rs 11 lakh crore. The Kisan Credit Cards have been extended to fisheries and animal husbandry farms. For fourteen agricultural crops, in what appeared impossible, the farmers will get a minimum support price (MSP) for kharif crops at 150 per cent of the cost of production.

To double the farmers' income and dairy infrastructure, development funds with an outlay of Rs 10,881 crore have been approved. For rural housing, the Awas Yojana has a total outlay of Rs 81,975 crore. The sanction of Rs 9000 crore has already taken place. A micro irrigation fund with a corpus of Rs 5000 crore has been created. A long-term irrigation fund with an initial corpus of Rs 20,000 crore has been created. Cumulative loans sanctioned under this have already touched Rs 57,487 crore.

Similarly, fisheries and aqua infrastructure development funds have been created. For the rural infrastructure development fund, the allocation is Rs 28,000 crore. There is an animal husbandry development infrastructure fund worth Rs 5020 crore. There have been large sanctions for research and education, the Pradhan Mantri Fasal Bima Yojana, the interest subsidy for short-term credit to be given to the farmers. The market intervention and price support schemes have an additional provisioning.

The effect

This year alone this investment will provide to rural India 321 crore person days of employment, 3.17 lakh kilometres of rural roads, 51 lakh rural homes, 1.88 crore toilets, 1.75 crore new electricity connected households. The unprecedented resources sanctioned to rural India are intended to bring a fundamental change in the quality of life in rural India. Each village will be connected with a pucca road. The target for pucca housing: each house to have electricity, each house to have a toilet, every poor family to have a gas connection. Every farmer to extend his activities from agriculture to dairy, animal husbandry and fisheries to get the benefit of farm insurance, to get a much higher MSP and under each of the above-mentioned programmes, to be a part of the intended success stories. The amount being spent on MGNREGA is much higher than what was spent by the UPA.

The other social welfare programmes

The other social welfare programmes of the government are intended to benefit the weaker sections, and those living in the rural areas are the prime target of these benefits. The success of the Jan Dhan programme has connected each home to the banks. It has facilitated the delivery of credit to the weakest. The low-cost insurance policies and the attractive Atal Pension Yojana has immensely benefited these sections. The MUDRA loans, 74 per cent of which have been granted to women entrepreneurs, have certainly benefited while providing a supplemental income to families with a modest income. Once the ambitious 'Ayushman Bharat' is implemented, hospitalisation for those 40 per cent at the bottom of the ladder will be possible where the expenditure is up to Rs 5 lakh a year for each year per family. The total amount sanctioned this year for the implementation of the low-cost food scheme under the Right to Food Programme is Rs 1,60,000 crore.

How does this cumulatively work out?

What does the entire investment being made for conferment of benefits to rural India, to India's farmers and to other deprived sections of the society mean in the long run for our people? We will witness increased incomes, increased social security, an improved quality of life, higher income from agriculture and better healthcare. Already investment in these areas is incurring a higher rural consumption. The construction sector is growing by 11 per cent because those with higher incomes in rural areas are improving their housing. Cement and steel sales have increased. All the auto companies, particularly those whose target sales are in rural areas, have witnessed a much greater purchasing power in rural India which is leading to a significant improvement in their sales.

India's growth at a fast pace is likely to continue as per assessment of all credible agencies. Obviously, a high trajectory growth leads to a higher revenue. Prime Minister Narendra Modi has shaken up the traditional thinking process and ensured that rural India and the less privileged get the first right to resources. If this and increased expenditure continue for the next decade, the impact on India's rural poor would be very significant. This benefits all, irrespective of religion, caste or community. The Congress provided India's poor with slogans. Prime Minister Modi has given them resources. This will ensure faster growth and lead to a faster reduction in poverty.

Agenda 2019: The Leadership Issue

Posted on 11 March 2019

The schedule for the Lok Sabha elections has been announced. The next ten weeks will witness a clash of ideas and ideologies, competitiveness amongst candidates and a battle for leadership. There are several issues which occupy the agenda space in an election. Today, I deal with one of the principal issues which occupies foremost relevance in the 2019 general elections – the issue of leadership.

The incumbent prime minister

India has witnessed several general elections where the incumbent prime minister has faced an anti-incumbency. Anti-incumbency is a phenomenon where unhappy people vote an incumbent out. The Opposition succeeds by default. However, if the comfort level and the confidence with the incumbent is high, his performance, leadership, ethics and integrity have been tested, the incumbent succeeds.

The country assessed Shri Narendra Modi as the chief minister of Gujarat for a period of fourteen years. He emerged a strong leader, a politician of utmost integrity with development orientations and a nationalistic vision. He ensured that those who work with or under him also adopt the ethics which are expected from people in public offices. He withstood a false and vicious campaign against him. The facts in the campaign proved false in every legal battle. He did not allow himself to be bogged down by the hostile campaign. He laid down his own developmental agenda for the state and won three successive Lok Sabha elections and three Assembly elections. He communicated directly with the people. He stands out as a communicator. He created and nurtured a new leadership in Gujarat. The Gujarati population all over the world identifies with him. He inspired them.

He entered the 2014 electoral race when the country saw indecisiveness, a collapse of leadership, a policy paralysis and when integrity was a big casualty. The people rewarded him with a comfortable mandate.

How does a nation assess him after five years?

He has proved to the world that India can be administered with integrity and honesty. India is capable of tough decisions in order to ensure growth to enable India to secure itself. India occupies the high table in the world. It has become the fastest-growing economy. He ensured an economic model where the advantage of the additionality of resources emerging from the fast-growing economy is spent on infrastructure or transferred to the poor, particularly in the rural areas. He did not give slogans, but he transferred actual resources to bring down poverty levels and added to the ease of living.

Even his critics are bewildered by the evolution of his national security doctrine. He has evolved India from a nation which only defended itself domestically against terror through intelligence and security network and isolated Pakistan at the global level to a nation which is capable of destroying terror at the points of its origin. The success of the surgical strikes of 2016 and the air strikes of 2019 points to this direction.

Within the NDA there are no leadership issues. There is absolute clarity. Shri Narendra Modi leads the NDA and will be the prime minister in the event of an NDA victory. His leadership is nationally accepted, his ratings are very high. His track record speaks for itself.

Let us look at the other side

What was promised to be a 'mahagathbandhan' is turning out to be a 'gathbandhan' of several conflicting gathbandhans. It is a self-destructive 'coalition of rivals'. The BSP and the SP will contest against the Congress but eventually join hands. So will the Trinamool and the Congress–left alliance in West Bengal. However, in Kerala the Congress and the left will contest against each other. The PDP and the National Conference tried to form the government together with the support of the Congress in Jammu and Kashmir. Today they are rivals in an election and on the dangerous agenda of either 'autonomy' or 'pre-1953 status' but could join hands with the gathbandhan. The Biju Janata Dal, the TRS and the YSRCP are not with the gathbandhan.

The leadership issue is an absolute puzzle. The Congress president, Shri Rahul Gandhi, is an inadequate leader. He has been tried, tested and has failed. His lack of understanding of issues is frightening. He aspires to be the leader of this chaotic pack.

Mamata Didi is positioning herself as the 'sutradhar' of this alliance. She won't concede a single seat either to the Congress or to the left in West Bengal but will want them to be her pillion riders if she drives the vehicle. Her instinctive comments on policy issues are retrograde.

Behan Mayawati, the leader of the BSP, was wiped out in the last Lok Sabha elections. She changed her strategy. She wants a strong

BSP and a weak Congress. She holds her cards close to her chest. She will open them only after the results are declared. She has had a strategic 'alliance of compulsion' with the SP in Uttar Pradesh but the scars of her historical conflict with its allies have not washed away. Leaders with flexible ideologies think that they are acceptable to all. The Opposition alliance is unclear – it is absolutely fragile. None of the political parties is capable of winning a significant number of seats. The alliance will not have a stable nucleus. It has a set of highly ambitious, self-centred and maverick leaders. Barring the Congress and the left, most of them have done political business with the BJP in the past. Their ideologies and commitment to their constituents are widely different.

The contest

The contest is between a leader in whose hands the country is developing and secure and multiple leaders, each trying to outwit the other. He is trusted. Against him is no one projected leader. The others can only promise a temporary government if we go by the past precedents. One can be certain of chaos. The choice is clear – it is either Modi or chaos.

Agenda 2019: Modi Hai Toh Mumkin Hai

Posted on 14 March 2019

Prime Minister Narendra Modi has during the last five years demonstrated his indefatigability by literally working round the clock. Not only has he proved to be a quick learner, adapting easily to foreign policy, economic and strategic issues, his clarity and determination have facilitated quick decision-making even in complicated matters. On policy issues, he sits for hours together with his team, ministers and officers of various departments of the government and takes decisions in relation to important matters. He sets targets only to beat them. His image as a doer is now recognised by most Indians. Many India-observers across the world have marvelled at India's pace of taking decisions and implementing them. The BJP, therefore, has chosen an effective slogan for the forthcoming elections: Modi Hai Toh Mumkin Hai – Modi makes it possible.

Some of the important landmarks in this direction have been summed up below:

- For the first time in history, for five years in a row, India has been the fastest-growing major economy in the world – a 'sweet spot' in the global economy.
- In the last five years, neither direct nor indirect tax rates have increased. On the contrary, they were reduced. Those with a net income of up to Rs 5 lakh have been exempted from income tax. Before every meeting of the GST Council, the nation speculates as to which taxes are going to be reduced. Small businesses up to a turnover of Rs 40 lakh are GST exempted. Those with a turnover up to Rs 1.5 crore can pay 1 per cent GST. Affordable housing is now taxed at 1 per cent. While reducing the burden of taxes, the tax base has expanded and the collections have grown exponentially.
- In a period of twenty months, the smoothest implementation of the GST has taken place. The Constitution amendment, the taxation laws subordinate to it, the regulations and the tariffs have all been decided unanimously by the Parliament and the GST Council respectively. Nobody imagined that India would reduce the rate of taxation and increase the tax collections.
- In 2014, seven kilometres of highways were built every day. Today that figure is thirty kilometres per day, i.e., more than

ten thousand kilometres a year. India has become the largest highway developer in the world.

- In 2014, only 38 per cent rural homes were connected with sanitation. Today 99 per cent rural homes are connected with sanitation.
- 91 per cent of all villages are connected with rural roads. The expenditure on rural roads has been increased three times.
- Fifty crore of the poorest people in India have been assured hospital treatment up to Rs 5 lakh a year per family under the Ayushman Bharat Scheme. The scheme was implemented on 23 September 2018 and as of yesterday 15.27 lakh patients have been treated on a cashless basis.
- Eight crore households of the poorest BPL households are being provided with cooking gas stoves and cylinders. India's poor have graduated from the ancient system of cooking to an ecologically friendly and a more modern system.
- All willing households (100 per cent) in India have been electrified.
- About 35 crore bank accounts under the PMJDY (Pradhan Mantri Jan Dhan Yojana) have been opened, connecting every household to the banking system. This is the largest ever financial inclusion scheme in the world.
- More than 16 crore loans under the Pradhan Mantri Mudra Yojana have been given to encourage self-employment and job creation. 54 per cent of the beneficiaries are SC/ST/OBC/ Minorities, 72 per cent of the beneficiaries are women.
- In 2014, India had sixty-five functional airports with commercial flights. Today there are 101 airports with commercial flights. This figure is likely to increase by another fifty very soon.
- Indian Railways have now entered the era of superfast 160 kilometres per hour trains and locomotives which are domestically manufactured. Very soon the dream of bullet trains will be

realised. The quality of facilities in rail travel have improved significantly.

- The Insolvency and Bankruptcy Code (IBC) has changed the pattern of creditor–debtor relationship. It has now become possible for the creditors, banks and financial institutions to throw the defaulting management out of control and eventually realise their debts.
- The Aadhaar – the Unique Identity Number – has made it possible that the benefits given by the state to all weaker sections reach them directly and instantaneously without any pilferage.
- In addition to building rural infrastructure, farmers for 22 crops have been assured an MSP of cost plus 50 per cent. Besides a subsidised Crop Insurance Scheme, 12 crore small and medium farmers will get Rs 6000 annually as income support. As of yesterday, 2.77 crore farmers have received the first instalment.
- In addition to a Rs 75,000 crore income support to farmers, Rs 60,000 crore is being spent on MGNREGA. This transmits resources to the rural economy.
- Cheap and subsidised food grain is being provided to the extent of Rs 1.84 lakh crore. No Indian will sleep hungry.
- Every BPL family in rural India will have a house by 2022. Fifty lakh houses are built every year.
- The unorganised sector labour, including farmers, will now be entitled to Rs 3000 pension under a scheme where the government contributes 50 per cent. This will benefit ten crore families.
- Inflation, which was 10.4 per cent under the UPA government, is down to less than 2.5 per cent today.
- The prime minister and the government have shown to the world that it is possible to run an honest government in India.
- For the first time in history, a 10 per cent reservation for the economically weaker sections of the non-reserved categories has been given in public employment and educational institutions.

- India has demonstrated, both through the surgical strikes of 2016 and air strikes of 2019, that merely dealing with terrorism within the country will not suffice. It is willing to adopt unconventional methods of attacking terror at the point of its origin.

The above are only an illustrative list of the kinds of strides India is making. Has any government done more? It was the same governmental machinery, the same political system, the same implementation instruments that the government had at its disposal. It is both the motivation and the leadership which made the vital difference. It is precisely for this reason that India will witness an election where the people will get an opportunity to endorse Prime Minister Modi's leadership, decisiveness, integrity and performance. Indeed, he makes it possible.

Prime Minister Modi's Evolving National Security Doctrine

Posted on 12 March 2019

The Jamaat-e-Islami (JeM) terrorist attack in Pulwama has brought back into focus the key issue of national security. India is a land of patriotic people. We have a history of valour and sacrifice. India struggled for Independence but with its head held high. We still find it difficult to digest the humiliation of 1962. We remember the 1965 and 1971 wars and the 1999 Kargil war with a sense of honour and satisfaction. Indians believe that the country must be secured. The entire nation has in one voice condemned terrorism, which cost us the lives of two of our former prime ministers, besides our security personnel and citizens.

Dangers of linking the battle against terrorism and insurgency with votebanks

Conventionally, India has condemned any form of terrorism and insurgency in one voice. When a misguided section of the Muslim community globally took to terrorism in order to voice their issues, Indian Muslims predominantly refused to be a part of that philosophy. Fortunately for us, that trend continues to date. Unfortunately, a few misguided modules did emerge in India. They were dangerous but our security forces overcame most of them.

The Terrorist and Disruptive Activities [Prevention] Act (TADA) was legislated when late Shri Rajiv Gandhi was in power. It was used and abused, but it continued as a law. After the 1993 Mumbai bomb blasts it was widely used against the terrorists, and a communal campaign started against this. TADA was dubbed as anti-minority. A campaign for its revocation started. The Narasimha Rao–led Congress government repealed TADA. India, which was most adversely impacted by terror, was without an anti-terror law which would act as a strong deterrent and which contained both procedural and substitutional provisions to deal with crime relating to terror. The government led by Shri Atal Bihari Vajpayee legislated Prevention of Terrorism Act (POTA). It took the government a joint session of both Houses of Parliament to approve the law. The Congress promised to repeal the law. The distinction between an anti-terrorism and an anti-minority law is significant. The Congress and its allies tried to obliterate that difference. And then the Congress started going soft on terror. It started an appeasement of terror.

When the Batla House encounter took place and terrorists were killed, the Congress leaders dubbed it a fake encounter. The terrorists, they claimed, were innocent. When the guilty of the 1993 Mumbai bomb blasts, the 26/11 attack on India's commercial capital and the Parliament attack case were to be executed, many Congressmen started appealing for amnesty. The 'disruptionists' who prefer to call themselves 'left liberals' fought a legal battle to save the terrorists.

The low point in the Congress party's attitude towards separatism and terror was reached when a combination of separatists, jihadis and Maoists ganged up to raise slogans like 'Desh ke tukde tukde' at New Delhi's JNU, and Congress President Rahul Gandhi stood shoulder to shoulder with them to defend their right to free speech and champion the cause of breaking India to pieces. He deviated from the Congress legacy of not associating with these extremists. Once the identification of Congressmen with the Maoists and the separatists was signalled by Rahul Gandhi, it was natural for Congressmen and their friends to support the cause of the 'urban Maoists' who were allegedly conspiring to assassinate India's prime minister. It is, therefore, not surprising that the new government in Chhattisgarh, the hub of left-wing extremism, has now taken several decisions, including the appointment of committees to effectively examine the 'misuse' of police powers against the Maoists. The battle against terror has been weakened on account of the Congress party and its mahagathbandhan friends diluting the fight against terror and insurgency for the sake of votes.

Kashmir and terror

The state of Jammu and Kashmir was a foremost victim of terror. The people of Jammu and Kashmir are the worst sufferers. Pakistan never reconciled to Jammu and Kashmir being an integral part of India. It waged wars but lost them. It resorted to encouraging cross-border insurgency and supporting domestic terrorists. The Congress had no structured plan during the ten years of UPA on how to deal with the problem.

Prime Minister Narendra Modi inherited this as a legacy issue. He experimented the conventional method of trying to soften the relationship with Pakistan in the hope that wiser sense would prevail, but Pakistan responded with Pathankot, Uri and Pulwama. He encouraged the mainstream political parties of the Valley to be a part of the national coalition in Kashmir but, unfortunately, the double talk of support from Delhi and the pressure from the Jamaat-e-Islami were to the detriment of anti-separatists policy.

Pulwama and Balakot

The terrorist strike of Pulwama which cost India the life of forty-one CRPF jawans shook the conscience of the whole country. Our security forces have already liquidated some of the major terrorists involved in the Pulwama attack. Post the Uri attack, our forces and the government have intelligence information with regard to the existence of terrorists training camps along the Line of Control. The Army, in September 2016, conducted the surgical strikes with utmost precision. There was no casualty on the Indian side and those camps were destroyed. We had crossed the LoC for the first time since the 1971 war.

Our security forces and the government again had information through intelligence agencies with regard to a huge terrorist training camp of the JeM in Balakot. On 26 February 2019, the Air Force conducted air strikes and destroyed the camp, causing severe losses of the terrorist infrastructure comprising men, material and premises.

With these two actions Prime Minister Modi had evolved India's internal security doctrine. Do we fight the terrorists merely on the strength of intelligence information, preventing attacks and diplomatically isolating Pakistan? In such cases, will we be able to ensure 100 per cent success. The odds are loaded against us on this ground. Even if the terrorists succeed only once a year, they make their point. Our intelligence and security have to succeed a 100 per cent. That is a big challenge. Alternatively, the surgical and air strikes evolved a policy that we must attack terror at the point of its origin. In both cases we succeeded. Pakistan realised that there was a severe cost involved if the state continued to patronise terror. The world welcomed our proactive approach. Pakistan was diplomatically isolated. Its traditional friends were not willing to stand up and defend it.

Political battle

The BJP-led government, both at the Centre and in Chhattisgarh, had a consistently strong position against left-wing extremism. From JNU to Chhattisgarh, the Congress has struck a deal with them. There are increasing instances of left-wing extremists actively encouraging Kashmiri jihadis in the Kashmir Valley. The Congress does not oppose the idea of a proactive approach in destroying terror at its point of origin. It is disturbed with regard to the political fallout of this pro-active approach on the image of Prime Minister Modi. The Congress is one with the government on condemning Pulwama but is disturbed about Balakot. Thus, it repeatedly rubbishes the surgical strikes. It contends that they have either taken place in the past also or they never took place under Prime Minister Modi. On the air strikes, their conduct is even more dubious. While giving lip sympathy to the Indian Air Force for the first two days, they started a multipronged attack. They questioned the success of the strikes. They started demanding proof of terrorists having died at Balakot. They even contended that the strike had taken place not against terror but to ensure the BJP's victory in the forthcoming elections. This was a self-goal by the Congress in domestic politics. This was also playing into the hands of Pakistan, where statements of Congress leaders, including Rahul Gandhi, were played out on television channels of the Pakistani government cited these statements to bolster their own falsehood.

This raises the final question. When India battles ultra-left and jihadi terrorists, when it is faced with serious threats of cross-border terrorism, how does India respond? This is a choice before the electorate in the 2019 general elections. Can an overground ally of left-wing extremism be put in power at New Delhi? Can those who have weakened the battle against terror for the cause of votebank politics be trusted? Should those who have played into Pakistani hands not be taught a severe lesson in these elections? Unhesitatingly, the answer to the above question is a big yes. This country is safe and secure under the NDA government led by Prime Minister Modi.

Part Two

What the BJP Got Right: Reforms 2014–19

2

The BJP's Key Reforms Under Modi

The Narendra Modi government has overseen sweeping social reforms that are expected to leave their mark for generations. The basic thrust has been to reach every ordinary family and change its life, whether through cooking gas, a bank account, a toilet, or an easy-to-obtain loan. From Swachh Bharat, aimed at changing daily habits to Smart Cites, aimed at showcasing what a future India could look like, Modi has tried both to deliver and to encourage Indians to expect more – both from themselves and from their governments. In essence, the prime minister has renewed Indians' faith in themselves and their nation's potential for greatness.

Two Successful Initiatives of the Central Government

Posted on 15 September 2018

There has, in the past, been a general distrust of government schemes. The principal reason for this is that either the benefits don't reach the target or that the projected parameters are never achieved. However, there are schemes with a difference. The Swachh Bharat Abhiyan is arguably the most successful one.

Swachh Bharat Abhiyan

When the prime minister of India, Shri Narendra Modi, announced the Swachhata campaign in his Independence Day Speech of 2014, some believed that the scheme would be a photo-opportunity with very little progress. In the history of independent India, this is one scheme which the people of India snatched away from the government and converted into a 'people's movement'. When the scheme was announced, the rural sanitation coverage of India was 39 per cent. The prime minister announced a target that India be made 'open-defecation-free' when we celebrate the 150th birth anniversary of Mahatma Gandhi in 2019. The symbolism was appropriate since Gandhiji had given a lot of emphasis on swachhata. As we have completed nearly four years of the scheme, 39 per cent rural sanitation coverage has increased to a phenomenal 92 per cent. This was not an easy goal to achieve. This involved a behavioural change in the people. Many in the rural areas were initially reluctant.

But this people's movement has today transformed into a women's movement with rural women playing a leading role in the programme. We all knew that the dignity of women demanded the privacy of toilets. However, women of India are now stepping beyond their roles as mere beneficiaries of this programme, becoming leaders of it today. For example, the construction of toilets has always been a male bastion. In many states, however, thousands of rural women have been trained as masons and, with the assistance of self-help groups, are now becoming the primary force in driving a state to be declared free from open defecation. Women becoming bread earners through the construction of toilets has added to the family income.

The hygiene in the utilisation of toilets is also a preventive healthcare scheme. Global experts believe that the SBM will have saved over three lakh lives in the country by the time we become open-defecation-free in 2019. Toilets in several parts of India have been named 'izzat ghar'. This is for the first time that the subject matter in the toilet-construction campaign has taken centre stage in the national agenda. It has become a subject matter of popular discussion. The government of India has made available all the funds required for making this scheme a success. This scheme will go a long way in improving the quality of life of India's rural population, particularly women.

With rural roads, rural electrification, rural Awas Yojana, toilets and a cooking gas connection with food grain provided at a modest cost, the quality of life of India's rural poor will get a quantum jump. Additionally, when the Ayushman Bharat, which provides up to Rs 5 lakh per family per year as hospitalisation expense, is fully implemented, this will change the quality of life of India's rural population.

Revision of amount paid to Anganwadi workers and helpers

The central government has announced the decision to enhance the compensation paid to the Anganwadi workers and the Asha workers. The Anganwadi workers are the mainstay of the National Nutrition Mission. There are approximately 12.9 lakh Anganwadi workers and 11.6 lakh Anganwadi helpers in position. These benefits would be available to these 24.9 lakh Anganwadi workers and their families.

The remuneration of the Anganwadi workers has been raised from Rs 3000 to Rs 4500 per month; the mini Anganwadi workers from Rs 2250 has been increased to Rs 3500. Remuneration of Anganwadi helpers has been increased from Rs 1500 to Rs 2250 per month.

These workers will also get an incentive of Rs 500 per month and Rs 250 per month respectively on the basis of the real-time monitoring of performance. The government had earlier made a significant increase in the cost norms for both pregnant and lactating mothers and for severely malnourished children.

This has been a long-term demand of the Anganwadi workers and their helpers to give them a reasonable remuneration. Governments in the past have always refrained from giving benefits to these 2.5 million workers ostensibly on revenue consideration. Notwithstanding the pressure on the Budget, the government has given almost a 50 per cent hike in the first go to these workers. This will go a long way in addressing the grievance of these workers.

100 Days of Ayushman Bharat

Posted on 1 January 2019

The Ayushman Bharat Scheme, which was launched on 23 September 2018 has completed 100 days. These 100 days have witnessed the most significant steps in improving healthcare for the poor ever since Independence. India's healthcare system was always lacking. Besides inadequacy of healthcare institutions proportionate to India's population, there were many other challenges. Besides important state-supported institutions, the private institutions have now been established mainly around large metropolitan towns or Tier-I or Tier-II cities.

Many public and private hospitals are of global quality. Their charges, if we compare to the cost elsewhere in the world, are extremely competitive, but for a large part of India's population, these are considered beyond reach. Government employees and those in other public institutions are generally supported by governmental healthcare programmes. Those in the armed forces are supported by the healthcare provided in those institutions. Some private sector corporates have a healthcare provision as part of their service conditions. Still, 62.58 per cent of the Indian population has to pay their healthcare bills themselves. Most find it unaffordable. Low healthcare insurance penetration, low financial protection and high out-of-pocket expenses pose major challenges.

The Ayushman coverage

Born out of this necessity is the government's scheme of Ayushman Bharat/Pradhan Mantri Jan Arogya Yojana (PMJAY). The Yojana was launched on 23 September 2018. It has completed 100 days today. This Yojana covers 10.74 crore poor families, i.e., over 50 crore people. Forty per cent of India's population is covered by this scheme. These weaker sections can avail of a medical scheme which covers hospitalisation charges spread over 1350 hospitalisation packages for a sum of Rs 5 lakh per year for the whole family. Thus, if any member of the family requires to be hospitalised, charges up to Rs 5 lakh will be picked up by the financial management under Ayushman Bharat. The scheme is paperless and cashless.

Launch of the scheme and its implementation has been relatively problem free.

Post Ayushman Bharat

In the first 100 days, 6.85 lakh patients have been provided hospital treatment; 5.1 lakh claims have availed of the scheme, for which payment has been released. This averages 5000 claims per day for the first 100 days. No patient has had to pay a single rupee. Thus, once awareness of the scheme increases, it is anticipated that in the next few years, almost 1 crore plus families will benefit each year. The total number of hospitals covered by this scheme are both government hospitals and private hospitals presently numbering 16,000 and increasing steadily. More than 50 per cent of the implementing hospitals are in the private sector. Thus, a patient can enrol himself in an empanelled hospital and get himself hospitalised up to charges of Rs 5 lakh in a totally cashless and paperless manner.

This scheme is a game changer in healthcare. Many people from the weaker sections avoided hospital treatment in order to avoid the burden of an unbearable payment. Today 40 per cent of India's poorest are assured of a treatment in a hospital at the cost of public expenditure. This scheme also supports the hospitals as an institution by ensuring patients for them. This will lead to more hospitals (especially in Tier-II and Tier-III cities), and those with better equipment. Health sector jobs are set to increase. PMJAY will help create an accountable health system because beneficiary feedback is an integral part of its implementation.

From infrastructure creation to rural roads to building houses for the poor, providing them with electricity, toilets, gas connection and now healthcare have only been possible after initiatives taken by the prime minister and the government have resulted in a higher tax base and greater revenue collection.

Benefits of Aadhaar and Where It Stands Today

Posted on 6 January 2019

The idea of having a Unique Identity Number (UID) for every citizen of India was conceived by Shri Nandan Nilekani during the UPA government. Unquestionably, the credit goes to him for conceiving, initiating and implementing the idea. Aadhaar, however, was non-statutory. There was no law governing it. This triggered a serious legal challenge. The UPA itself was a divided house. While Shri Nandan Nilekani pushed hard, a senior minister blocked it. The prime minister was indecisive. The enrolment continued, though at a very moderate pace.

The BJP, while in Opposition, had some reservations particularly with regard to non-citizens being enrolled. Immediately after the formation of the government, a presentation was made to the Hon'ble prime minister by Shri Nandan Nilekani where I was also present.

At the conclusion of the presentation, the prime minister consulted the others present and, decisive as he is, immediately took the decision to go ahead with the idea of Aadhaar.

The legal hurdle

The UPA legislation was inadequate. It provided for the methodology by which the UID would be issued. It did not contain adequate safeguards on privacy. It did not mention for which purpose the UID would be used. The NDA government re-examined the issue and the legislation was completely changed. The pith and substance of the new law was that the government spends a large part of the public resources in subsidising the poor. This subsidy became an indefinite amount which is given to an unidentified section of the people. There are many claimants who don't exist. Several others are not entitled to it. There are several cases of duplication, and thus, the unique identity based on biometrics would eliminate these aberrations, and relief would travel only to the intended. This was the thrust of the new law. After the new law was passed in Parliament it was challenged before the Supreme Court. The Supreme Court upheld the whole concept of unique identity and rejected the challenge that it violated the right to privacy. It held that Aadhaar meets the concept of constitutional trust, limited government and good governance and empowers marginalised sections of society. It also introduced several safeguards to ensure that it is not misused. The judgement of the Supreme Court added balance to the concept of Aadhaar.

The performance

The Aadhaar (Targeted Delivery of Financial and other Subsidies, Benefits and Services) Bill, 2016, was passed by the Parliament on 16 March 2016. It was notified on 26 March 2016. Several other Sections of the Act which had initially not been notified were notified on 12 September 2016. In the last twenty-eight months over 122 crore Aadhaar numbers have been issued. 99 per cent of the population of India above the age of 18 stands covered.

Many state Support Schemes, including some by the DBT (direct benefit transfer) mechanism, have been linked to Aadhaar. 22.80 crore of PAHAL and Ujjwala beneficiaries are given cooking gas subsidies through DBT in their Aadhaar linked bank accounts; 58.24 crore ration card holders stand linked; 10.33 crore MGNREGA card holders get wage payment through DBT in their bank accounts. So do the 1.93 crore beneficiaries and other beneficiaries of the National Social Assistance Programme (NSAP).

The income tax department has already linked 21 crore PAN card holders with their Aadhaar numbers.

To date, 2579 crore authentications have been undertaken. Every day 2.7 crore authentications are done. UIDAI has the capacity of 10 crore transactions to be authenticated per day.

The government estimates that Rs 90,000 crore has been saved in the last few years till March 2018 by the use of Aadhaar. Several duplicate beneficiaries, non-existent beneficiaries and fake beneficiaries have been eliminated. The Digital Dividend Report prepared by the World Bank estimates that India can save Rs 77,000 crore every year by the use of Aadhaar. The savings through Aadhaar can fund three schemes of the size of Ayushman Bharat.

In most schemes the DBT takes place to the 63.52 crore beneficiaries' bank accounts that had been linked with the unique identity as on 15 December 2018. The total number of subsidy transactions through Aadhaar are almost about 425 crore. The total amount of subsidy transferred through Aadhaar now equals Rs 1,69,868 crore. With the elimination of middlemen, the benefits go directly to the bank accounts. This is a unique technology implemented only in India. The money saved through Aadhaar is money fruitfully employed for the poor elsewhere.

Aadhaar is a game changer. Its evolution tells the same story. The UPA, because of its contradictions and indecision, remained half-hearted about Aadhaar. Instead of taking credit for it, Congress lawyers challenged it in court and appeared as the anti-technology, anti-Aadhaar faces. A decisive prime minister made it possible.

Two individuals deserve a special credit. Shri Nandan Nilekani, who started it, and Dr Ajay Bhushan Pandey, who subsequently provided it with direction and expansion. He masterminded the government strategy to repel the legal challenge.

How the Poor and the Middle Class Benefited Most From the Modi Government Policies

Posted on 11 January 2019

The Constitutional Amendment Bill to provide reservation to the economically weaker sections has been passed by both Houses of Parliament. It will soon become a part of India's Constitution. Caste in India was considered a key determinant of social or historical oppression as in the case of the Scheduled Castes and Scheduled Tribes or a determinant of social and educational backwardness as in the case of the Other Backward Classes. Poverty, however, is a secular criterion. It cuts across communities and religions. Poverty as a criterion for a carve-out does not in any way contravene the basic structure of the Constitution.

In its Preamble, the original Constitution (unamended) mentions Equality of Opportunity and Justice for all whether political, social or economic to be ensured by the state. The Preamble expresses the intent of the Constitution framers. It is an aid to the interpretation of what constitutes the basic structure. The carve-out amongst the general non-reserved categories for 10 per cent of their poor does not in any way get restricted by the 50 per cent reservation embargo placed by the Supreme Court. In the Indra Sawhney case, the Supreme Court had categorically mentioned that 50 per cent criteria applies only to the caste-based reservations envisaged in Article 16(4) of the Constitution.

Nonetheless, the prime minister's decision to force an agenda for poverty-based reservation is the single greatest recognition/concern for the poor across the general categories and the need to eliminate poverty. The principal opposition party showed only lip sympathy for the measure and grudgingly supported it while poking holes in the same.

The pro-poor economic measures

The Modi government has promised a house for every rural poor. Currently about 50 lakh houses are being built per year in rural India. By 2022, every poor family will have a roof on its head. Most Indian villages have been connected by a pucca road. State funding has been increased from Rs 9000 crore annually (pre-UPA) to Rs 27,000 crore during NDA. Each village has been electrified and all willing dwelling households, including those who cannot afford an electricity connection, have been provided with the same. Rural sanitation has moved up from 39 per cent to over 98 per cent. The mode of cooking has been altered from coal and wood to cooking gas. The poor are being provided the same under the Ujjawala Scheme. The MGNREGA expenditure has crossed Rs 60,000 crore, almost twice of what was being spent by the UPA.

The universal health scheme – Ayushman Bharat – is targeted at 40 per cent of India's population who are at the lowest point of the economic ladder. Each one of them can get hospital treatment free with the coverage up to Rs 5 lakh annually per family.

For the farmers, besides doubling the expenditure on interest subvention, completing the 99 unfinished irrigation schemes, giving the farmer a crop insurance scheme, the government has expressed its intention to help the farmer by fixing the MSP for the notified crops at 50 per cent higher than cost. The farmers, of course, need greater support and the government is committed to the same.

I have already highlighted the pro-labour steps that the government has taken in terms of improving/liberalising the provisions of gratuity, bonus, minimum wage increase, ESI, social sector pension, Anganwadis and Asha workers etc.

Middle class

For India's middle class, in the last five years, not a single tax has been increased. Indirect taxes have been merged into one in the GST. The GST is the single most important 'consumer friendly measure' in India. Taxes of most commodities have been brought down. Commodities have been made cheaper, even though the revenue sacrificed now, after the rates revision, would be close to Rs 1 lakh crore.

Similarly, in every Budget, the lower end of the taxpayers have got relief both directly and indirectly. Even though the taxation slab is Rs 2.5 lakh, those with an earning up to Rs 3 lakh need not pay any tax. A Rs 40,000 standard deduction has been given to all employees. Similarly, all investments in housing, insurance and other saving instruments have been increased in the last four years. The cost of this to the exchequer is almost Rs 97,000 crore per annum. This is the first time that during the five-year tenure of a government a Rs 2 lakh crore annual tax rebate for both direct and indirect taxes has been given to the middle class taxpayer without a single tax being increased.

The subsidy for housing for the middle class has been liberalised. Inflation during the five-year tenure has been kept between 3–4 per cent as against 10.4 per cent during UPA-2. The government staff has benefited from speedy implementation of the Seventh Pay Commission, the Services have benefited from the implementation of the OROP (One Rank One Pay), the pensioners have benefited from the New Pension Scheme. The government contribution being increased from 10 per cent to 14 per cent and greater part of rebate being given to the entire amount of 60 per cent which can be withdrawn at the time of superannuation.

There is a method for economically empowering the poor. Their purchasing power has improved. This helps trade and businesses and impacts positively on the economy. This is the first five-year tenure of a government where India has consistently remained the fastest-growing economy in the world. This indeed helps every Indian – the poor, the neo-middle class, the middle class and, of course, the large business community.

Political Stability, Decisive Leadership and a Clear Mandate – Their Relationship With Growth

Posted on 15 January 2019

India's post-Independence economic study can be divided into two parts, with 1991 as a cut-off line. The regulated economy restricted India's potential for forty years. From 1951–52 to 1990–91, India's GDP grew by 4.2 per cent per annum. The per capita income grew by 2 per cent each year. The Consumer Price Index for almost a two-decade period from 1969–70 to 1990–91 rose by 8.2 per cent. The fiscal deficit of the central government from 1980–81 to 1990–91 for a ten-year period was an average of 6.5 per cent. Our external debt was 28.7 per cent of the GDP at the end of the pre-liberalisation period.

The liberalisation of the economy not only improved the GDP growth rates but also brought millions of people out of poverty and improved the quality of life of a large number of Indians.

Post-liberalisation, it is important to analyse the GDP growth and the inflation data relatable to various governments under various prime ministers. The data reads as under:

Period	GDP Growth (%)	Inflation (%)	Prime Minister
1991–92 to 1995–96	5.1	10.2	P.V. Narasimha Rao
1996–97 to 1997–98	5.8	8.1	H.D. Deve Gowda I.K. Gujral
1998–99 to 2003–04	5.9	5.4	Atal Bihari Vajpayee
2004–05 to 2008–09	6.9	5.7	Manmohan Singh
2009–10 to 2013–14	6.7	10.1	Manmohan Singh
2014–15 to 2018–19	7.3	4.6	Narendra Modi

While analysing the above chart, two important facts have to be kept in mind. First, that the average GDP growth of 7.3 per cent during the five years of Prime Minister Narendra Modi is on a much larger base than that of his predecessors. The growth rates are higher. A higher growth rate on a larger base has a multiplier effect. Second, during the five years of UPA-2, inflation varied between 12.2 per cent and 8.4 per cent. In 2013–14, the UPA government left behind an annual inflation figure of 9.4 per cent. It took time for this figure to be moderated. In the five years of Prime Minister Narendra Modi, the inflation figure has been 5.9 per cent, 4.9 per cent, 4.5 per cent, 3.6 per cent and 3.9 per cent. Once it was moderated in the first year of the present NDA government, it has consistently been kept in check. The Modi government fixed a Statutory Inflation Target of 4 per cent +/– 2 per cent as the range of inflation.

When Prime Minister Modi came to power, India was the tenth largest economy in the world in GDP terms. Presently, the fifth, sixth and seventh economies, namely the United Kingdom, France and India, are within a very narrow range. A marginal fluctuation of currency values alters the size of the economies. India, of course, is projected to grow at 7.5 per cent next year. This will conclusively ensure that India, at the end of the next financial year, could possibly be the fifth largest economy in the world.

Needless to say, India's fiscal discipline during the past five years has been amongst the best as compared to any preceding period. The McKinsey Institute reports that the size of India's middle class is growing very fast from 14 per cent in 2005 to 29 per cent in 2015. It is estimated to go all the way to 44 per cent in 2025.

With the kind of transfer of resources to rural India which have been made in the past five years, a huge aspirational class is emerging even in the rural areas.

This is an indication of the social profile, purchasing power and the quality of life Indians are going to have in the decades to come. To ensure that this happens as projected, it is a prerequisite that India gets a decisive leadership, consistency in policy direction and a strong and stable government. An unworkable alliance with maverick leadership whose longevity is suspect can never achieve this.

Today India is the fastest-growing major economy in the world. Still we are not satisfied with a 7–7.5 per cent growth rate. We are increasingly becoming impatient and want to break the 8 per cent barrier. Ease of Doing Business rankings for five years have improved from 142nd position to 77th position. We now have to get into the top 50, if not still lower.

Who should be India's prime minister, if India were to achieve this? Should he/she be constrained by his/her rival aspirants who have reluctantly supported him/her out of mere dislike for a common opponent, or does India need a prime minister with a clear mandate as in 2014? Only such a prime minister can deliver growth and satisfy the nation's aspirations.

Does the Bareilly Nikah-Halala Not Shock Your Conscience?

Posted on 8 February 2019

Some incidents are so unconscionable and repulsive that they shake the conscience of the society and compel it to take remedial measures. Injustice perpetuated by personal laws is a glaring example of this.

Many communities, over the last several decades, have brought incremental but significant changes in their personal laws. The object and direction of these changes has been that gender equality is ensured, rights of women and children are protected and the right to live with dignity is ensured. Some practices which survived for centuries and were so obnoxious (such as Sati and Untouchability) are now considered unconstitutional.

A recent case from Bareilly has shocked my conscience. It relates to the obnoxious practice of Nikah-Halala in Islamic personal law. A lady who was married in 2009 was divorced twice by her husband through Triple Talaq, once in 2011 and subsequently in 2017. The family prevailed upon the husband to accept her back. On both occasions, she was sedated and asked to undergo Nikah-Halala, on the first occasion with her father-in-law and on the subsequent occasion with her brother-in-law. They both raped her. Almost a similar case was reported by the PTI on 2 September 2018 as having taken place in the Sambhal district of Uttar Pradesh. That in the twenty-first century there could be such gross violation of the dignity of women in the world's largest democracy should make every head hang in shame. After raping this lady, both the father-in-law and brother-in-law used the weapon of Triple Talaq to divorce the victim so that she could be accepted by her husband.

If Triple Talaq had not been a permitted mode of divorce in

India, would this incident emanating from a no-fault-impulsive divorce have taken place? The Supreme Court has already declared instant talaq as unconstitutional and yet in the absence of a deterrent it can at best amount to a civil wrong with no penal consequences. A number of Muslim men and conservatives are choosing to even ignore the Supreme Court judgement.

Unfortunately, when human conscience should have been repelled while reading this news in the morning newspapers, the Congress president, Rahul Gandhi, and his coterie, while addressing a minority convention, promised to withdraw the bill pending in the Parliament penalising Triple Talaq. History has repeated itself, neither as a satire nor as a tragedy. It has repeated itself with a mindset of cruelty. The late Rajiv Gandhi committed a monumental mistake in legislatively overturning the Shah Bano judgement of the Supreme Court which guaranteed maintenance to all Muslim women. He allowed deserted women to be driven to poverty and destitution. Thirty-two years later his son has taken another retrograde step to drive them not merely into destitution but also to live a life which is an antithesis of human existence. The Muslim woman in Bareilly has been forced into an animal existence.

Votes are important, so is fairness. Political opportunists only look at the next day's headlines. Nation builders look at the next century.

The Fourteen Iconic Reforms of Prime Minister Narendra Modi's Government

Posted on 18 March 2019

Five years is not a long period in the life of a nation. It can, however, be a turning point in its direction towards progress. 1991 was an important watershed in Indian history. Prime Minister

P.V. Narasimha Rao was confronted with an economic crisis. The economic situation compelled reforms. Many in the Congress party lacked the conviction to support reforms. After the initial two years from 1991 to 1993, the Congress party became apologetic about the reforms. That is probably the reason why the efforts to erase the memory of Shri P.V. Narasimha Rao from the Congress party's contemporary history is still a 'work in progress'.

The National Front government partly rationalised direct taxes. The first NDA government took key decisions with regard to infrastructure creation and prudent fiscal management. Bold policies on telecom and national highways made significant impacts on the economy. The UPA governments between 2004–14 got stuck in slogans rather than economic expansion. They created 'Rights' without a major increase in resources being provided to implement those rights. Subsequently, the government got marred in corruption and wasted its tenure in a cover-up exercise. Prime Minister Modi's government was elected when India was already a part of the 'Fragile Five' and the world was predicting that India's 'I' will be knocked off from the 'BRICS'. The government had no options. It was committed to reforms. 'Reform or Perish' that was the challenge before the Indian economy. Therefore, the government systematically and consistently introduced several reforms spread over a five-year period which will go down in India's economic history as the 'Second Generation' of reforms that were much needed. I discuss herein some of the significant steps that the government took.

Taxation reforms

India was substantially a tax non-compliant society. Taxation departments of the government were a source of harassment which dissuaded people from coming into the tax net. Our tax rates were abnormally high. The interface between the assessing officers, businessmen and inspectors needed to be substantially cut down. The last five years will be considered momentous in this journey. No taxes have been increased. In fact, after sixty-seven years of increase, tax rates have moved downwards. In a bold step spread over a five-year period, income up to Rs 5 lakh has been exempted from income tax. Even deductions available to the taxpayers have been increased to encourage and incentivise savings. The GST has enforced one tax across the country, eliminated barriers and made inspectors disappear. Both income tax and GST returns are filed on the net and assessments are done on the net. No interface, no corruption. Queries are raised on the net and responses are given on the net. The number of assessees filing returns with reduced tax rates in income tax has risen close to double in the five-year period. The GST will increase the assessee base in the first twenty-one months of its implementation by almost 80 per cent. The ideal tax policy of simplification, no interface, lower rates and higher collections has been implemented.

The measures against black money

From the legislation of black money law, through the laws dealing with the confiscation of property of fugitives and extinguishing their civil rights, significant taxation measures to curb black money have been taken by the government. The double taxation prohibition treaties with Mauritius, Cyprus and Singapore have been rewritten. International agreements have been entered into for a real-time exchange of information relating to assets held by Indians in their jurisdiction.

The insolvency and bankruptcy code

Indiscriminate lending by public sector banks during the UPA government had created large NPAs. The banking system was under stress. It was unable to support growth. Existing schemes and systems were not working. The IBC changed the debtor–creditor relationship. Defaulting managements are removed from management and debtor companies are going in for resolutions with either new promoters taking over or by sale of assets. Banks have finally started recovering their bad debts. No one can cheat the banks and get away.

Aadhaar

The implementation of Aadhaar has given a unique identity number to every Indian. It is a historic step towards using technology and digitisation of governance. The result is that without any pilferage or middlemen, the beneficiaries of all government programmes belonging to the central government, the state government or even the local bodies can now get their benefits in bank accounts directly. In this area we are ahead of any other country in the world.

Demonetisation

Demonetisation has proved to be a significant step towards formalisation of the Indian economy. It compelled people to deposit their high currency cash into the banking system, account for the deposits by paying taxes or otherwise. It brought a behavioural change in how India spends its money. The real test of demonetisation is: has it led to higher tax collections and higher digital transactions? The unequivocal answer is yes.

Inflation

The average inflation during UPA-2 was about 10.4 per cent. The average inflation during the NDA has been less than 4.5 per cent. In fact, it has been much lesser in the last three years. Today the CPI inflation is below 2.5 per cent.

No discretions

The NDA eliminated all discretions which governments, bureaucrats and politicians had. There is no power in any individual or group of individuals to grant favours, largesse or contracts to individuals. Systems have been established and all contracts can only be awarded through a market mechanism.

Cooperative federalism

The Fourteenth Finance Commission recommended 42 per cent as the share of the states in devolution of the taxes collected by the Centre. It was a significant increase by 10 per cent of what the Thirteenth Finance Commission had recommended. The central government immediately agreed. The states are fiscally much stronger today. In the GST Council, the states have a two-third vote and the central government has a one-third vote.

Agriculture and rural infrastructure

For the first time, resources have been spent in a major way in rural areas. Rural roads, housing, sanitation, electrification, cooking gas, all have been added to our infrastructure. The farmers now get 50 per cent plus their cost through MSP, a subsidised crop insurance scheme, a Rs 75,000 crore income support system by payment of Rs

6000 each to small and marginal farmer annually and Rs 60,000 crore through MGNREGA.

Urban infrastructure

I will separately give details in other articles on the creation of urban infrastructure. National highways, rural roads, port connectivity, number of airports, surplus power, modernisation of the Indian Railways, more resources for urban infrastructure, significant resources for rural infrastructure have been the hallmarks of infrastructure improvement in the last five years.

Ayushman Bharat

India has seen a major change in healthcare,. Today Ayushman Bharat ensures that 40 per cent of the poorest Indians – 50 crore people get a free hospitalisation up to an expenditure of Rs 5 lakh a year. In the first few months, nearly 16 lakh people have been treated. Today, with 40 per cent support by Ayushman Bharat and 38 per cent support by insurance schemes of either government employers or corporate bodies, 78 per cent of India is health-insured. Our target is to make it a 100 per cent.

Financial inclusion

In financial inclusion India has become a global leader. About 35 crore bank accounts under the PMJDY were opened and every poor household has been connected to the banks. As against 58 per cent of the households in 2014, today every willing household is connected to the banking system. Crores of poor people have got an accident and life insurance at a normal and negligible cost under the subsidised government schemes. More than 16 crore MUDRA loans have been given to small entrepreneurs for creating avenues of self-employment. The Indian example in financial inclusion is globally quoted as a role model.

Investment and Make in India

The stressed banking system that the UPA left behind had its impact on the investment cycle. From a worrisome situation on the investment front, today fixed capital formation, which is an indication of investment, has moved up to about 14 per cent. Foreign direct investment has been liberalised and procedures simplified so as to ensure that India becomes the preferred destination for investment.

Social sector investments

Swachh Bharat, which has connected 99 per cent rural homes to sanitation, became the flagship success story. The education of the girl child, reduction in dropouts from schools, increased remuneration for those employed in the formal sector such as, Asha in Anganwadi, and other such workers has had a tremendous economic impact. So will be the impact of the 10 per cent reservation in jobs and college admissions for the economically weaker sections. The minimum wages have been increased by about 45 per cent. The gratuity limit has been increased from Rs 10 lakh to Rs 20 lakh. Income eligibility for bonuses has been increased from Rs 7,000 to Rs 21,000. The impact on middle-income groups by implementation of the Seventh Pay Commission, the OROP and increasing government share from 10 per cent to 14 per cent in the New Pension Scheme has helped the salaried class. The contributory pension scheme for the 10 crore informal-sector workers is a new first for India. It will make India a pensioned society.

I have outlined above only fourteen game-changing decisions of the government which impacted the economy. The economy expanded at a rate faster than any other country in the world. Our revenues went up and we ensured that the benefits of prosperity and the first right to the exchequer going to the poor are maintained. It will be our endeavour to maintain this direction in future also.

Agenda 2019 – Part 9: The NDA Government's Economy Report Card versus Its Predecessors

Posted 19 March 2019

The irony of a large number of Opposition leaders is that they specialise only in politicking and sloganeering rather than understanding the world of development and economy. One of the fake campaigns against the present government has been on the question of economic data. The Central Statistical Organisation (CSO), which handles data management, always maintains an arm's length distance from the government and functions professionally and independently. Our data is maintained as per the best global practices. The World Bank and the International Monetary Fund have always commented favourably while accepting our data. The recent statement by the 108 purported economists needs to be analysed. Most of them have, over the last few years, repeatedly signed the memorandums of manufactured political issues against the present government. Compulsive contrarians can hardly be objective.

We need to analyse as to where we stand in terms of the economy. The period 2014–19 has witnessed the fastest ever growth of the GDP in India for a five-year term of any government. It has been a period of fiscal consolidation. The following chart will give the exact comparison of how the economy has performed during this period as against the earlier period.

	Indicator	1951-52 - 1990-91	1991-92 - 2013-14	2009-10 - 2013-14	2014-15 - 2018-19	2018-19
1	Growth of real GDP (per cent)	4.2	6.1	6.7	7.7	7.0
2	Growth of real per-capita GDP (per cent)	2.0	4.3	5.0	6.2	5.7
3	Inflation-CPI (per cent)- from 1969-70 onwards	8.2	7.8	10.1	4.5	3.50 (Apr'18-Feb'19) 2.70 (Feb '19)
4	Fiscal Deficit (Centre) - per cent of GDP from 1980-81 onwards	6.5	4.8	5.4	3.7	3.4
5	External debt end period – per cent of GDP	28.7	23.9	23.9	20.0	
6	Current Account Deficit per cent of GDP from 1970-71 onwards	1.1	1.2	3.3	1.5	-2.7

Notes:

1. GDP and GDP growth from 2005-06 onwards is at base year 2011-12 and before 2005-06 is on base year 2004-05.

2. Inflation for 2018-19 is for April, 2018 – Feb., 2019. Current Account Balance for 2018-19 is for first half of the year.

3. External debt is at end period. For 2014-15 to 2018-19 the end period taken is March, 2018.

4. Inflation figures are based on CPI-IW for the period 1969-70 to 2011-12 and CPI-combined (New series of CSO) for the period after 2011-12. (Base years of 1960 for 1969-83, 1982 for 1984-2005; and 2001 for 2006-2011 are used under CPI-IW)

Source: National Accounts Statistics of CSO, RBI, Budget 2019 and Labour Bureau. Data from these sources are taken for the Economic Survey as well.

An analysis of the above table clearly reveals that the five year GDP has been 7.5 per cent – the fastest amongst the major economies of the world. Inflation has been broadly under control. Fiscal deficit has gradually slided down. The external debt as a percentage of the GDP is on the decline and there is significant improvement in the current account balance of the government.

GDP and fiscal prudence

- **Inflation**: Inflation during the period 2009–14 was 10 per cent plus. During the period 2014–19, it will come down to an average of about 4.5 per cent. In fact, the last three years' average is much lower. Presently it is close to 2.7 per cent.
- **Jobs**: The recent survey of MSME published by the Confederation of Indian Industry in March 2019 covers 1,05,345 firms

of varying sizes across sectors and geographies. The survey indicates 'a growth of 13.9 per cent in net jobs created over the last four years at 3.3 per cent per annum (compounded growth rate).' The survey further states: 'given that the total workforce size according to the labour bureau is estimated at 450 million (projected for 2017–18), the overall job additions work out to 13.5–14.9 million per annum.' The above fits in with the trends given by the EPFO data by S.K. Ghosh and Pulak Ghosh. All these data indicate the general trend of jobs increasing in India, which match the 7.3 per cent average growth rate of GDP. Normally a high growth rate leads to a higher job creation. This can be negated only if the productivity levels suddenly go up. In India, it is unlikely. There is no social dissatisfaction in terms of popular agitations or protests. Thus, the fake campaign of job losses in India deserves to be rejected.

If we consider the rate of growth of GDP, investment in infrastructure and accompanying economic and labour reforms for the last five years along with the underlying structure of the Indian economy, it would be amply clear that there have been several sources of employment growth and creation of gainful employment opportunities.

MoSPI has been bringing out employment-related statistics using payroll reporting. EPFO data shows that 72.32 lakh new subscribers were added to EPFO between September 2017 and December 2018. This would not be possible without an increase in jobs in the formal sector. This is corroborated by a study by Mohandas Pai, which calculated that 1.08 crore jobs have been created in just three professions in 2017 – CAs, lawyers and doctors.

The faster pace of constructions of National Highways and rural roads under PMGSY are estimated to have generated 178.8 crore person – days of work (as per an IIT Kanpur study).

New entrants in the e-commerce and technology space like Uber, Ola, OYO have generated a large number of direct and indirect employment activities. About Rs 7.99 lakh crore has been sanctioned under MUDRA, out of which 28 per cent loans are to new entrepreneurs. It would be preposterous to contend that the fastest-growing economy in the world is actually losing jobs and that even (as on 19 March 2019) the 17.1 crore Mudra loans created no jobs through self-employment.

- **The Insolvency and Bankruptcy Code**: It is estimated that in the last two years about three lakh crore NPAs have been recovered on account of enactment of IBC either through the IBC process or through the pre IBC provisions. The ability of banks to support growth has increased. The amalgamation of banks is giving way to stronger lending institutions.
- **Some social indicators**: The LPG coverage across the nation was 55 per cent in December 2014 and had increased to 93 per cent. Ayushman Bharat has provided hospital healthcare to 10.74 crore families totalling about fifty crore beneficiaries. Rural sanitation has increased from 39 per cent in 2014 to 99 per cent as of today.
- **Infrastructure indicators**: Rural roads were built in 2013–14 at 69 km per day. It has increased to 134 km per day in 2017–18. The same is the position with the National Highways, where today 25 km per day (more than 10,000 km a year) are being built. Currently the Metro service operates in fourteen cities and its length is 645 km. India's first High Speed Rail will be completed in 2022–23 covering a distance of 500 km between Ahmedabad and Mumbai. India's air traffic in the last four years has seen the largest ever growth. Today we have 102 functional airports. We have moved towards near total rural electrification. The construction sector, which traditionally creates significant

jobs, is growing in double digits. Yet, if the critics are to be believed, this growth did not create jobs.

- **Electronics manufacturing**: The Indian electronic sector has made significant advances in the last five years. From Rs 1,80,000 crore manufacture of electronics in India pre-2014, we have now touched Rs 3.87 lakh crore of manufacturing. The five years of the NDA government will see the growth of the electronic sector close to rupees five lakh crore. From almost a negligible manufacturing of mobile phones in India in 2013–14, today we are the second largest producer of mobile phones in the world. An incredible contrarian data shows that this did not create jobs.
- **Ease of Doing Business**: From a low of 142 in 2014, our ranking in the first four years of the government has improved to 77. This is the fastest ever growth of 65 places in our ranking. In areas such as, 'Construction Permits', we have improved our rank by 129 places. In 'Trading Across Borders (customs)', we have improved 66 ranks. We have similarly improved in other areas such as 'Starting a Business', 'Getting Credit', 'Getting Electricity in a Country'. We still need to improve under certain sectors such as 'Enforcement of Contracts'.
- **Rural Infrastructure and Agriculture**: Today India spends Rs 1,84,000 crore on the right to food for the poor people by providing them subsidised food. India spends Rs 75,000 crore in income support to our farmers. It further spends Rs 60,000 crore on the Rural Employment Guarantee, the highest ever. We have tripled the expenditure on rural roads. We have made substantial headway in rural electrification, sanitation and cooking gas. On healthcare, through Ayushman Bharat, we have launched the largest and the most successful healthcare scheme for the poor people. We are supporting farmers with over rupees twelve lakh crore of credit, interest subvention, subsidised crop insurance,

subsidised fertiliser and seeds and increased MSP and income support system. I believe that these measures when combined with enhanced investments in rural India over the next ten years will help us to bring the quality of rural life closer to those in the cities.

I have given some details of economic development in India over the last five year using empirical evidence. The evidence clearly shows rapid progress in the economic fortunes of all Indians irrespective of caste or creed. Only those who failed to develop the Indian economy despite being in power for several decades cannot witness the reality that is staring in their faces. The whole world, including the IMF and the World Bank, regard India as the fastest growing major economy in the world. The 130 crore Indians believe it. Only the compulsive contrarians don't!

Triple Talaq Without Social Security

Posted on 31 July 2019

Both Houses of Parliament have approved the Triple Talaq Bill. The new law seeks to criminalise those who, in defiance of the law, still resort to this practice and drive their wives to destitution. I had an opportunity to listen to the debate in both the Houses. Strong arguments were presented on both sides. There are some basic principles to be kept in mind while analysing this issue.

No social security for women in India

Those who champion the case of liberalising marriage and divorce laws must realise two basic facts. India is a developing society. Even though weaker sections are being provided certain facilities by the government, the concept of social security does not exist in India. The second important fact is that in a divorce proceeding, no person can take advantage of his own wrong.

Christianity traditionally did not accept the idea of an easy divorce. The conservatives were opposed to the idea of divorce. However, with the economic evolution of developed countries along with the creation of a social security net, laws in the developed world started liberalising. In most cases, negotiated settlements take place between the wife and the husband. The husband has to pay a huge amount of alimony or maintenance. In many societies, divorce is accompanied with sharing of assets. We, in India, are still in a stage where sharing of assets is extremely rare, maintenance levels are extremely low and post a divorce, unless she is working or employed, the wife is driven either to dependency or destitution. On basic principles of humanity, justice and fair play, would it be right, irrespective of religion, to give to the husband a unilateral right to end the marriage? The fear of the husband uttering three words will always keep the wife subjugated and bear the injustice.

Divorce, in India, takes place either by consent of both parties on agreed terms or one of the parties approaches the court for divorce on the grounds that the spouse has committed a 'matrimonial misconduct' (the grounds for divorce in Indian law). Most cases end in a settlement with a reconciliation or a divorce where the wife is provided either monthly maintenance or a large lump-sum of money which will maintain her. The basic principle of matrimonial law is that no person can take advantage of his own wrong. The Sharia law was an exception. The husband may have wronged the wife and still, despite his own matrimonial misconduct, divorce her by uttering three words to dissolve the marriage. This is against all cannons of humanity, justice and fair play. If this practice is adopted by others, many women would be driven to destitution.

The politics of this bill

This bill has exposed all those who consider themselves 'liberals'. A liberal should ordinarily be hostile to the idea of discrimination and injustice perpetuated by an oral divorce. In this case, not one spoke in favour of the bill which is ending the injustice. They raised weak arguments so that the fundamentalists amongst the Muslims are kept happy. Let us assume the reverse of the present situation. What if such a provision existed in Hindu law? Liberals, leftists, women's organisations and perhaps even the judiciary would have been shocked with such a provision and would have attempted for either a repeal of the law or it being declared unconstitutional. These people stand exposed because what they have attempted to raise are farcical objections. They wanted to continue and defend an obsolete practice which promotes injustice.

Rights versus rituals

The fundamental rights in India's Constitution and the right to practise and propagate one's religion are in the same chapter of the Constitution. How do you reconcile provisions of personal law which violate fundamental rights? What would be the harmonious construction so that these provisions can coexist?

I have consistently held the opinion that there must be a recognised distinction between two aspects which stem out of religious interpretations. The first is the 'rituals' of a religion. Rituals cannot be decided by the law. They remain squarely within the right to practise one's religion. However, fundamental rights belong to all. One section of the society cannot be denied these rights. What affects the right of a citizen – in this case the Muslim wife – cannot be determined by a religion. After the Constitution came into force, rights emanating from birth, rights of a minor, rights in relation to marriage, divorce, succession, adoption, rituals etc., belong to every citizen. They should necessarily be compatible with fundamental rights.

Granting an arbitrary right to a husband to orally and instantaneously divorce his wife does not deal with any ritual which is in the domain of religion. In a society governed by a Constitution and the rule of law, prima facie, this practice of oral divorce violates both the right to equality and the right of a woman to live with dignity. It is long overdue that the courts re-examine whether the rights being deprived to a citizen on the grounds of personal law violate the constitutional guarantees.

The deterrent effect

Those with short-sighted vision have repeatedly argued that since the Supreme Court has declared the practice as unlawful, then why punish a husband who is indulging in an unlawful act. If the Triple Talaq right used by him is unlawful and does not exist, then why send him to jail? The Supreme Court, by striking down the practice of Triple Talaq, has merely made a declaration of the law. This declaration has to be followed by a legislation which punishes the offending spouse for indulging in this cruel act despite it being declared unlawful. Many conservatives would still practise this irrespective of what the court has said. There is data available post the judgement which establishes that this is actually happening on the ground.

Besides being tried for the offence in a court, obviously the husband will have to pay maintenance to his wife. Both these will have a strong deterrent effect on those who want to use the weapon of Triple Talaq. They will think a hundred times before using it due to the onerous consequences of its illegality. I have no doubt that once an example is made out of some people, the fear of its consequences will lead to minimising this practice. If this law is not enacted, the judgement of the Supreme Court will turn into a futile academic exercise where the practice is illegal, however, if you still indulge in it no penal consequence visits you.

Why make a civil contract into a criminal offence?

Demanding dowry, indulging in bigamy or polygamy, indulging in cruel behaviour (including mental cruelty) are all criminal offences. A bounced cheque or a defamation may be a civil wrong but both have penal consequences in criminal law. Merely to oppose a progressive legislation, one does not have to invent a new jurisprudence.

The Congress party has ruled this country for a long time. During this period, it has amended several personal laws to make them acceptable to the changing social mindset. But when it comes to the Sharia, it is scared. Its stands in both the Shah Bano case and now in the legislation emanating from the Shayara Bano case, have given a clear evidence of its intent. It does not mind Muslim women being driven to destitution. After all, the fundamentalist votebank is at a higher priority than justice being conferred to the female gender.

3

The BJP's Campaign Against Black Money and How it Marked a Turning Point Against Corruption

The NDA's campaign against black money is just one of many measures to eliminate corruption and tax evasion in order to clean up the system both at home and globally through international cooperation. Compare this with the Congress party and the *National Herald* scandal in which they have acquired properties worth a huge amount without spending anything and used tax-exempted income for a non-exempted purpose or the chit fund fraud in West Bengal. Prime Minister Modi's five-year tenure will be regarded by future political historians as a turning point where a movement to free India from corruption began.

Confidentiality Clauses and the Battle for Tracing Black Money Outside India

Posted on 2 November 2014

The world is increasingly moving towards a more structured and organised struggle against illegal money parked in tax havens or even otherwise transacted at foreign soil. Originally the tax havens were completely non-cooperative. However, international pressure has compelled some of them to relax the rigidity against non-disclosure.

Almost all countries which entered into Double Taxation Avoidance Treaties or have a domestic legislation, as in the case of the US, that has an extra-territorial application, insist that information parted to the receiving state would be subject to confidentiality clauses. The confidentiality clauses make it incumbent that disclosure would be made only after prosecution is filed before a charging court. Thus, the issue is not whether, but when disclosure can be made. The debate is not between disclosure and non-disclosure of confidential information. It is between unauthorised disclosure in violation of tax treaties and disclosure as per tax treaties. An unauthorised disclosure in violation of tax treaties entails that the disclosure is made for collateral purposes. It is usually not accompanied by any evidence or proof. But when a disclosure is made in pursuance of a charge sheet in a court of law where a criminal prosecution is filed, it would certainly be a disclosure substantiated by adequate proof and evidence.

A disclosure in violation of tax treaties helps the account holder. The reciprocating state would treat this as a violation of a tax treaty and refuse to provide any evidence in support of the unauthorised account. The holder of the unauthorised account in the absence of any proof and confirmation from the reciprocating state would get the benefit in any investigation or prosecution and then claim that 'I stand vindicated'. In fact, a premature disclosure would additionally alert the account holder to prepare some documentation or a sham defence. It may even enable him to destroy evidence.

India has to take a conscious call. Does it want to be a part of the global coalition which is moving in the direction of automatic sharing of information or not? Does it ensure all information is supported by substantial evidence and proof or only wishes to remain restricted to sloganeering? In the recent meeting of about fifty countries in Berlin where automatic sharing of information was proposed, India could not participate since a prevalent view is that confidentiality clauses are unconstitutional under Indian law. This view requires reconsideration. An automatic exchange of information would relate both to authorised and unauthorised movement of money. Why should any information with regard to authorised movement of money be made public? Why should information even in relation of unauthorised movement of money be made public only for political or collateral purposes? Why should the account holder be alerted in advance? It should be put to an authorised use with collection of evidence and filing of prosecution.

The US has legislated the Foreign Account Tax Compliance Act, 2010 (FATCA). The FATCA contains a confidentiality clause. It makes it mandatory for foreign financial institutions (FFIs) to register with the appropriate authority and exchange information. The foreign financial institutions are required to enter into agreement with the US Internal Revenue Service. Alternatively, foreign governments can sign agreements with the US government – the mandatory exchange of information subject to confidentiality clause being necessary. FATCA mandates the deduction and withholding of tax equal to 30 per cent on a US source payment to recalcitrant FIIs or FFIs in non-compliant countries which do not meet the requirements of FATCA. Such 30 per cent withholding will also be imposed by other FATCA compliant countries against non-compliant countries. The consequences of not signing the agreement with the US under FATCA would be disastrous. It will negate the efforts being undertaken by our government to revive the Indian economy.

The Reserve Bank of India has already informed the government of India about the serious and adverse consequences of non-compliance of FATCA by India. Several countries have already subscribed to FATCA.

An unauthorised disclosure of information is fraught with both investigation and economic consequences. They can sabotage the investigation. They can attract sanctions in the form of withholding taxes. It is obvious that in a choice between unauthorised disclosure and disclosure as per treaties, the latter is both a fair and beneficial proposition. It will help in collection of evidence and exposure of a wrongdoing in accordance with law and fair procedure. A disclosure without evidence would ensure that evidence is never available.

Notwithstanding its clarity, why should someone with adequate understanding of the subject, demand a disclosure in violation of the treaty. The Congress party's stand is understandable. It does not want evidence to be forthcoming in support of the names available with SIT. Are some others ill informed, just indulging in bravado or are they Trojan horses? I am sure the SIT which has been entrusted by the Supreme Court with the investigation, will succeed in bringing out the truth while realising the full implications of the subject matter.

The NDA government has had an exemplary record in this matter. The first decision of its cabinet meeting was to accept the Supreme Court direction in constituting the SIT. It has complied with every decision of the SIT. It made available all the names in its possession to the SIT on 27 June 2014 itself. It will continue to support the SIT fully and unequivocally in search of truth.

The NDA Government's Campaign Against Black Money

Posted on 4 October 2015

No society can indefinitely sustain a system where income earners consider tax evasion to be a way of life. Regrettably our high taxation regime in the past eventually ended up encouraging tax evasion. When states tax their people reasonably, they can persuade them to honestly declare their incomes. The early decades after Independence witnessed India with high taxation rates, prompting people to evade. The capacity of the state to detect evasion was less than adequate. Over the years, India has slowly started moving towards moderate rates of taxation. It has been a conscious strategy of the NDA government to put more money in the pockets of middle- and low-income groups by raising exemption limits and incentivising savings through fiscal policy. This will encourage consumption and bring more money into the system. Consumption increases the volumes of indirect taxation. To make India a more investment friendly destination, I had announced in the 2015 Budget that the rate of corporate tax would be brought down to 25 per cent over the next four years and most exemptions, other than those which incentivise savings, would eventually be phased out. The present government under the leadership of Prime Minister Shri Narendra Modi stands by this commitment.

How the campaign played out abroad

The government has formulated a conscious strategy to deal with the menace of black money. At the very first meeting of the Union cabinet, after the swearing in of the government, we implemented the direction of the Supreme Court to constitute an investigation team headed by two retired judges of the Supreme Court who would monitor the entire efforts against black money. The UPA government had tried to evade the Supreme Court direction on one pretext or the other for over three years. The government swung into action and accelerated all the income tax assessments against those with regard to whom information about holding illegal money abroad in Liechtenstein and in the HSBC bank at Geneva, were available. Most assessments have been completed and wherever illegalities are being found, criminal prosecutions have been launched against beneficiaries of these bank accounts.

A total peak balance of about Rs 6500 crore in these accounts has been assessed. The government, thereafter, proposed a law for imposition of taxation on undisclosed assets held outside the country. Since this tax was being imposed for the first time, a ninety-day compliance window was offered to those wanting to disclose their unlawful assets. The compliance window ended on 30 September 2015. A total tax at the rate of 30 per cent and penalty at the rate of 30 per cent has to be paid by the declarants before 31 December 2015. Those who chose to declare between this period would not be prosecuted under the new black money law. Six hundred and thirty-eight persons have declared their income amounting to Rs 3770 crore. These declarants can now sleep well.

For those who have undisclosed foreign assets but have failed to file such a declaration will now be subjected to penal provisions of this law. They will be liable to pay 30 per cent tax and a penalty of 90 per cent, thus leading to confiscation of the assets plus more. In addition, they will be liable to prosecution where they can be sentenced up to ten years. This law will create a deterrent in future against the flight of capital from India.

The assessed income of Rs 6500 crore in HSBC and the Rs 3770 crore declared during the compliance window should not be treated as income under any immunity scheme. The comparison of these amounts with amnesty schemes relating to domestic black money is ill-conceived. The campaign against domestic black money has to be separately dealt with for which government is independently taking steps.

In order to encourage international cooperation in the matters of tax evasion, the government has taken a series of steps. The prime minister took the initiative at the G-20 meeting in order to bring about international cooperation in tackling unlawful assets held by the residents of one country on foreign soil. The G-20 initiative is intended to lift the veil of secrecy in banking transactions and in real time inform domestic taxation authorities about transactions of their citizens internationally.

The government has signed an understanding with the US under FATCA wherein the United States and India would disclose to each other any real-time transaction in accounts with financial institutions, by its citizens in foreign territories. This cooperation would also extend to all those countries which would become signatories to global standards on Automatic Exchange of Information being developed under the mandate of G-20. The revenue secretary led a team of Indian officials and has held extensive discussions with Swiss authorities. Discussions have also been held at the ministerial level. Switzerland has agreed to provide India with proof relating to several HSBC accounts where India can give some evidence over and above the stolen data, which was delivered to India through France.

It is expected that over the next two years this international cooperation will be worked out and information with regard to illegal assets held abroad, subject to certain conditions, would be available to each of the demanding nations. Thus, those with illegal assets abroad, who have failed to make declaration, would now stand the risk of information relating to them eventually reaching the Indian taxation authorities.

Domestic black money

The bulk of black money is still within India. We, thus, need a change in national attitude where plastic currency becomes the norm and cash an exception. Being seized of this problem, the government has been working with various authorities in order to incentivise this change. The opening of a large number of payment gateways, internet banking, payment banks and the emerging reality of e-commerce will prompt the use of banking transactions and plastic money significantly. The JAM Trinity and the Direct Benefit Transfer of subsidies to the accounts of beneficiaries of various government schemes will also be a step ahead in this direction. Each of the 180 million beneficiaries of the Jan Dhan accounts has been provided with RuPay cards, which will encourage them to use plastic currency and get familiarised with it. The MUDRA Yojana, over the next few years, has a target of sixty million people (which means six crore families out of 25 crore families in India) to become entrepreneurs. Loans being made available to them by the banks can only be withdrawn from the ATMs by use of MUDRA credit cards which are being provided to them. More and more of their transactions will be through plastic currency or through the banking channel.

The government is at an advanced stage in considering the requirement of furnishing PAN card details if cash transactions beyond a certain limit are undertaken. The monitoring regime of income tax has been strengthened and its capacity to access information and apply technology-driven analytical tools to expose evasion, has been enhanced. Its ability to detect large cash withdrawals, or large cash transactions which enter the system, is being strengthened. The GST regime, once introduced, will also be a landmark step in this direction. Thus, for commodities like gold where the initial purchase by the exporter is after the payment of custom duty, the subsequent transactions which are mostly in cash, can easily be found out.

The government's policy is rationalisation of tax structures, taxing at reasonable rates, placing more money in the hands of small earners, encouraging and promoting the use of plastic money by all sections of society and creating deterrence for those who continue to use unaccounted money.

Why the Congress Is Wrong

Posted on 10 December 2015

The Congress party, for the past few days, has disrupted both houses of Parliament. Its Goebbelsian propaganda is that the party's leadership is a victim of political vendetta. What then are the facts?

A company was created for the purpose of starting a newspaper *National Herald*. The company got allocation of prime land in several parts of the country. The land was meant to be used for the newspaper business. Today, there is no newspaper. There is only land and built up structures which are being commercially exploited.

A political party is entitled to collect funds for its political activities. For that purpose, it gets an exemption from payment of income tax. Rupees ninety crore from amongst the funds collected by the Congress party are given to the newspaper company. Prima facie, it can be said that there is a breach of the provisions of the Income Tax Act in as much as an exempted income is used for a non-exempt purpose.

The Rs 90 crore debt is then assigned to a Section 25 company for a paltry amount of Rs 50 lakh. Tax exempted money effectively gets transferred to a real estate company. The real estate company now acquires 99 per cent of the shareholding of the former newspaper company. Effectively, the Section 25 company substantially controlled by the leaders of the Congress party now owns all the properties acquired for a newspaper publication, and for virtually no consideration, the Section 25 company owns all the assets. This profit will become huge taxable income in its hands.

Since 2012, as a private citizen, Dr Subramaniam Swamy, has alleged a breach of trust. It is the duty of every citizen to report an offence when it comes to his notice. Any citizen can set the process of criminal law into motion. A Trial Court issued summons on Dr Swamy's complaint. The accused leaders of the Congress party moved the Delhi High Court for quashing, which granted them an interim protection. Eventually, the Delhi High Court dismissed the petition of the accused. The accused now have two alternatives. They can either challenge the order in the Supreme Court or appear before the Trial Court and contest the case on merits.

The facts are clear. By a series of financial transactions, the leaders of the Congress party created a 'Chakravyuh' for themselves. They have to find their own exit route out of the Chakravyuh. They have acquired properties worth a huge amount without spending anything. They have used tax-exempted income for a non-exempted purpose. They have transferred the income of a political party to a real estate company. They have created huge taxable income in favour of the real estate company.

The government, so far, has not taken any punitive action. The enforcement directorate has not issued any notice to them. The income tax authorities will follow their own procedure. The criminal court, meanwhile, has taken cognizance of the offence. The High Court has agreed with the trial court. The battle has to be fought legally. But the results of legal battles are always uncertain. The Congress is, therefore, crying foul and calling it political vendetta. Is that a charge against the courts? The government has passed no order in relation to the disputed transactions. There is equality before the law. No one is above the law. India has never accepted the diktat that the queen is not answerable to the law. Why should the Congress party and its leaders not contest the notice before the court? The government cannot help them in the matter, nor can the Parliament. Why then disturb the Parliament and prevent the legislative activity from continuing? The answer to the Congress party's leadership landing up in a Chakravyuh is to fight their battle legally and not disrupt Parliament. By disrupting democracy, the financial web created by the Congress leaders cannot be undone.

The Kleptocrats Club

Posted on 5 February 2019

Mamata Banerjee's disproportionate overreaction to the CBI wanting to interrogate the Kolkata Police Chief has flagged several issues for a public discourse, the most important being that a Kleptocrats Club now aspires to capture the reigns of India.

The chit fund fraud and its investigation

The West Bengal chit fund fraud was unearthed in 2012–13. Its investigations were handed over to the CBI by the Supreme Court. The court monitored these investigations. The CBI has interrogated and even arrested some people. Many have been granted bail. If a police officer is also required to be interrogated, how does it become a 'super emergency', an 'assault on Federalism', or 'destruction of institutions'? What is the strategy behind the chief minister's disgraceful and disproportionate reaction? What is her strategy in inviting all other leaders belonging to every opposition to join her on the dharna? It would be a gross error to assume that she did this because of a routine investigation involving a police officer. She did it to defocus from other opposition aspirants for the highest office and to project herself as the nucleus of India's Opposition. Her speeches attack Prime Minister Modi, but her strategy is aimed to defocus some of her other colleagues in the Opposition and hog the centre stage.

Can a state assault federalism?

Federalism is not a slogan. It is a delicate balance of the Centre–state relationship. Our Constitutional framework clearly defines the sharing of functions between the Centre and the state. It does not permit an overlap. There are central agencies and organisations which conduct legitimate investigation in states. Today the CBI is being brutally prevented by physical force and detention of its officers from investigating a crime legally within its jurisdiction in the state of West Bengal. It is a textbook-illustration of a state government assaulting Federalism. Can a state government prevent the income tax department from collecting taxes in a state? Can another state government prevent the NIA from proceeding to arrest a terrorist located in the state? Can the enforcement directorate be prevented from investigating or arresting a smuggler or money launderer physically located in a state? Obviously, the answer is No. If any of these are visible, it would be a case of the state assaulting Federalism. The prevention of a central investigating agency discharging a function given to it by the Supreme Court is a direct assault on federalism.

Mamata Banerjee's dubious allies

Technology has been a great enabler in detection of improper monetary transactions. Traceability of transactions has become simpler and the footprints of illegality can be traced. This has empowered all investigative agencies both at the Centre and state governments to unearth financial crimes including corruption.

When Mamata Banerjee decided to sit on a dharna she received support from many Opposition parties. There is an important commonality between them. They are all in the Opposition and aspire to be in power. Most of them, or their affiliates are today being investigated, prosecuted and in some cases have also been convicted for crimes of corruption. Her ally from Bihar represents the party of the convicted. The friend from Andhra Pradesh runs a party of contractors, 'thekedaars' and money launderers. Her two friends from Uttar Pradesh represent a scandalous legacy of corruption. Her anarchic brother from the Delhi government is at his wits' end because the penny stock companies of his ministerial colleagues have been found out. Curiously, the AICC president somersaulted his position from Saradha being a scam to shoulder-to-shoulder support to the scamster. This somersaulter belongs to the first family of the Congress party where most members of the family are on bail.

It has been argued in the past that the Opposition is going in for a non-ideological, short-lived coalition. India cannot afford instability. It has also been argued that the choice in the next election will be either Modi versus Chaos or Modi versus Anarchy. Mamata Banerjee's latest acrobatics are the best evidence of the kind of governance India's Opposition can provide. But more importantly, those who have lent support to the West Bengal Dharna are those who are battling serious allegations of economic improprieties, criminal misconduct and even corruption. Can New India be run by this Kleptocrats Club?

Is Prime Minister Modi's First Five-Year Tenure a Turning Point in Corruption?

Posted on 13 March 2019

Till 2014, India was considered, by both domestic and international investors, one of the most corrupt nations in the world. India's credibility on the issue of corruption was at rock bottom. The banking system had been siphoned-off during the UPA by those who benefitted from 'phone banking'. India had one of the lowest taxation bases in the world. Evasion was not considered morally or commercially imprudent. It was a normal business practice that the promoter's equity in a new project would be 'manufactured' from the bank debt and then round-tripped either through the Mauritius route or through Kolkata shell companies. Spectrum, mineral and other largesse were delivered on the strength of ministerial discretions. Rent-seeking was an established norm. Cash was the preferred mode of political funding. Many found it convenient to keep assets abroad, particularly in tax havens. Most defence transactions were tainted by middlemen close to the power centres.

From the Bofors gun deal to the HDW Submarine purchases, the Airbus transaction, the AugustaWestland deal, the fertiliser scam, the footprints of the Indian National Congress and its leaders were everywhere.

The new normal

Prime Minister Modi's five-year tenure will be regarded by future political historians as a turning point where a movement to free India from corruption began. The government and its ministers have conclusively proved that it is possible to run an honest government in India. Not a single charge of any substance has been made against the government. Frustrated with the clean image of the prime minister and his government, Congress leaders resorted to fake allegations but were snubbed both by the courts and the CAG. The message, loud and clear to all, is that a 'new normal' has now been established in India. If you don't pay back the banks, you will be out of management. If you escape the country, you will be extradited back. If you indulge in round-tripping, you will be found out. Lakhs of shell companies have been closed down. International treaties have been rewritten. The Mauritius, Cyprus and Singapore routes which enabled round-tripping have been closed down. Treaties have been entered with various countries for a real-time exchange of information with regard to assets held by Indians abroad. Ministerial discretions have been abolished. The spectrum, coal mines and other minerals are now allocated through a market mechanism. So are government contracts. The government maintains an arm's-length distance from the IBC process in the NCLT. The new promoters are decided by the Committee of Creditors through a transparent bidding process. There has not even been a whisper of allegations that in any of these cases political interference has taken place.

India is today building ten thousand kilometres of National Highways per year. Not one contract has been impugned having been allotted on any collateral consideration. New airports are being allocated by tendering processes. The government has even formulated a scheme to ensure that even political funding through electoral bonds is done by tax-paid money.

Where are the middlemen?

Prior to May 2014, Delhi was a city flooded with middlemen. They have been rendered jobless. Some have escaped the country. The corridors of North Block and Udyog Bhawan, which were flooded with businessmen and industrialists, are today vacant. As a finance minister, not a single person till date has approached me for file-pushing. The message is clear – this government works. It cannot be pushed. The prime minister told the bankers in 2015 that not a single call will come to him from either South Block or North Block. We have lived up to that promise. The bank boards have now professionals on them. The days of loan pushers on bank boards are over. All senior executives, CEOs of Public Sector Banks are now appointed through a professional mechanism of the Bank Board Bureau.

The impact on ease of doing business

The Environment Ministry was the hub of all corruption. Files were stacked on tables and not cleared indefinitely. Files even travelled with some ministers. Today, all applications are online. The permissions are granted or refused online. There is no scope for pushing files. It is not without reason that India's ratings for ease of doing business have improved from a horrible 142 to seventy-seven. Last year the largest single improvement was done in the matter of building and construction permits. The new byelaws framed by the government and adopted by most municipalities now provide an online grant of building permits and permissions to be done within a definite period of time.

The use of technology in taxation

Besides the municipalities, the taxation department was notorious for harassment and corruption. On the direct tax front, returns are now filed online, queries are addressed online, and assessment orders are passed online. Even the refund is communicated and delivered online. This year 99.6 per cent of all personal income tax returns filed have been accepted as they are. The CBDT is now working on a project where returns would be assessed, and orders delivered within days of the return being filed. There is no interface between the assessing officer and the assessee. Assessees no longer know the name of their assessing officer. They do not send him gifts. The GST has been designed to give the benefit of input credit. This necessarily involves the inputs being purchased from registered dealers or through banking transactions. This is leading to a more gradual formalisation of the economy. For the first time, we have had a government for five years which has not increased any taxes. On the contrary, it has reduced many taxes and yet significantly increased the tax base and the tax collections. This has enabled greater spending for defence, poverty-alleviation and infrastructure.

The Kumbh (2019) versus the Commonwealth Games (2010)

A textbook illustration is a comparison between the recently concluded Kumbh at Prayagraj and the 2010 Commonwealth Games. The Commonwealth Games are remembered more for corruption than for the number of medals India won. Projects were delayed; many were incomplete even when the games came to a close. There was mass-scale corruption. Many went to jail and their criminal cases are still pending.

The Kumbh 2019 is an excellent illustration of how public funds are effectively and honestly used. A total amount of Rs 4200 crore has been spent. Eight kilometres of ghats, 1.2 lakh toilets, residential camps, pandals to house twenty-four crore pilgrims have been constructed besides improving the city infrastructure. All of 683 projects were completed in time. This year's Kumbh is regarded as the best ever organised.

The Direct Benefit Transfer

Former prime minister, the late Shri Rajiv Gandhi had stated that only 15 per cent of the amount released by the central government reaches the beneficiaries. Corruption consumes the balance 85 per cent. The Centre would transfer money to the state. The state would send the money to the Collector, who would then use the machinery of the Tehsildar and the Panchayat Head to hand over the state support to the beneficiary. There was pilferage all the way. Aadhaar as a unique identity has ensured Direct Benefit Transfer (DBT), which ensures that payments under hundreds of schemes reached the bank of the beneficiary straightway without middlemen. The money is then used by the ultimate beneficiary.

What is the methodology that the prime minister and his government framed to ensure this moral transformation of India?

- No discretions with ministers or civil servants in commercial matters. Decision to be taken by market mechanisms.
- Fairness in awards of contract, natural resources and largesse.
- Banks to operate independently without any political interference.
- Anti-black-money steps such as the black money law dealing with unlawful assets abroad, placing both direct and indirect tax system on the digital platform, reducing personal interface, lowering the rates, increasing the tax base through compliances and ensuring that anti-evasion measures are strictly implemented.
- The DBT has ensured that benefits travel directly to the targeted.
- The investigative agencies have to be fair, clean and professional. This has now been implemented.

India has understood that corruption follows the law of Newton's gravitational pull. It travels from top to bottom and not the other way round. If the leader at the top is honest and has the capacity to ensure similar ethical standards from his colleagues, the moral authority of the government to ensure integrity travels through the system.

Those who operated improperly in the system are getting to realise that it is safer to be clean. That is the difference between Prime Minister Narendra Modi's NDA government and its predecessor UPA.

Tailpiece

While I was finalising this blog, an online site carried a detailed analysis of the unjust enrichment of the extended Gandhi family. While on the subject of cleaning public life, a relevant issue which many people raise is about several Indian politicians and their extended families who seem to live well without working. The expose with regard to the extended Gandhi family provides you with an answer. While conventionally many may have relied on straightway corruption through bribery, a new methodology has now been established.

Wheeler-dealers and fly-by-night operators give you the privilege of 'sweetheart deals'. With very little investment, windfall profits are thrust on a few privileged ones to enable them to create a capital. 'Political equity' results in buying goodwill. It enables you to influence decisions. When exposed, the beneficiaries hide behind the shield of 'clever business decisions.' If the 'capital creation' of the Congress party's first family is subjected to a forensic audit, facts will speak for themselves. Those who live in glass houses should not throw stones.

Legitimate Action Against Corruption Is Not Vendetta

Posted on 10 April 2019

It has become a routine practice to call any action against corruption as political vendetta. Claim of vendetta has never been a legitimate defence in corruption. Those who commit such large acts of corruption have to be judged on the merits of the action itself.

In all states large amounts sanctioned by the central and state governments for public works, roads, housing, schools, dispensaries, panchayat facilities and several other public infrastructure are created by Public Works Departments (PWDs). These works are carried out by the PWD through contractors. Similarly, large amounts are sanctioned for the mid-day meal scheme which encourages poor children to attend schools and towards other schemes intended to provide a composite diet to pregnant women. In the public space evidence has come in relation to Karnataka where allocations made for public welfare to the PWDs were being round-tripped by engineers for a political purpose. In Madhya Pradesh, an institutional mechanism has been created where money that is meant for development and social welfare of the weaker sections are now being channelled into politics.

Regrettably, none of the two state governments have replied to the allegations on merits. An argument is being given by them as to why they are being singled out and their political rivals are not being searched. Is there a right to equality that no action can be taken till the opponents are charged? Revenue departments act objectively on the basis of material available and take action when they are satisfied that a case of search operation is made out.

The fact that money is meant for the most vulnerable section of the society – namely, poor children or pregnant women belonging to the economically weaker sections are siphoned out – shows the mind frame of those indulging in such an act. They do not even spare those who live in destitution. This is the hypocrisy of Indian politics. After inflicting such injustice, they have the audacity to speak of Nyay.

4

The Indisputable Success of Demonetisation

With the return of Rs 15.28 lakh crore to the formal banking system, almost the entire cash holding of the economy now has an address. No longer is it anonymous. Apart from pushing the economy towards greater formalisation, India has moved on to a much cleaner, more transparent and honest financial system. If not the current generation, the next generation will see November 2016 as a turning point when the country began to feel proud of living by a fairer and more honest system.

A Year After Demonetisation

Posted on 7 November 2017

8 November 2016 would be remembered as a watershed moment in the history of Indian economy. This day signifies the resolve of this government to cure the country from 'dreaded disease of black money'. We, the Indians, were forced to live with this attitude of *chalta hai* with respect to corruption and black money and the brunt of this was faced particularly by the middle class and lower strata of society. It was a hidden urge of the larger section of our society for a long period to root out the curse of corruption and black money, and it was this urge which manifested in the verdict of the people in May 2014.

Immediately after taking up responsibility in May 2014, this government decided to fulfil the wish of the people in tackling the menace of black money by constituting SIT on black money. Our country is aware how even a direction from the Supreme Court on this issue was ignored by the then government for number of years. Another example of lack of will to fight against black money was the delay of twenty-eight years in implementation of the Benami Property Act.

This government took decisions and implemented the earlier provisions of law in a well-considered and planned manner over three years to meet the objective of fight against black money. These decisions span from setting up of SIT to passing of necessary laws for foreign assets to demonetisation and to implementation of GST.

When the country is participating in Anti-Black-Money Day, a debate was started on whether the entire exercise of demonetisation has served any intended purpose. This narrative attempt to bring out positive outcomes of demonetisation in short-term and medium-term with respect to stated objectives.

RBI has reported in its Annual Accounts that Specified Bank Notes (SBNs) of an estimated value of Rs 15.28 lakh crore have been deposited back as on 30 June 2017. The outstanding SBNs as on 8 November 2016 were of Rs 15.44 lakh crore value. The total currency in circulation of all denominations as on 8 November 2016 was 17.77 lakh crore.

One of the important objective of demonetisation was to make India a less cash economy and thereby reduce the flow of black money in the system. The reduction in currency in circulation from the base scenario reflects that this intended objective has been met. The published figure of currency in circulation for half year ending September 2017 is Rs 15.89 lakh crore. This shows year on year variation of (–) Rs 1.39 lakh crore; whereas year on year variation for the same period during last year was (+) Rs 2.50 lakh crore. This means that reduction in currency in circulation is of the order of Rs 3.89 lakh crore.

Why should we remove excess currency from the system? Why should we curtail cash transactions? It is common knowledge that cash is anonymous. When demonetisation was implemented, one of the intended objectives was to put identity on the cash holdings in the economy. With the return of Rs 15.28 lakh crore in the formal banking system, almost the entire cash holding of the economy now has an address. It is no more anonymous. From this inflow, the amount involving suspicious transactions based on various estimates ranges from Rs 1.6 lakh crore to Rs 1.7 lakh crore. Now it is with the tax administration and other enforcement agencies to use big data analytics and crack down on suspicious transactions.

Steps in this direction have already started. The number of Suspicious Transaction Reports filed by banks during 2016–17 has gone up from 61,361 in 2015–16 to 3,61,214; the increase during the same period for Financial Institutions is from 40,333 to 94,836 and for intermediaries registered with SEBI the increase is from 4,579 to 16,953.

Based on big data analytics, cash seizure by the income tax department has more than doubled in 2016–17 as compared to 2015–16; during search and seizure by the department Rs 15,497 crore of undisclosed income has been admitted which is 38 per cent higher than the undisclosed amount admitted during 2015–16; and undisclosed income detected during surveys in 2016–17 is Rs 13,716 crore which is 41 per cent higher than the detection made in 2015–16.

Undisclosed income admitted and undisclosed income detected taken together amounts to Rs 29,213 crore; which is close to 18 per cent of the amount involved in suspicious transactions. This process will gain momentum under Operation Clean Money launched on 31 January 2017.

The exercise to remove the anonymity with currency has further yielded results in the form of:

- 56 lakh new individual tax payers filing their returns till 5 August 2017 which was the last date for filing returns for this category; last year this number was about 22 lakh.
- Self-Assessment Tax (voluntary payment by tax payers at the time of filing return) paid by non-corporate tax payers increasing by 34.25 per cent during 1 April to 5 August in 2017 when compared to the same period in 2016.

With increase in tax base and bringing back undisclosed income into the formal economy, the amount of advance tax paid by non-corporate tax payers during the current year has also increased by about 42 per cent during 1 April to 5 August.

The leads gathered due to data collected during demonetisation period have led to identification of 2.97 lakh suspect shell companies. After issuance of statutory notices to these companies and following due process under the law, 2.24 lakh companies have been de-registered from the books of the registrar of companies.

Further actions were taken under the law to stop operation of bank accounts of these struck off companies. Actions are also being taken for freezing their bank accounts and debarring their directors from being on the board of any company. In the initial analysis of bank accounts of such companies, following information has come out which is worth mentioning:

- Of 2.97 lakh struck-off companies, information pertaining to 28,088 companies involving 49,910 bank accounts show that these companies have deposited and withdrawn Rs 10,200 crore from 9 November 2016 till the date of strike off from RoC.
- Many of these companies are found to have more than 100 bank accounts – one company even reaching a figure of 2,134 accounts.
- Simultaneously, income tax department has taken action against more than 1150 shell companies which were used as conduits by over 22,000 beneficiaries to launder more than Rs 13,300 crore.

Post demonetisation, SEBI has introduced a Graded Surveillance Measure in stock exchanges. This measure has been introduced in over 800 securities by the exchanges. Many a time inactive and suspended companies are used as harbours of manipulative minds. In order to ensure that such suspicious companies do not languish in the exchanges, over 450 such companies have been delisted and demat accounts of their promoters have been frozen; they have also been barred to be directors of listed companies. Around 800 companies listed on erstwhile regional exchanges are not traceable and a process has been initiated to declare them as vanishing companies.

Demonetisation appears to have led to an acceleration in the financialisation of savings. In parallel, there is a shift towards greater formalisation of the economy in the near term aided by the introduction of GST. Some of the parameters indicating such a shift are given below:

- The corporate bond market has started reaping the benefits of additional financial savings and transmission of interest-rate reduction. The corporate bond market issuance grew to Rs 1.78 lakh crore in 2016–17, the year-on-year increase was Rs 78,000 crore. With other sources of issuance in capital market the incremental variation was almost Rs 2 lakh crore in 2016–17 while it was Rs 1 lakh crore in 2015–16.
- This trend is further substantiated by the surge in primary market raising through public and rights issues. There were eighty-seven issues of public and rights for raising equity involving an amount of Rs 24,054 crore during 2015–16; in the first six months of 2017–18 itself there were ninety-nine such issues amounting to Rs 28,319 crore.
- Net inflow into mutual funds during 2016–17 increased by 155 per cent during 2016–17 over 2015–16 reaching 3.43 lakh crore. Net inflows in mutual funds from November 2016 to June 2017 were about Rs 1.7 lakh crore as against Rs 9,160 crore during the same period in the year before.
- Premia collected by life insurance companies more than doubled in November 2016; the cumulative collections from November 2016 to January 2017 increased by 46 per cent over the same period of the previous year. The premium collections witnessed 21 per cent growth for year ending September 2017 over the corresponding period in the previous year.

With a shift to a less-cash economy, India has taken a big leap in digital payment during 2016–17. Some of the trends are given below:

- 110 crore transactions valued at around Rs 3.3 lakh crore and another 240 crore transactions valued at Rs 3.3 lakh crore were carried out through credit cards and debit cards respectively. The value of transaction for debit and credit cards was Rs 1.6 lakh crore and Rs 2.4 lakh crore respectively during 2015–16.

- Total value of transactions with Prepaid Payment Instruments (PPIs) has increased from Rs 48,800 crore in 2015–16 to Rs 83,800 crore in 2016–17. Total volume of transactions through PPIs has increased from about 75 crore to 196 crore.
- During 2016–17, National Electronic Funds Transfer (NEFT) handled 160 crore transactions valued at Rs 120 lakh crore, up from around 130 crore transactions for Rs 83 lakh crore in the previous year.

With a higher level of formalisation, it has brought out related benefits to workers who were denied social security benefits in the form of EPF contribution, subscription to ESIC facilities and payments of wages in their bank accounts. A large increase in opening of bank accounts for workers, enrolment in EPF and ESIC are added benefits of demonetisation. More than 1 crore workers were added to the EPF and ESIC system post-demonetisation, which was almost 30 per cent of the existing beneficiaries. Bank accounts were opened for about 50 lakh workers to get their wages credited in their accounts. Necessary amendment in Payment of Wages Act was done to facilitate this.

The reduction in incidence of stone pelting, protests in J&K and Naxal activities in LWE-affected districts are also attributed to the impact of demonetisation as these miscreants have run out of cash. Their access to Fake Indian Currency Notes (FICNs) was also restricted. During 2016–17, the detection of FICNs for Rs 1000 denomination increased from 1.43 lakh pieces to 2.56 lakh pieces. At the Reserve Bank's currency verification and processing system, during 2015–16, there were 2.4 pieces of FICNs of Rs 500 denomination and 5.8 pieces of FICNs of Rs 1000 denomination for every million pieces notes processed; which rose to 5.5 pieces and 12.4 pieces, respectively, during the post-demonetisation period. This shows almost doubling of such detection.

In an overall analysis, it would not be wrong to say that country has moved on to a much cleaner, more transparent and honest financial system. Benefits of these may not yet be visible to some people. The next generation will view post November 2016 national economic development with a great sense of pride as it has provided them a fair and honest system to live in.

Demonetisation and Its Impact on Tax Collection

Posted on 30 August 2018

The Reserve Bank has twice released its reports stating that the demonetised notes of Rs 500 and Rs 1000 have been substantially deposited in the banks. A widely stated comment has been that just because most of the currency came back into the banks, the object of demonetisation has not succeeded. Was the invalidation of the non-deposited currency the only object of demonetisation? Certainly not. The larger purpose of demonetisation was to move INDIA from a tax non-compliant society to a compliant society. This necessarily involved the formalisation of the economy and a blow to black money. How has this been achieved?

- When cash is deposited in the banks, the anonymity of the owner of the cash disappears. The deposited cash is now identified with its owner, giving rise to an enquiry into whether the amount deposited is in consonance with the depositor's income. Accordingly, post-demonetisation about 1.8 million depositors have been identified for this enquiry. Many of them are being fastened with tax and penalties. Mere deposit of cash in a bank does not lead to a presumption that it is tax paid money.
- In March 2014, the number of income tax returns filed was 3.8 crore. In 2017–18, this figure has grown to 6.86 crore. In the last

two years, when the impact of demonetisation and other steps is analysed, income tax returns have increased by 19 per cent and 25 per cent. This is a phenomenal increase.

- The number of new returns filed post-demonetisation have increased in the past two years by 85.51 lakh and 1.07 crore.
- For 2018–19, advance tax in the first quarter has increased for personal income tax assesses by 44.1 per cent and in the corporate tax category by 17.4 per cent.
- Income tax collections have increased from the 2013–14 figure of Rs 6.38 lakh crore to the 2017–18 figure of 10.02 lakh crore.
- The growth of income tax collections in the two years pre-demonetisation was 6.6 per cent and 9 per cent. Post-demonetisation, the collections increased by 15 per cent and 18 per cent in the next two years. The same trend is visible in the third year.
- The GST was implemented from 1 July 2017, i.e., post-demonetisation. In the very first year, the number of registered assesses has increased by 72.5 per cent. The original 66.17 lakh assesses have increased to 114.17 lakh.

This is the positive impact of demonetisation. More formalisation of the economy, more money in the system, higher tax revenue, higher expenditure, higher growth after the first two quarters.

Formalisation of the Economy

Posted on 8 November 2018

Today we complete two years after demonetisation.

Demonetisation is a key step in a chain of important decisions taken by the government to formalise the economy.

The government first targeted black money outside India. Asset holders were asked to bring this money back on payment of penal tax. Those who failed to do so are being prosecuted under the Black Money Act. Details of all accounts and assets abroad which have reached the government resulted in action against the violators.

Technology has been used for both direct and indirect taxes to facilitate filing of returns and expanding the tax base.

Financial inclusion was another important step to ensure that even weaker sections became part of the formal economy. Jan Dhan Accounts have resulted in most people being connected to the banking system. The Aadhaar Law has ensured that direct benefit transfer of government support system reaches the bank accounts directly. The GST has further ensured that in the matter of indirect taxes, the tax procedures become simple. It is now becoming increasingly difficult to evade the tax system.

The role of cash

India was a cash dominated economy. Cash involves anonymity in transactions. It bypasses the banking system and enables its possessors to evade tax. Demonetisation compelled holders of cash to deposit the same in the banks. **The enormity of cash deposited and identified with the owner resulted in suspected 17.42 lakh account holders from whom the response has been received online through a non-invasive method.** The violators faced punitive actions. Larger deposits in banks improved the lending capacity of the banks. A lot of this money was diverted to the mutual funds for further investments. It became a part of the formal system.

The misconceived argument

An ill-informed criticism of demonetisation is that almost the entire cash got deposited in the banks. Confiscation of currency was not an objective of demonetisation. Getting it into the formal economy and making the holders pay tax was the broader objective. The system required to be shaken in order to make India move from cash to digital transactions. This would obviously have an impact on higher tax revenue and a higher tax base.

Effect on digitisation

The Unified Payment Interface (UPI) was launched in 2016, involving real-time payments between two sets of mobile holders. Its transactions have grown from Rs 0.5 billion in October 2016 to Rs 598 billion in September 2018. The Bharat Interface for Money (BHIM) is an app developed by NPCI for quick payment transactions using UPI. It is currently used by 1.25 crore people. The value of BHIM transactions has gone up from Rs 0.02 billion in September 2016 to Rs 70.6 billion in September 2018. The share of BHIM transactions in overall UPI transactions is about 48 per cent in June 2017.

The RUPAY card is used both at the Point of Sale (PoS) and for e-commerce. Its transactions have increased from Rs 8 billion before demonetisation to Rs 57.3 billion in September 2018 for PoS and from Rs 3 billion to Rs 27 billion in e-commerce.

Today Visa and Mastercard are losing market share in India to the indigenously developed payment systems of UPI and RUPAY cards whose share have reached 65 per cent of the payments done through debit and credit cards.

Impact on direct taxes

The impact of demonetisation has been felt on the collection of personal income tax. Its collections were higher in financial year 2018–19 (till 31 October 2018) compared to the previous year by 20.2 per cent. Even in corporate tax the collections are 19.5 per cent higher. From two years prior to demonetisation, direct tax collections have increased 6.6 per cent and 9 per cent respectively. In the next two years, post demonetisation the increase by 14.6 per cent (part of the year before impact of demonetisation in 2016–17) and an increase of 18 per cent in the year 2017–18.

Similarly, in the year 2017–18, the tax returns filed reached 6.86 crore, an increase of 25 per cent over the previous year. This year, as on 31 October 2018, 5.99 crore returns have already been filed, which is an increase of 54.33 per cent compared to the previous year till this date. The new filers added this year are 86.35 lakh.

In May 2014, when the present government was elected, the total number of income tax returns filers was 3.8 crore. In the first four years of this government, it has increased to 6.86 crore. By the time the first five years of this government are over, we will be close to doubling the assessee base.

Impact on indirect taxes

Demonetisation and implementation of the GST curbed cash transactions in a big way. An increase in the digital transactions is visible. This formalisation of the economy has led to the tax payer base increase from 6.4 million in the pre-GST regime to 12 million tax payers in the post-GST regime. The actual consumption of goods and services being recorded as part of the tax net has now increased. This has given a buoyancy to the indirect tax growth in the economy. This has benefited both the Centre and the states.

Every state, post-GST, is getting a mandatory 14 per cent increase in taxation each year. The fact that assessees have to now declare their business turnover not only impacts the indirect tax calculations, but also ensures that income tax arising out of them is disclosed in the tax assessments. In 2014–15, the indirect tax to GDP ratio was 4.4 per cent. Post-GST it has climbed up by at least 1 percentage point to 5.4 per cent.

Despite an annual income tax relief of Rs 97,000 crore given to the smaller tax payers and a Rs 80,000 crore relief given to the GST assesses, tax collections have gone up. Rates of taxes, both direct and indirect, have been reduced, but tax collections have gone up. The tax base has expanded. GST rates on 334 commodities which were paying an effective 31 per cent tax pre-GST have witnessed a tax reduction.

The government has used these resources for better infrastructure creation, in the social sector and rural India. How else could we visualise villages being connected by road; electricity in every home, 92 per cent coverage for rural sanitation; a successful Awas Yojana; a cooking gas connection in eight crore poor homes. Ten crore families are covered under Ayushman Bharat, Rs 1,62,000 crore is being spent on subsidised food, 50 per cent increase in MSP for farmers and a successful Crop Insurance Scheme. It is the formalisation of the economy which has led to 13 crore entrepreneurs getting Mudra Loans. The Seventh Pay Commission was implemented within weeks and the OROP was finally implemented.

More formalisation, more revenue, more resources for the poor, better infrastructure and a better quality of life for our citizens.

5

The Story of GST and How We Made It Work

The story of the Goods and Services Tax (GST) is a long and winding one. Though pioneered by the Congress, its MPs have tried to obstruct its passage through mindless dissent. Yet the BJP government managed one of the smoothest switchovers ever in one of the largest ever tax reforms in the country. The positive impact of the GST on direct tax is already visible. It is also helping the country's indirect tax base to expand. Notwithstanding some inevitable teething problems, the whole country became a single market.

Dissent or Disruption – The Congress Party's Position on GST

Posted on 2 August 2015

The report of the Select Committee on the GST has been submitted to the Rajya Sabha. The Constitution Amendment Bill has already been approved by the Lok Sabha. The Select Committee has recommended a five-year compensation to the states which suffer any revenue loss on account of the introduction of the GST.

History

The proposal for the introduction of GST was first mooted by Shri P. Chidambaram in his Budget Speech for the year 2006–07. After detailed deliberations and negotiations in the Empowered Committee of State Finance Ministers, the 115th Constitution Amendment Bill, 2011 was introduced by Shri Pranab Mukherjee, the then finance minister. It was referred to the Parliamentary Standing Committee which submitted its report in August 2013. The bill, however, lapsed with dissolution of the Fifteenth Lok Sabha.

Thereafter, the NDA government again held negotiations with the Empowered Committee and after an overwhelming consensus, introduced a bill incorporating certain changes which had also been recommended by the Parliamentary Standing Committee. The near unanimous recommendations of the Empowered Committee, which were entirely supported by Congress-ruled states, enabled the preparation of the eventual bill to amend the Constitution which was introduced by me as 122nd Constitutional Amendment Bill.

Rationale

The rationale of the bill is to simplify the complex indirect tax structure in the country. The present system involves multiplicity of taxes, absence of uniform rates of taxation, and the cascading effect of 'Tax on Tax'. It is also an impediment in the seamless transfer of goods and services across the country. The GST simplifies the indirect tax regime. It seeks to reduce cost of production, inflation, multiplicity of taxes and uneven taxation rates. Significantly, it also creates an ecosystem for seamless movement of goods and services across the country and cuts down transaction costs. It will broaden the tax base, result in better tax compliance and eventually increase the country's GDP. The GST resulting in better compliance will improve the revenue of the states and certainly do justice to a large number of lesser-developed states in the country. It is for this reason that most state governments and regional parties are supporters of the GST.

The Congress dissent

Three members of the Congress party have circulated a note of dissent to what is otherwise a consensus report of the Select Committee. I wish to comment on each of the points raised by the Congress party in its note of dissent.

- The Congress members have proposed that a rate of GST be fixed in the Constitution as not exceeding 18 per cent. This suggestion was not in the bill proposed by Shri Pranab Mukherjee. Even when Shri P. Chidambaram negotiated with the Empowered Committee, this suggestion did not exist. The rates of taxation are usually not fixed in the Constitution, more so when we live in a dynamic world. The rates have to be recommended by the GST Council depending on various factors such as economic conditions, revenue buoyancies etc., and incorporated in the GST laws. There may be some rationale to the rate recommended by the Congress party. However, this decision has to be taken by the GST Council and cannot be a part of the Constitution itself. The rates will vary depending on a host of factors.

- The Congress has further proposed that the expression 'supply' should not apply to goods and services supplied by one unit of a firm to another unit of the same unit of the firm. There was no such proposal in either Mr Pranab Mukherjee's bill nor in the proposal approved by Mr Chidambaram. In any case, GST charged on supply of goods and services would be liable to VAT and not have any cascading effect.
- The Congress proposes that the share of local bodies in the revenue buoyancy should be a part of the proposed constitution amendment. This goes contrary to the 73rd Amendment to the Constitution which provided for setting up state Finance Commissions which have the responsibility of making such recommendations. In any case, neither Mr Pranab Mukherjee nor Mr Chidambaram had accepted any such proposal.
- The Congress has further proposed that a state or a Union Territory with or without a legislature having a population not exceeding twenty lakhs should be given a special status. This was never Mr Pranab Mukherjee's or Mr Chidambaram's proposal. In any case, the provision for special category approval is based on a host of factors. Congress wants Goa to be a special category state under GST, but Goa has the highest per capita income in the country.
- The Congress has further proposed that electricity, tobacco products and alcohol for human consumption should be given the same treatment as petroleum in the amendment bill. This was not a proposal mooted by any of the Congress finance ministers. A consensus with the states would be effectively broken if this

suggestion of the Congress is accepted. Petroleum has been included in the GST but the GST would be levied and charged on the product only when the GST Council so decides.

- Congress has further proposed that the voting representation of the states in the GST Council, which has been kept at two-third should be increased to three-fourth. This would effectively reduce the Centre's voting power from one-third to one-fourth. This is contrary to the decision that Mr Chidambaram specifically took on 30 July 2013. The majority required in the GST Council for taking a decision is three-fourth. In fact, the Congress proposal would mean that if all the states get together and decide that the Centre should have a lower GST rate, they could deplete revenues of the Centre almost completely. India is a Union of states. Is it the Congress proposal that the Union should cease to economically survive? Is it their proposal that the Centre should have no say in the system of national taxation? The Congress appears to have made this proposal without adequate application of mind.
- The Congress has further proposed that any dispute with regard to GST should be adjudicated by a GST Tribunal chaired by a person who has been a Judge of the Supreme Court or chief justice of a High Court. The power of deciding the modalities of adjudication and settlement of disputes in the present bill is with GST Council. Political issues have to be settled politically and not by judges. The original proposal for setting up a Dispute Redressal Tribunal was rejected by the Standing Committee and the Empowered Committee of the State Finance Ministers. The UPA government accepted the suggestion of the Standing Committee. It is only an afterthought that the Congress has chosen to revive the proposal.
- The Congress party has asked for deletion of a two years transient provision which provided for an additional tax of 1 per cent to be credited to the exporting state. This provision has been added

in order to allay the fear of the manufacturing states which felt that they would initially lose some revenue. This is based on a unanimous decision of the Empowered Committee to which all Congress ruled states have agreed.

It was the Congress-led UPA government that proposed the GST in the 2006–07 Budget. The Constitution amendment was piloted by the UPA. The changes suggested by the Empowered Committee and the Standing Committee were accepted by the UPA government. The present government has not made any significant modifications to the same except to bring a consensus between manufacturing and the consuming states. The state governments belonging to the Congress party have consistently supported the proposal. Is it only out of an obstructionist attitude that the Congress party has adopted a negative role? Since Parliament is not functioning and there is no way to clarify these points before the same, I am constrained to place the above facts in public domain.

The Congress party and its leader may be upset with the government for political reasons. They may be upset with the electorate for the 2014 verdict. The Congress party should accept and seriously introspect after having ruled the country for the longest period of time, that negativism hurts the country. Should its obstructionist tendencies inflict an economic injury on the country?

The GST Experience

Posted on 1 July 2018

It has been one year since the country's switchover to a new indirect taxation system – the Good and Services Tax. One single tax replaced seventeen taxes and multiple cesses imposed by the central and the state governments. This had obviously necessitated every assessee to file multiple returns, have an interface with multiple inspectors and assessing authorities, suffer the cascading effect of having to pay tax even on the tax component already paid, having to pay tax separately in every state when movement of goods took place, to suffer the inordinate delays of multiple checkpoints and obstacles, and being fed up with the taxation system devises measures on how to bypass the tax system.

The very foundational idea of the Goods and Services Tax was not original. It had been experimented in several countries of the world. The Indian model had to be devised keeping several facts in mind. An indirect tax, unlike a direct tax, is regressive. In a country where diverse sections of population with different paying capacities, everybody pays the same rate of tax, the rate cannot be different for the wealthy and the not so wealthy as in the case of a direct tax. But in the selection of the commodities which are tax-free or less taxed, a differential could be made in a society like India. Secondly, India had multiple markets, each constituting a different market which needed to be consolidated. Thirdly, the essence of Indian federalism had to be respected. India is a Union of states where both the Union and the states have to be fiscally strong. A weak Union is detrimental to both national sovereignty and growth and weak states won't be able to deliver development. India is not a confederation of states and, therefore, strengthening of state revenues cannot be at the cost of central revenues. If the Union does not survive, what will happen to India i.e. Bharat – the Union of States?

The flawed UPA model of GST

My friends in the UPA and the Congress party occasionally raise questions as to why some chief ministers were not comfortable with the idea of GST during the UPA period. The fact is that almost everyone wanted the GST but not a single state was comfortable with the UPA's model of GST. There were two prime reasons for this.

Firstly, the UPA government lost the confidence of the states, including the Congress ruled states. In a move towards the single tax system, the UPA asked the states to abolish the CST. It promised the states that it would give them a compensation in lieu of the CST for a certain number of years. The states acted accordingly, abolished the CST and the central government owed the states several thousand crore as CST compensation. When the states demanded CST compensation, the Centre would look the other way. When I took over as the finance minister in May 2014, all the states, including the BJP ruled states, told me that they don't trust the central government because of what the UPA government had done. They will discuss GST only if past CST compensation is paid. I conceded that the UPA let-down of the states was unacceptable and in order to bridge the trust, despite pressures on the central revenue, I will clear the arrears of the central CST. I, accordingly, did that. The CST compensation was paid. The states were then willing to come to the table and move further on the GST.

The second reason why the UPA failed in its effort to bring the GST was that every state was apprehensive that during the transition period there would be a loss of revenue to the states. How would the states be compensated for the loss of revenue? Their demand seemed logical but UPA chose not to address it. The Constitution amendment proposed by the UPA had no provision for compensating the losing state. Manufacturing states like Tamil Nadu, Gujarat, Maharashtra and Karnataka were particularly apprehensive. They had raised a flag 'No Compensation No GST'. Having brought them to the negotiating table on the strength of the CST payment I agreed to pay to the states, after discussing in the GST Council, a 14 per cent increase of revenue for the first five years for any loss of revenue. The states jumped for this proposal and we succeeded in winning the trust of the states back for the GST enactment. Our positive commitment to the federal principles was unambiguously established.

The petroleum products issue

Both Rahul Gandhi and P. Chidambaram have repeatedly demanded that petroleum products be forthwith brought within the GST. When I speak to the Congress finance ministers in the states, they don't seem to be ready for it. But what was the UPA's own track record on petroleum products in the GST? The Constitution amendment proposed by the UPA permanently kept all petroleum products outside the GST. Thus, till such time that the Constitution was ever amended again (it is normally difficult to amend the Constitution), petroleum products would never be in the GST as per UPA. Having won the trust of the states, I used the inclusion of petroleum products as a bargaining issue with the states while conceding the CST and compensation payment to the states. I worked out a formula that petroleum products would be included in the Constitution amendment providing for the GST but the council can decide the date from which to bring them into GST. The states agreed. The UPA kept petroleum products permanently outside GST. On the contrary, we brought them back into the Constitution as levyable to GST and can gradually impose the GST when the GST Council so decides. For this I would continue to make my earnest efforts and, hopefully, when the states are more comfortable with the revenue position, it would be an ideal time to strike for a consensus between them.

The experience after one year

When the GST was to be launched on 1 July 2017, we were being advised by the Congress to postpone it. A reluctant government can never take reformist decisions. We went ahead. At the initial stage, we fixed the first set of rates. A large number of requests started coming from trades, industry and, therefore, we started rationalising the rates.

The initial few meetings of the GST Council started reducing the rates wherever it was desirable. If we look at the entire basket of goods and services, the rates today taken collectively are far lesser than under the previous taxation system. With the cascading effect of tax on tax going away, the liability in any case came down.

To develop a consensus, we passed the Constitution amendment enabling the GST unanimously. All legislations enabling the GST were passed unanimously. The rules were put before the GST Council. They have been approved unanimously. We have held twenty-seven meetings of the GST Council so far where every decision has been taken by consensus and unanimity. All the rates are fixed through consensus on the recommendation of the Rates Committee. Whenever there are contrarian views in the Council, a representative group of ministers of the state is constituted to work out a via media and we try to evolve consensus one way or the other.

I do realise that the delicate federal balance in India has to be maintained. The GST Council is India's first experience at cooperative-federalism-based decision-making authority. We cannot afford to risk a failure and, therefore, it is functioning to arouse confidence amongst all states. The meetings have always been consensus-based. The only area where unanimity seems to be lacking is the television bites that some ministers give after the meeting, which may be necessary for their own political position. I am willing to live with the experience of a healthy debate and unanimity within the Council and a show of dissent outside the Council meetings.

We have had amongst the smoothest switchovers in one of the largest tax reforms in the country. All the checkposts disappeared overnight. The system of input tax credit ensures that disclosures are made. The GST has encouraged enormous voluntary tax registration. Detailed calculations done in this year's economic survey show that as of December 2017, about 1.7 million registrants were those who fell below the GST threshold but nevertheless chose to be part of the GST. Similarly, more than 50 per cent of those who could have chosen to opt for the simpler composition scheme chose to register under the regular GST scheme.

To ensure further compliance, the e-Way Bill has been put in place. Once the invoice matching starts, evasion would become extremely difficult. The assessee's life has become easier. He files his returns online and his interface with multiple authorities is gone. The return filing process is also being simplified. The group of ministers has already worked out that mechanism. The overall weighable of the tax basket has come down. As the tax base increases, our capacity to rationalise taxes and slabs will increase further.

The very small businesses have been protected. Those with turnover of less than Rs 20 lakh don't pay GST. Those with a turnover up to Rs 1 crore can compound their GST with a payment of 1 per cent tax on the turnover and file a quarterly return.

A single slab

Rahul Gandhi has been advocating a single slab GST for India. It is a flawed idea. A single slab GST can function only in those countries where the entire population has a similar and a higher level of paying capacity. Being fascinated by the Singapore model is understandable but the population profile of a state like Singapore and India is very different. Singapore can charge 7 per cent GST on food and 7 per cent on luxury goods. Will that model work for India? Since GST is a regressive tax, the poor have to be given a substantial relief. Thus, most food items, agricultural products and the products used by the aam aadmi have to be tax exempt. Some others have to be taxed at a nominal rate. The others could be taxed higher. Eventually, as the collections improve, many more items from the 28 per cent category can possibly come down. Only sin products and luxury goods can remain there. There would also be a scope again, depending on the collection going up, to merge some of the mid category slabs but for that we have to see the progress of the new tax regime and the possible upward movement in the collections.

The tax effect

The impact of the GST on direct tax is already visible. Those who have to disclose business turnovers are now having to disclose their income for the purposes of the income tax. The direct tax collection has, therefore, picked up as per the initial indications. When we look at the GST performance in the first nine months, from July 2017 to March 2018, and add the entire amount collected – the CGST, SGST, IGST and the composition cess – we will get the sum total of the GST collection. In the very first nine months, the total amount collected is Rs 8.2–11 lakh crore if annualised, yielding a revenue growth of 11.9 per cent i.e. a tax buoyancy of 1.22, which has historically been achieved very rarely for indirect taxes and despite rates being lowered for consumers. As more and more anti-evasion steps will be put in place, the tax buoyancy will increase further. The GST will strengthen the country's tax base for the medium term, adding up to an additional 1.5 percentage points of GDP.

Today the states are getting a 14 per cent increase on the tax base of 2015–16 with the help of the compensation cess. Eventually, when the blocked IGST is gradually released to the Centre and the states, even without the compensation cess, most states would cross the 14 per cent growth target. It may also be borne in mind that even today the compensation requirement is minimal and the current level of compensation cess about Rs 7000 crore monthly are more than adequate to ensure that the states are compensated for any loss of revenue. Significantly, the GST is expanding the tax base of the less developed consuming states which will provide more resources for them to devote for development purposes.

The indirect tax base is expanding. There is a seamless flow of goods and services across the country. The 'doing of business' has become simpler. The switchover has taken place without any major disruption. The IT system after initial teething trouble is functioning much better. For all of this, I want to express my heartfelt thanks to and appreciation for the efforts of Revenue Secretary Shri Hasmukh Adhia, all the officers of the CBIC and revenue and tax departments of the Centre and all the states, officials of GSTN, and Chief Economic Adviser Arvind Subramanian.

There is always scope for improvement. Key areas of future action will include further simplifying and rationalising the rate structure and bringing more products into the GST. I am confident that once revenue stabilises and the GST settles, the GST Council will look into these carefully and act judiciously.

The biggest success of the GST has been that the GST Council has proved to be an extremely effective and powerful decision making federal institution. The finance ministers of the states have created history in the matter of federal governance. It has indeed been my privilege to have got the cooperation of each one of them. Thank you, finance ministers, for having collectively made the GST a historic transformation and an experience worth it for the country.

Eighteen Months of the GST

Posted on 24 December 2018

The GST was implemented w.e.f. 1 July 2017. It hasn't completed eighteen months of implementation as yet. The GST has been at the receiving end of a lot of ill-informed and motivated criticism. What has been its real performance?

The pre-GST regime

India had the worst indirect tax system anywhere in the world. Both the Centre and the state government were entitled to levy a set of taxes. There were seventeen taxes levied. An entrepreneur, therefore, faced seventeen inspectors, seventeen returns and seventeen assessments. The rate of taxation was exorbitantly high. The standard rate of VAT and excise was 14.5 per cent and 12.5 per cent respectively. To this could be added the CST and the cascading effect of tax on tax. The standard rate thus became 31 per cent on a large number of commodities. The assessee had only two options – either to pay a high rate of tax or evade it. Tax evasion was prevalent to a large extent. India comprised of multiple markets. Each state was a separate market because the rate of tax could be different. Interstate sales became inherently inefficient because trucks had to wait for hours and days at the state borders.

The GST impact on 1 July 2017

From the date of its implementation, the GST changed the situation radically. All seventeen taxes were combined into one. The whole of India became one market. The interstate barriers disappeared. Entry into the cities became open with the abolition of the entry tax. States were charging an entertainment tax ranging from 35 per cent to 110 per cent. This came down radically. Two hundred and thirty-five items were being charged at either 31 per cent tax or even higher. All except ten such items were brought down immediately to 28 per cent. The ten items were brought down to an even lower rate of 18 per cent. Multiple slabs were fixed transiently in order to ensure the tax of no commodity goes up radically. This contained the inflation impact. Most aam aadmi items were placed in the 0 or 5 per cent tax bracket. Returns became online, assessments will be online, multiple inspectors had disappeared. The states were guaranteed that for the first five years they will be ensured a 14 per cent annual revenue increase.

The revenue trends

A frequently made comment has been that the revenue position has been disappointing. The comment is based on an inadequate understanding of both the targets and the revenue increase. The targets set for the state in the GST regime is unprecedently high. Even though GST commenced on 1 July 2017, the base year for revenue increase has been calculated is 2015–16. For each year a 14 per cent increase is guaranteed. Thus, even when eighteen months have not passed since the launch of GST, on this day every state has a target of improving its revenue with three 14 per cent increases compounded annually over the base year of 2015–16. This is close to a 50 per cent being reached in the second year itself.

It is almost an unachievable target. Yet six states have already achieved it, another seven are within a striking distance of achieving it and only eighteen are still more than 10 per cent away from achieving it. By the third, fourth and fifth year, as in the case of VAT, the ability to increase revenues and closing the gap will substantially increase. Those states which do not achieve the target of 14 per cent are paid out of the compensation cess. The requirement of compensation cess in the second year is expected to be much lower than the first year. This increase in the tax collection has to be factored keeping in mind the significant rate reduction which has taken place in the GST. The reduction in monetary terms amounts to about Rs 80,000 crore per year. Notwithstanding the substantial tax reduction, the GST collection in the first six months of this year has shown a significant improvement as compared to the first year. The average monthly tax collected in the first year was Rs 89,700 crore as compared to Rs 97,100 crore per month in the second year.

The rate rationalisation

We were faced with a situation with a large number of commodities being taxed heavily in the pre-GST regime. The Congress legacy of indirect tax was a 31 per cent tax. We transiently put them in the 28 per cent slab. As the revenues kept increasing, we started bringing down the rates. Most of the commodities have seen tax reduced. Today, barring tobacco products, luxury vehicles, molasses, air-conditioners, aerated water, large TVs, and dish washers, all twenty-eight items have been transferred from 28 per cent to 18 per cent and 12 per cent. Only cement and auto parts are items of common use which remain in the 28 per cent slab. Our next priority will be to transfer cement into a lower slab. All other building materials have already been transferred from 28 per cent to 18 per cent and 12 per cent. The sun is setting on the 28 per cent slab.

Of the 1216 commodities which are used, broadly 183 are taxed at zero rate, 308 at 5 per cent, 178 at 12 per cent and 517 at 18 per cent. The 28 per cent slab is now a dying slab. Restaurants are being levied a tax compounded under the composition of turnover at 5 per cent. Assessees with turnover up to Rs 20 lakh are exempted from tax payment. Assessees up to Rs 1 crore turnover can get a composition by paying 1 per cent tax. The composition scheme for small service tax assessees is under consideration. Cinema tickets tax which was 35 per cent to 110 per cent has been brought down to 12 per cent to 18 per cent. The GST has helped in controlling inflation. Evasion has also come down.

The net effect

Lower rate of taxes, increased tax base, higher collections, easy for trade and least interface in assessments with a significant part of the tax rationalisation over, the growth percentage in the years to come will increase. The transformation has been done over a period of eighteen months. Any abrupt transformation could have been either detrimental to revenue or to trade.

The GST Council

The GST Council has had thirty-one meetings. It is India's first experiment with the federal institution. It is a body that has behaved with utmost responsibility. Several thousand decisions, including legislative drafting, rules drafting, notifications, fixing initial rates and rationalising rates have all been taken unanimously with consensus. The political noise outside is inconsistent with the harmony inside the Council.

A personal thought with regard to the future

With the GST transformation completed, we are close to completing the first set of rates of rationalisation – phasing out the 28 per cent slab except in luxury and sin goods. A future road map could well be to work towards a single standard rate instead of two standard rates of 12 per cent and 18 per cent. It could be a rate at some midpoint between the two. Obviously, this will take some reasonable time when the tax will rise significantly. The country should eventually have a GST which will have only slabs of zero, 5 per cent and standard rate with luxury and sin goods as an exception.

Those who oppressed India with a 31 per cent indirect tax and consistently belittled the GST must seriously introspect. Irresponsible politics and irresponsible economics is only a race to the bottom.

Why Agriculture, Rural Development and Healthcare Require a GST Council Type Structure

Posted on 20 March 2019

Yesterday, 19 March 2019, the GST Council held its thirty-fourth meeting. The GST was enabled by a Constitution Amendment which was unanimously approved by both the Houses of Parliament. Several legislations to implement the GST were passed by the Parliament. Laws relating to the state GST (SGST) were approved by all the state legislatures.

The GST has enabled a single indirect tax in the whole country. Its implementation, compared to several other countries in the world, has been extremely smooth. Some initial teething trouble are to be expected. Everyone learns from experience. Not only did the GST consolidate multiple taxes and multiple cesses, it eliminated barriers in the country overnight. The whole of the country became a single market. Inspectors were eliminated, taxes were reduced and the interface between the assessee and the department was reduced. The online filing of returns and assessment was the order of the day. The input tax credit prevented the cascading effect of tax on tax and ensured that the back chain in manufacturing and services was done through authorisation. A more efficient system detected leakages and improved the revenue collections. States have been guaranteed, for the first five years, a 14 per cent increase in annual revenue. For the first time since Independence, consumers have witnessed a continuous reduction of taxes.

The decision-making process of the Council

Chairing the Council in its initial years has been one of my most satisfying experiences. The quality of participation of state finance ministers and their supporting civil servants was extremely high. The debates in the Council were on issues of substance. There was no populism. Concern for revenue, consumers, industry and trade dominated the discourse. They concentrated on simplifying procedures. Members shed their political colours outside the meeting venue. To satisfy their political constituencies, some spoke outside the meeting but inside there was an atmosphere of positive suggestions. At times conflicting views and thereafter the consensus.

Thousands of decisions have been taken in the Council. These range from framing of new regulations, circulars, notifications and tariff fixation. Council was always prepared, based on market reports, to make changes wherever required.

The states effectively had a two-third voting right and the central government had a one-third voting right. All decisions had to be approved by at least three-fourth majority. This necessarily meant that the Centre and the states had to work together. Yet the Council set an incredible precedent which recognises the delicate balance of India's federalism by taking all decisions through consensus and not once putting any decision to vote. I hope this continues in future. The decision-making culture involved extensive discussions flagging various viewpoints and, thereafter, formulating the consensus. A consensus is never imposed, it evolves. Where consensus was not possible, the matter was not pursued.

The lessons from the GST Council

The GST Council has become India's first federal institution. Its working is a role model in other areas where federal institutions are needed in India. It displays the maturity of India's democracy and politics. When larger national interest requires, decision makers can rise to the occasion. It negates the popular impression that politicians of different shades of opinions will always be divided on party lines. It has worked to the benefit of industry, trade, consumers and has become the single most important tax reform in Independent India. The question, thus, is why can't this experiment be replicated elsewhere?

Agriculture, rural development and healthcare

Agriculture, rural development and healthcare are areas where, in larger national interest, the GST Council experience needs to be replicated. Both the central and the state governments have several schemes working for the betterment of the farmer. The agricultural sector needs a major support. Both the Centre and the states spend a large part of their budget in the sector. Similarly, the process of developing rural infrastructure and improving the quality of life in villages has now started. A lot more needs to be done in both agriculture and rural development. Should the Centre and the states only be competing and not supplementing each other's efforts? Should they not be pooling their resources to ensure that no overlap or duplication takes place and that the interest of the largest number is protected and enhanced?

The same is equally true on healthcare. Primary health centres, hospitals, health schemes for treatment of poor patients, supply of medicines at an affordable cost are all intended by both central and the state governments to ensure that affordable healthcare is available to the people. For those who cannot afford healthcare, it is available at the cost of the central and some state governments. Is overlap of expenditure necessary or should it be pooled and spent in an optimum manner?

Are elected governments intended to non-cooperate with each other or must they work on the principle of 'Bahujan Hitay Bahujan Sukhay'. West Bengal, Delhi, Odisha are amongst the states which have refused to implement Ayushman Bharat where every poor family gets up to rupees five lakh of hospitalisation support annually. Rajasthan, Madhya Pradesh, Delhi, Karnataka and West Bengal are non-cooperative in the PM Kisan scheme where small and marginal farmers get Rs 6000 income support annually. Is this in public or national interest? Is it necessary to act against the poor and allow the compulsion of competitive politics to take over?

Society has great faith in the wisdom of men and women. The country hopes that the wisdom prevails over transient political requirements.

Two Years After GST

Posted on 1 July 2019

Today, the GST regime enters its third year. The monumental restructuring of one of the world's clumsiest indirect tax system was not an easy task. The challenges to implement the GST were compounded by some outlandish and exaggerated comments of the not so well-informed. It would, therefore, only be fair to look back the last two years and analyse the implementation and the impact/consequences of the GST.

The pre-GST regime

In a federal structure, both Centre and states were entitled to impose indirect tax on goods. The states had multiple laws which entitled them to impose taxation at different points. There were twin challenges. Firstly, to get the states to agree because some of them felt they were losing their fiscal autonomy to tax and, secondly, to develop a consensus in the Parliament. The states were scared of the fear of the unknown. The critical point which enabled the government to persuade the states was to cushion them with a 14 per cent annual increase from the tax base of 2015–16 for a period of five years.

The GST merged all these seventeen different laws and created one single taxation. The pre-GST rate of taxation as a standard rate for VAT was 14.5 per cent, excise at 12.5 per cent and added with the CST and the cascading effect of tax on tax, the tax payable by the consumer was 31 per cent. The entertainment tax being levied by the states was from 35 per cent to 110 per cent. The assessee had to file multiple returns, entertain multiple inspectors and additionally face inefficiency – trucks being stranded at the state boundaries for days altogether.

The GST changed this scenario completely. Today, there is only one tax, online returns, no entry tax, no truck queues and no interstate barriers.

Consumer- and assessee-friendly

After two years, one can confidently argue, without fear of contradiction, that GST proved to be both consumer- and assessee-friendly. The high taxation of pre-GST era pinched the consumers' pocket and acted as a disincentive against tax compliance. The last two years have seen each of the meetings of the GST Council reducing the tax burden on consumers as the tax collections improved. An efficient tax system certainly leads to better compliance. The 31 per cent tax, which was temporarily 28 per cent, has seen the largest single reform. Most items of consumer use have been brought in the 18 per cent, 12 per cent and even 5 per cent category. Only luxury and sin goods remain in addition to some white goods. A sudden reduction of all categories can lead to a massive loss of government revenue leaving the government without resources to spend. This exercise had to be done in a gradual manner as the revenues increased. Cinema tickets, earlier taxed at 35 per cent to 110 per cent, have been brought down to 12 per cent and 18 per cent. Most items of daily use are in the 0 or 5 per cent slab. The loss to the revenue on account of this reduction collectively has been more than Rs 90,000 crore annually.

Widening tax base and higher revenue

The assessee base in the last two years has increased by 84 per cent. The number of assessees covered by the GST were around 65 lakh. Today they are at 1.20 crore. This obviously leads to higher revenue collections. In the eight months of 2017–18 (July to March), the average revenue collected per month was Rs 89,700 crore per month. In the next year (2018–19), the monthly average has increased by about 10 per cent to Rs 97,100 crore. The fear of the states today is that for the first five years they get a guaranteed 14 per cent increase. The lurking doubt is what will happen after five years? Every state has been paid its share of tax as also from the compensation fund, if necessary. We have just completed two years of GST. Already after the second year, twenty states are independently showing more than a 14 per cent increase in their revenues and the compensation fund in their case is not necessary.

Simplification and compliance

Businesses up to an annual turnover of Rs 40 lakh are GST exempt. Those with a turnover up to Rs 1.5 crore can make use of the composition scheme and pay only 1 per cent tax. There is now a single registration system which works online and the procedures for the trade and business are reviewed and simplified regularly.

A response to certain misconceived ideas

Many warned us that it may not be politically safe to introduce the GST. In several countries, governments lost elections because of the GST. India had one of the smoothest transformation. Within the first few weeks of the implementation, the new system settled down. There were a few protests in Surat. The issues were resolved. The BJP won all the Assembly seats in the Gujarat poll in Surat. In 2019, the BJP won the Surat seat by the highest margin in the country. Those who argued for a single slab GST must realise that a single slab is possible only in extremely affluent countries where there are no poor people. It would be inequitable to apply a single rate in countries where there are a large number of people below the poverty line.

The direct tax is a progressive tax. The more you earn, the more you pay. An indirect tax is a regressive tax. In the pre-GST regime, the rich and the poor, on various commodities, paid the same tax. The multiple slab system not only checked inflation, it also ensured that the aam aadmi products are not exorbitantly taxed. Illustratively, a Hawai chappal and a Mercedes car cannot be taxed at the same rate. This is not to suggest that the rationalisation of slabs is not needed. That process is already on. Except on luxury and sin goods, the 28 per cent slab has almost been phased out. Zero and 5 per cent slabs will always remain. As revenue increases further, it will give an opportunity to policy makers to possibly merge the 12 per cent and 18 per cent slab into one rate, thus, effectively making the GST a two-rate tax.

The role of the GST Council

The GST Council is India's first statutory federal institution. The Centre and the states jointly sit and decide. Both have pooled their fiscal rights in a collective forum to create one common market. My own experience of two years while chairing the GST Council, was that finance ministers of states, notwithstanding the political position their parties take, have displayed a high level of statesmanship and acted with maturity. The Council worked on the principle of consensus. This has added to the credibility of the decision-making process. I am sure this trend will continue in future.

6

Cutting the Gordian Knot on Article 370: Only the BJP Had the Will and the Vision

Article 370 and Article 35A discriminate against all those in Jammu and Kashmir who are Indian citizens but not 'state subjects'. They cannot vote or contest Assembly or Panchayat elections, they cannot get a government job, they cannot acquire property and their children are not entitled to admission to colleges. In short, these residents of the state are not entitled to the fundamental rights enshrined in the Indian Constitution, protecting them against discrimination on the basis of religion, caste, race or place of birth and equality of opportunity in government employment and reservations. Should a provision like Article 35A, which exists only because of Article 370, have a place in any civilised society? It is oppressive, discriminatory and violative of fundamental rights.

The Anti-Daughter Position in Jammu and Kashmir

Posted on 2 December 2013

Yesterday Shri Narendra Modi and Shri Rajnath Singh addressed a huge rally in Jammu and Kashmir. Jammu and Kashmir's integration with India has been an essential part of the ideology of the Bharatiya Jana Sangh and now the BJP. The BJP believes that Dr Shyama Prasad Mukherjee's vision of complete integration of Jammu and Kashmir was the correct vision for India.

The Nehruvian vision of a separate status has given rise to aspirations for the pre-1953 status, self-rule and even azadi. The desire of proponents of these three ideas has weakened the constitutional and political relationship between Jammu and Kashmir and the rest of the country. The journey of separate status has been towards separatism and not towards integration. It would be incorrect for anyone to interpret BJP's challenge for a debate on this issue as a softening of stand on Article 370.

Erroneous beliefs

The state laws in Jammu and Kashmir were consistently interpreted for over five decades to mean that a daughter in Jammu and Kashmir would lose her status as a permanent resident of the state as also the special rights and privileges available to her if she married outside the state. This was based on an erroneous belief that a wife followed the domicile of the husband. A large number of women in Jammu and Kashmir questioned the constitutional validity of this provision. A full bench of the High Court of Jammu and Kashmir, by a judgement dated 7 October 2002, reinterpreted the law and by a majority judgement held that a daughter marrying outside the state would not lose her status as a permanent resident. The

National Conference government which was in power in the state was represented in this case by its advocate general, M.A. Goni, who vehemently opposed the plea of the daughters.

The judgement records:

> Ld. Advocate General Mr M.A. Goni contended that a female descendent of a permanent resident of the state on marriage to a non-permanent resident of the state would lose the status of a permanent resident of the state and would not be permanent resident of the state as defined under section 6 of the state Constitution. He submitted that by marrying a non-permanent resident, a female descendent of a permanent resident of the state will not only lose the property which she may have acquired in the state before marriage as permanent resident of the state but she would also lose all special rights and privileges like employment in the state government, right to scholarship or any other such privileges as the government may provide. He further submitted that the status of the wife or the widow depends on the status of the husband and in case she ceases to reside in the state and takes permanent residence outside the state she would lose the status acquired by marriage with a permanent resident of the state.

This was the categorical position of the government of Shri Omar Abdullah's party, the National Conference. Dissatisfied with this judgement, the National Conference government filed an SLP in the Supreme Court.

In 2003, the PDP government in alliance with the Congress party was formed in the state. The PDP government followed an alternative strategy. They withdrew the SLP and introduced The Jammu and Kashmir Resident (Disqualification) Bill 2004 which attempted to statutorily nullify the progressive majority view taken by the High Court. The bill was enthusiastically supported by the PDP and the National Conference. It sought to withdraw the status of a permanent resident from a daughter who married outside the state. The bill was passed by the Legislative Assembly.

In March 2004, Shri Atal Bihari Vajpayee, the then prime minister suggested that the state government should find a solution to this problem. The PDP and the National Conference linked it to the upholding the special status of the state guaranteed under Article 370 of the Constitution.

After being passed by the Legislative Assembly, this bill was taken to the Legislative Council. It ran into some trouble with the chairman of the Legislative Council adjourning the house without voting and referring it back to the Assembly where it again got stuck. Recently, moves have again been made to re-enact the bill.

In 2010, a PDP member again introduced this bill as a private member's bill in the Legislative Council. Competitive statements have been made by leaders of the National Conference that they are committed to bring this bill. Special status and Kashmiri identity have been pitted against women's rights. Can Chief Minister Shri Omar Abdullah ignore a dubious track record of his party on this issue and indulge in discourteous tweets on the subject? It must be accepted by one and all that such discriminatory provisions which also compromise the right to live with dignity, have no place in Indian law.

The Problem With Articles 370 and 35A in Jammu and Kashmir

Posted on 4 December 2013

Narendra Modi's speech in Jammu invited Omar Abdullah's response. After a long time, Article 370 is being seriously debated in this country. An ill-informed debate had earlier linked the issue of Article 370 to a secular versus non-secular debate. Article 370 has nothing to do with secularism. My own study on the subject has revealed a very interesting dimension as to how Article 370 can turn into an instrument of oppression and discrimination against Indian citizens.

Article 370 is a special provision created only in relation to the state of Jammu and Kashmir. It is a temporary provision. It relates to the distribution of power between the Centre and the state. The central list in relation to Jammu and Kashmir was a small one. Most powers were vested in the state legislature. If any power had to be transferred from the Centre to the state, it required the concurrence of the state. Article 370 states as under:

370. Temporary provisions with respect to the state of Jammu and Kashmir

Notwithstanding anything in this Constitution

(a) The provisions of Article 238 shall not apply in relation to the state of Jammu and Kashmir.

(b) The power of Parliament to make laws for the said state shall be limited to

  (i) Those matters in the Union List and the Concurrent List which, in consultation with the government of the state, are declared by the president to correspond to matters specified in the Instrument of Accession governing the accession of the state to the Dominion of India as the matters with respect to which the Dominion Legislature may make laws for that state.

  (ii) Such other matters in the said Lists as, with the concurrence of the government of the state, the president may by order specify.

Explanation: For the purpose of this article, the government of the state means the person for the time being recognised by the president as the maharaja of Jammu and Kashmir acting on the advice of the council of ministers for the time being in office under the maharaja's proclamation dated the fifth day of March 1948.

(c) The provisions of Article 1 and of this Article shall apply in relation to that state.

(d) Such of the other provisions of this Constitution shall apply in relation to that state subject to such exceptions and modifications as the president may by order specify:

Provided that no such order which relates to the matters specified in the Instrument of Accession of the state referred to in paragraph (i) of sub clause (b) shall be issued except in consultation with the government of the state: Provided further that no such order which relates to matters other than those referred to in the last preceding proviso shall be issued except with the concurrence of that government.

Pursuant to the provisions of Article 370 (1) (d) the president of India by an order (not legislation) notified the provisions of Article 35A of the Constitution. The provisions of Article 35A read as under:

35A: Notwithstanding anything contained in this Constitution, no existing law in force in the state of Jammu and Kashmir, and no law hereafter enacted by the legislature of the state

(a) Defining the classes of persons who are or shall be, permanent residents of the state of Jammu and Kashmir or

(b) Conferring on such permanent residences any special rights and privileges or imposing upon other persons any restrictions as respects

(i) Employment under the state government.

(ii) Acquisition of immovable property in the state.

(iii) Settlement in the state.

(iv) Right to scholarships and such other forms of aid as

> the state government may provide, shall be void on the ground that it is inconsistent with or takes away or abridges any rights conferred on the other citizens of India by any provisions of this part.

There are, thus, citizens of India who have not been conferred the status of state subjects. The phrases 'state subjects' and 'permanent residents' are used interchangeably. Millions of people migrated to India in 1947. Those who settled in other parts of India have all the constitutional guarantees available to them. They are entitled to all fundamental rights available under the Constitution of India to the citizens. The unfortunate ones who migrated to the state of Jammu and Kashmir have been conferred citizenship of India. They can vote in national elections. They can hold property anywhere in India.

However, they have not been conferred the status of being state subjects under Article 6 of the Jammu and Kashmir Constitution. Being citizens of India, they are discriminated against. They cannot vote or contest elections of the Assembly, Municipality or Panchayats in the state. They cannot get a job in the state. They cannot acquire property in the state. Their children are not entitled to admission to colleges as state subjects. The bright ones amongst them cannot even get scholarships or any other type of aid from the state. Article 35A of the Constitution of India executively inserted pursuant to Article 370(1)(d) excludes the provision of 'this part' of the Constitution. 'This part' of the Constitution refers to Part III.

The effect of this would be that laws inconsistent with fundamental rights would be valid qua these persons. These citizens of India are not entitled to the protection of Article 14 (equality), Article 15 (prohibition of discrimination on basis of religion, caste, race or place of birth), Article 16 (equality of opportunity in matters of public employment and reservations), the fundamental rights under Article 19 including the right to free speech and the right to life and liberty under Article 21. They are not entitled to the freedom of practice and propagation of religion under Article 25. They are also not entitled to protection of interests available to minorities under Articles 29 and 30. The non-state subjects, who are citizens of India, who live in Jammu and Kashmir by virtue of Article 35A, are denied these protections. The pre-2002 position in relation to daughters who marry outside the state that they would lose their right of inheritance is based on the authority to discriminate against citizens of India, between citizens of India and state subjects which Article 35A confers.

Should a provision like Article 35A which exists only because of Article 370 have a place in any civilised society? It is oppressive against citizens of India. It is discriminatory and violative of fundamental rights. Article 35A was inserted in 1954. On a bare reading, it violates the basic structure of the Constitution. I wonder if its constitutional validity will be challenged at some point of time.

On Dr Shyama Prasad Mukherjee's Anniversary: How Nehru's Intolerance Towards Dr Mukherjee's Views Led to a Constitution Amendment Restricting Free Speech

Posted on 6 July 2018

Today the nation remembers Dr Shyama Prasad Mukherjee, an eminent parliamentarian, statesman and the founder president of the Jana Sangh. Dr Mukherjee formed the Jana Sangh when the Congress was the dominant political party. He formed the Jana Sangh as an alternative ideological pole. Today the BJP has replaced the Congress as the key ideological pole in Indian politics. Today, as we pay homage to Dr Mukherjee, I recall a forgotten chapter where

Dr Mukherjee's advocacy of Akhand Bharat led Nehru to amend the Constitution restricting Dr Mukherjee's free speech.

Free speech and the Constitution

The Constitution guarantees to all citizens the right to freedom of speech and expression under Article 19(1)(a). Under Article 19(2), the state can make laws restricting the exercise of this right subject to certain conditions. The conditions on which this right could be restricted were very minimal as drafted by the Constituent Assembly. However, the first amendment to the Constitution in 1951 and the sixteenth amendment in 1963 imposed further conditions on the right to free speech. Whereas restrictions in the interest of sovereignty and integrity of India, public order or to prevent the incitement of an offence are understandable, the one that raises several questions relates to a restriction which can be imposed in the interest of friendly relations with foreign states.

This restriction did not exist in the original Constitution adopted in 1950. This was introduced by the first amendment to the Constitution in 1951 and approved by the Parliament which as a central Assembly was duplicating earlier as a Constituent Assembly. Needless to mention that this was prior to the election of India's first elected Parliament in 1952.

The circumstances which led to this amendment have been discussed in detail in the book *Republic of Rhetoric – Free Speech and the Constitution of India* authored by Abhinav Chandrachud. The book traces the history of the entire debate on free speech from the Constituent Assembly till the publication of the book in 2017. It is a piece of legal literature which lawyers and lawmakers need to read. After reading the relevant chapter of this book, I went through the entire Parliament debate and the Select Committee recommendations in 1951 which prompted this amendment.

Why this amendment?

The restriction is very broadly worded. It empowers the state to prohibit free speech if it adversely impacts friendly relations with foreign states. The state can even make the exercise of speech in this regard a penal offence. The same would be constitutionally justifiable. The world is consistently changing and so are global alignments. Erstwhile opponents become allies or vice versa. Relations between foreign states can be based, amongst others, on historical and cultural factors, geographical proximity, security considerations or even trade relations. There are several other considerations which can impact our relations with foreign states. A debate in any liberal democracy on the policy that the government of the day follows would be perfectly permissible. Governments can be cautioned or appreciated for the course that they follow. They can even be criticised. In the absence of debate and even criticism, there would be only one opinion expressed which is detrimental to a democracy. Why then was this provision introduced?

The partition of India led to a huge exodus of population from India to Pakistan and vice versa. After the first few months, the tense situation started calming down. But in 1949–50, where on the one hand the raiders had invaded the state of Jammu and Kashmir, on the other hand there were many communal riots in East Pakistan which led to Hindu refugees migrating from East Pakistan into West Bengal.

Prime Minister Nehru and Pakistani Prime Minister Liaquat Ali Khan signed an agreement which is popularly known as the Liaquat–Nehru Pact or the Delhi Pact. Ostensibly it was aimed at confidence-building measures and securing peace so that the minorities in both the countries are protected. East Pakistan had a 30 per cent Hindu population which was rapidly decreasing. There were many in India who were opposed to the very idea of Partition.

Amongst the leading opponents was Dr Shyama Prasad Mukherjee. He was one of the key advocates of a united India which he referred to as Akhand Bharat.

Two days before the Liaquat–Nehru Pact was to be signed in April 1950, Dr Mukherjee, who was industry minister in the First cabinet as a Hindu Mahasabha representative, resigned from the cabinet in protest and took a strong public position against the Liaquat–Nehru Pact. He spoke extensively in Parliament and outside, opposing the pact and advocating his philosophy of Akhand Bharat in brief. Pandit Nehru overreacted to Dr Mukherjee's criticism. He interpreted the very idea of Akhand Bharat i.e. united India, as an invitation to conflict since the country could not be reunited other than by war. He, therefore, advised Sardar Patel to consider what action would be taken.

After consultation with constitutional experts, Sardar Patel's opinion was that he could not prevent Dr Mukherjee from propagating his idea of Akhand Bharat under the Constitution and if the prime minister wanted him to stop this, the Constitution needed to be amended. Dr Mukherjee, on the contrary, claimed that Pakistan wanted a war and was already at war with us having captured a part of our legitimate territory of Jammu and Kashmir and, therefore, to suggest that his speeches on Akhand Bharat would lead to a war was not acceptable.

The Parliament proceedings

The bill to amend the Constitution which, amongst others, contained the restriction relating to friendly relations with foreign states was introduced in Parliament. There were some amendments which had been necessitated because of the judgement of the Supreme Court quashing the ban on certain publications. The bill was referred to the Select Committee of Parliament. Those days ministers could also be members of the Select Committee. The prime minister himself became a member of the Select Committee. The Select Committee submitted a report within a week along with a note of dissent. The report of the Select Committee was debated in the Lok Sabha on 29 May 1951.

Several senior members such as H.V. Kamath, Acharya Kripalani, Dr Mukherjee and Naziruddin Ahmad, amongst others, questioned the need for this amendment. They argued that such a provision did not exist in any Constitution in the world. It was too widely worded and could even prevent a legitimate debate of foreign policy issues. It was argued that the Constitution had been in force for only sixteen months and it may not be prudent to bring a hurried Constitution amendment. But Pt. Nehru was determined to go ahead. His principal response was, 'If you criticise a head of a state or a foreign state, that country may launch a war against us. This would adversely impact India's sovereignty.' He argued that, 'We cannot imperil the sovereignty of the whole nation in the name of some fancied freedom which puts an end to all freedoms.'

Dr Mukherjee argued that such widely worded amendment could prevent a legitimate debate on issues pending with Pakistan, not merely on the treatment of minorities or what was happening in Jammu and Kashmir, it would also prevent us from commenting on issues relating to evacuee property etc. The bill was eventually passed and it became a part of the Indian Constitution.

The paradox

Was it intolerance against Dr Mukherjee and his philosophy which triggered this Constitution amendment? The answer is obvious. Panditji and Dr Mukherjee were ideological opponents. Panditji had once commented that he would crush the Jana Sangh. Dr Mukherjee had retorted that he would crush the crushing mentality. Their views on Jammu and Kashmir were diametrically opposite. History and subsequent developments have vindicated Dr Mukherjee's position on Jammu and Kashmir.

Since this provision was not a part of the original Constitution and has come by way of an amendment it could be put to a challenge. I do seriously believe that it could be vulnerable to a challenge based on the basic structure theory. Unquestionably, free speech is a part of basic structure of the Constitution and if an amendment dilutes it through an unreasonable restriction, it will be liable for challenge on the grounds of violation of the basic structure.

But the major paradox today is that the essence of this amendment was that a mere speech advocating Akhand Bharat or of a united India is a threat to the country, it can be an incitement to war and, therefore, any talk of the same could be prohibited. It could even be made a penal offence. The paradox in our jurisprudential evolution is that we have applied a different yardstick to those who want to dismember India and commit an offence of sedition.

This debate recently came to the forefront during the Tukde Tukde agitation at the Jawaharlal Nehru University. The 1962 judgement of the Supreme Court in Kedarnath Singh's case was repeatedly cited. The Supreme Court held, while disagreeing with an earlier privy council's decision on Article 124A with regard to promoting dissatisfaction against the government established by the law was to be followed, the same would be inconsistent with Article 19(2). The court interpreted Article 124A of the IPC to mean that utterances would be punishable under section only if they intended to incite violence or had a reasonable tendency to create disorder or disturbance to public order by resorting to violence. A speech per se advocating disintegration would not be sedition unless the element of violence was apparent.

Where it would stand today

In the past seventy years, this country has witnessed a change in the situation where Pandit Nehru amended the Constitution so that the demand for Akhand Bharat could incite a war and therefore should be prohibited. On the contrary, we were all told that to advocate a breakup of the country without inciting violence is legitimate free speech.

The Rule of Law and the State of Jammu and Kashmir

Posted on 28 March 2019

The seven decade history of the state of Jammu and Kashmir confronts changing India with several questions. Was the Nehruvian course, on which the state had embarked, a historical blunder or was it the correct course to follow? Most Indians today believe that it is the former. Does our policy today have to be guided by that erroneous vision or out-of-the-box thinking which is in consonance with ground reality?

The Article 35A misadventure

Article 35A was surreptitiously included by a presidential notification in the Constitution in 1954. It was neither a part of the original Constitution framed by the Constituent Assembly, nor did it come as a Constitutional amendment under Article 368 of the Constitution which requires an approval by two-thirds majority of both Houses of Parliament. It came as a presidential notification and is a surreptitious executive insertion in the Constitution.

It gives the state government the right to discriminate between two state citizens living in the state on the basis of declaring some as permanent residents while leaving out the others. It also discriminates between permanent residents of the state and all other Indian citizens living elsewhere. Lakhs of Indian citizens in Jammu and Kashmir vote in Lok Sabha elections but not in assembly, municipal or panchayat polls. Their children cannot get government jobs. They cannot own property and their children cannot get admitted to governmental institutions. The same applies to those who live elsewhere in the country. The heirs of ladies marrying outside the state are disinherited from owning or inheriting property.

How Article 35A hurt the people of Jammu and Kashmir

The state does not have adequate financial resources. Its ability to raise more has been crippled by Article 35A. No investor is willing to set up an industry, hotel, private educational institutions or private hospitals since he can neither buy land or property nor can his executives do so. Their ward cannot get government jobs or admission to colleges. Today, there are no major national or international chains which have set up hotels in a tourism centric state. This prevents enrichment, resource generation and job creation. Students have to travel all over, including to Nepal and Bangladesh, to get college admissions. Engineering colleges and hospitals, including super-speciality facilities set up by the central government in Jammu are lying underutilised or unutilised since professors and doctors from outside are unwilling to go there. Article 35A has prevented investment and dismantled the state's economy.

Article 35A, which is constitutionally vulnerable, is used as a political shield by many but it hurts the common citizen of the state the most. It denies them a booming economy, economic activity and jobs.

Our disappointment with the mainstream parties of the Valley

Governments at the Centre have always desired that despite political differences we must allow more space to the mainstream parties in the Valley so that the separatist space is shrunk. Three families, since 1947, dominated that mainstream space. Two of them are based out of Srinagar and one in New Delhi. Regrettably, they let down the people of the state. The two major mainstream parties, even when they condemned terrorism, always did it with 'ifs' and 'buts'. It is only their absolute distancing from separatism, violence and terrorism that can create an alternative space. Being soft in criticising separatism does no good. It is for this reason that their own space has shrunk. This is the country's disappointment with them.

The present situation

Why should the rule of law that applies to the rest of the country not apply to the state? Should violence, separatism, mass stone-throwing, vicious ideological indoctrination be allowed on the plea that, if we check it, it will have a negative effect? It is this misconceived policy that has proved to be counterproductive. Today, the present government has decided that the rule of law in the interest of the people of Kashmir Valley and the larger interest of India, must equally apply to the state of Jammu and Kashmir.

The Jamaat-e-Islami, in the last several years, has indulged in ideological indoctrination which provided the manpower resource for separatism. It transformed the Valley from the liberal land of Sufism to hardcore Wahhabism. It has been banned. Hundreds of its activists have been arrested. Its offices have been sealed. Its activities have been significantly curtailed. The Jammu and Kashmir

Liberation Front (JKLF), which was working over-ground, has also been banned. Several of its people have been arrested. Separatists and Hurriyat leaders, as also several undeserving cases numbering in hundreds, have had their security withdrawn. You cannot advocate a break away from India and expect India to secure you.

The NIA has cracked down on terrorist funding. The income tax department has swung into action after seventeen years and discovered several sources of anti-national funding. The CBI is looking into 80,000 gun licences given in recent years.

All this has witnessed insignificant protests, no mass stone-throwing incidents, and a reduction in domestic recruitment to terrorist organisations. The past few months have witnessed the neutralisation of the largest number of militants.

Developmental activities

Today, government offices are opening and working regularly. Attendance has gone up. Several corrupt officials have been booked and are in prison. Nepotism in appointments has been done away with. There are no interviews conducted. They have been abolished. Multiple legislations have been passed and several legislative measures taken by the central government for SC/ST and weaker sections have been extended to the state. Forty-two thousand new posts have been created in the last six months.

Infrastructure projects, including the Mass Rapid Transit Corporation for both the cities of Jammu and Kashmir, the Ring Road for the two cities, an AIIMS in both the regions, an IIT and an IIM in Srinagar and Jammu respectively are projects which have been resolved in the last few months and are progressing further. The state has become 'open defecation free' with 100 per cent sanitation. Every house has already been electrified. Several long pending projects in three regions have been cleared. Fifty new colleges in the state have been sanctioned and 232 schools upgraded. A lot of decentralisation of finances has taken place.

More power has been given to the Ladakh and Kargil Autonomous Hill Development Councils. A Ladakh Division has been created. A new university has been established in Ladakh.

The separatists and the terrorists have been badly hit. The two mainstream parties are only giving television bytes and their activities are confined to social media. The people of the state are welcoming the steps taken. They wanted peace and freedom from violence and terror. The rule of law is being enforced in the Valley and is ensuring people a safe and peaceful life.

Ek Desh Mein Do Vidhan, Do Pradhan

Posted on 1 April 2019

The two mainstream parties in Kashmir are increasingly losing their identity. The separatists and the terrorists want a part of the state to segregate from India. India will never accept this. It has already given a loud and clear message to both separatists/terrorists and Pakistan that azadi is not a distant possibility. It is an impossibility.

The statements by the two parties say that the constitutional link between the state and the country is based on solemn assurance of Article 35A. If there is no Article 35A, it will break the link. Some have even gone further and argued that two constitutional provisions constitute the revocable link which has to be maintained.

The argument is completely unacceptable. Article 35A was not there in 1947 when the Instrument of Accession was signed in the month of October. In 1950, when the Constitution came into force, it was not there. It was only surreptitiously inserted in 1954. How can it be the essential Constitutional link? The challenge is being heard by the Supreme Court. Why intimidate the court which is hearing the matter? History is never reversed by court judgements. The argument of revocability is as absurd as a suggestion that if the Indian Independence Act was revoked by the British Parliament, we will lose our Independence.

The National Conference president's statement today that we will demand the revival of the post of Wazir-e-Azam and Sadar-e-Riyasat is only intended to create a separatists' psyche. Little do these demandeurs realise how much they are hurting the country as also their own people. The new India will never allow any government to commit such blunders.

Why Jammu and Kashmir and a New Approach to Terrorism Will Remain a Key Political Issue

Posted on 15 April 2019

During the course of the election campaign, whenever issues relating to the terror attack at Pulwama and the air strikes at Balakot are raised, India's Opposition is on the back foot. Why are national security and terrorism-related issues being made into subject matters of electoral debate? This is a question they raise.

India's Opposition argues that elections have to be fought on 'real issues' and not on issues of national security. It is my endeavour to argue that national security and terrorism are the most important issues which concern India in the long run. All other challenges are capable of early resolution.

The conventional election issues

Conventional election issues in India related to poverty alleviation, employment generation, improving growth rates, the quality of life of Indians, and the provision for quality healthcare and education, besides creating world-class infrastructure and improving the quality of rural infrastructure. There are also additional areas which relate to the quality of leadership and probity in public life and preserving and strengthening democratic institutions. With India, for the past five years maintaining the global 'bright spot' position as the fastest-growing major economy, there is a lot more revenue available to the state year after year to complete these unfinished tasks.

Compared to very slow poverty depletion till 1991, the period subsequent to that has seen faster depletion of poverty. The 2011 census mentioned the BPL figure of 21.9 per cent. By 2021, this figure should be comfortably below 15 per cent and in the decade thereafter we will probably see poverty substantially depleted to negligible levels. Urbanisation will increase, the size of the middle class will grow and the economy will expand manifold. These will add to the number of jobs and as the experience of past three decades has shown in the liberalised economy, every section of citizens will benefit. These are all challenges that India is capable of capturing and resolving over the next decade or two. The India of 2030 and the India of 2040 will present a completely different look with the socioeconomic profile of the population having substantially changed. In this changed India, there will be a lesser role of caste in politics, the quality of elected representatives will improve and obviously the standards of probity will be much tighter.

Terrorism and national security

While the other above mentioned issues are all capable of resolution, where does India stand on the issue of national security and terror? In Punjab, the north east and the south, peace has been established.

There is Maoist terror in the central parts of India. The region where it operates is restricted, its appeal is narrow. As the economic profile of India moves upwards, it will become extremely difficult for the Maoists to sustain their violent movement to overthrow democracy. The security 'might' of the state is far superior to handle this movement.

The same, however, can't be said of what is happening in the state of Jammu and Kashmir and the terrorism emanating from the region.

Kashmir and terrorism

The most important issue which thus confronts India in the short, medium and even the long term, is how we handle the state of Jammu and Kashmir and terrorism emanating from Pakistan and from within.

The Congress party can be identified with the creation of the problem itself. When Pakistan did not reconcile to Kashmir being a part of India, the Congress party wished the issue away. It was its historical blunder on account of which we lost one-third of our territory. Instead of working for total integration, the party wanted a loose and liberal constitutional connect between the rest of the nation and the state under an erroneous impression that such an arrangement would further the cause of integration.

Article 370 was disastrously thought out as a constitutional connect between the rest of the country and the state. Article 35A was surreptitiously introduced in 1954. It catered to a separatist psyche and legitimised discrimination. The National Conference–Congress relationship was a paradox. From total trust in Sheikh Sahab to his arrest in 1953, from his reinstallation in 1976 to the dismissal of the Farooq government in 1984 and installing a government headed by Ghulam Mohammad Shah were amongst the many pitfalls. The 1957, 1962 and 1967 and even 1988 elections were rigged elections, thereby leading to further alienation of the people. All warnings were ignored and the separatists virtually took over the state in 1989–90, leading to violent civil disobedience.

Atrocities were practised on the minorities, including the Kashmiri Pandits, the Sikhs and others, and an ethnic cleansing of the minorities was undertaken. The UPA wasted its ten years with a set of sham policies while the Jamaat-e-Islami and other fundamentalist organisations were busy transforming the liberal Islam of Sufism in the Valley to a more fundamentalist form of Wahhabism.

The NDA experimented with supporting a regime of the regional mainstream party in the state. Obviously, the experiment did not succeed since the PDP could not come out of the clutches of the Jamaat-e-Islami agenda. Thereafter, the central government, for the last few months, has sent out a clear message that terrorism will not be acceptable in the Valley. Terrorists are being liquidated in large numbers by our security forces. Their modules are being cracked up. The rule of law is effectively being imposed. The activities of the separatists have been curtailed. Terrorism from across the border is attacked at the point of origin. Our historical view on Article 370 and Article 35A continues to guide our vision.

Who is best suited to eliminate terror?

To an emerging economy, the cost of fighting terror and its perpetrators across the border is huge. Civilian lives are lost. Our security personnel are martyred. The security apparatus interferes with the lives of ordinary citizens. The aftermath of terror and all preventive action creates social tension and even strife. Development in the state of Jammu and Kashmir has suffered due to terror. Tourism has been adversely impacted. Both democracy and secularism have been casualties in the Valley. The cost of maintaining a large security force and equipment amounts to money meant for development and poverty alleviation being spent on fighting terror or its handlers.

How can Jammu and Kashmir, the attitude of Pakistan and terrorism not be important issues in India?

An important question before the country is: who is best suited to handle the issue of Jammu and Kashmir and terrorism? It obviously can't be solved by those whose policies created the problem and who are no longer willing to change their track. It can't be solved by those who linked battle against terror with votebank politics of their political parties. It can't be solved by those who believe that a loose constitutional connect will lead to integration even though the experience of seven decades is to the contrary.

This failed obsolete thought has to be rejected. The people of Jammu and Kashmir have to be at the centre point in our strategy. They deserve a special relationship with India; they deserve opportunities, peace and security of life; they need freedom from terror. A state free from terror itself will imply much less of a security presence.

Terror supported from across the border can't be fought either with velvet gloves or a policy of appeasement. The two regional parties have played a disappointing role. Of late, they are more strident in advocating secession of the state if firm measures are taken. The soft measures have not worked. The current leadership of the Opposition parties has hardly a roadmap except to tread on the path to disaster.

This challenge can obviously be resolved with a fresh approach which is uncompromising on terror, uncompromising in its determination to enforce the rule of law and committed to total integration. A strong government and a leader with clarity is alone capable of resolving the Kashmir issue. This will necessarily require a reversal of the historical blunders of the past.

The issue of Jammu and Kashmir and terror continues to remain the biggest challenge before India. It relates to our sovereignty, integrity and security.

Part Three

The Days of Dynasty Are Over

7

How the Congress Party Lost Its Way

A dynasty flourishes or declines in correlation to the charismatic power of the personality at the head. The earlier Congress leaders were able to carry the party on the strength of their leadership. The recent crop lacks both personal chemistry and ideology. Bereft of ideas and will, they are mere epigones who resort to fake issues and slogans even emptier than the 'garibi hatao' of Indira Gandhi in the 1970s.

The Diversionary Tactics of the Congress

Posted on 20 December 2013

The Congress party has not realised the challenges that it faces. It has no answers to reviving the economy or cleansing itself from the allegations of corruption. It further does not know how to politically deal with Narendra Modi. Rather than its organisation being strengthened and the charisma of its leaders being built up, it believes that Modi can be politically countered either by the CBI or by outlandish comments of its leaders. Home Minister Shri Sushil Kumar Shinde's statement that the Centre is considering the appointment of a Commission of Enquiry on the alleged snooping charges, only establishes that the Congress party has failed to learn the lessons from its electoral defeat.

The 2G spectrum allocation was a monumental fraud. The Congress believes it has resolved the issue through a cover-up report of the Joint Parliamentary Committee. Even the notes of dissent submitted by the Opposition MPs have not been considered. The Adarsh scam involved a loot of public property by private persons. The Congress CM of Maharashtra, Ashok Chavan, had to resign on the issue. Today, the Congress believes that it has resolved the issue by denying the sanction to prosecute Ashok Chavan and by the cabinet rejecting the report of the Enquiry Committee probing the Adarsh scandal.

The Congress party had highlighted the issue of alleged snooping on a lady by the Gujarat police. The lady's family has already clarified that it was a security measure on their own request. Notwithstanding that clarification, the Gujarat government has appointed a commission of enquiry headed by a retired judge to look into the whole issue. The commission at present is functioning. Rather than deal with the problems of economy and corruption, the home minister's statement that the government is considering the appointment of a commission of enquiry by the central government on the same issue comes as a surprise. Notwithstanding the constitutional impermissibility of the central government appointing a commission on the issue, the Congress party has merely reaffirmed that it is not concerned with the problems facing the country. It believes that petty, vindictive politics alone suits its modus operandi.

With a JPC cover-up of the 2G spectrum allocation scam, the country needs a Commission of Enquiry to look into the whole issue. The report of the committee which examined the Adarsh scam has to be implemented and the guilty prosecuted. State governments of Rajasthan and Haryana need to probe allegations of land scandals involving a key member of the first family of the Congress party. Rather than clear itself from the charges of corruption on all these issues, the Congress party feels that by diverting attention away from the principal issue, it can get a political advantage. Such moves will serve no useful purpose.

Why Is the Congress So Demoralised?

Posted on 13 January 2014

I have in the past few weeks made two comments which I wish to refer to. Firstly, that the Congress has lost the will to effectively fight the 2014 election. It is squeezing itself out of the contest. Secondly, with the result of the elections to the state Assemblies declared on 8 December 2013, the UPA government has evolved from a lame duck to a dead duck. Notwithstanding these two comments, political experience dictated that the Congress will at least make an effort to fight back. Resilience, after all, is an essential aspect of Indian politics.

I am, however, surprised at the complete collapse of the Congress to fight back in adversity. Except for routine functioning of the government such as meetings, file clearance or approval of routine items at the weekly meetings of the union cabinet, paralysis has completely engulfed the government. Even the arrogant responses and the exaggerated tweets of some of the ministers have disappeared. The blame game has started. Some union ministers privately refer to the non-political approach of the Prime Minister's Office and the others maintain a position of 'the boy doesn't listen to anybody'.

We in the BJP have been in power only in 1997, 1998 and 1999. We supported a government for a brief period from the outside in 1989. For the remaining time we have been in Opposition. Our lowest point was when we got two seats in Lok Sabha in 1984. Notwithstanding the debacle we did not compromise on ideology. We did not lose heart. We did not wait a day before deciding to fight back. Even in 2004, when we lost the election, we went down fighting and were proud of our performance. The communist parties have remained confined to only a few states. Their strength at the national level is limited and yet they continue their politics with a sense of purpose.

Why is it that the Congressmen find themselves so demoralised today? Is it because they have been in power for too long and cannot survive without being in office? Is it because of arrogant behaviour, scams and misuse of institutions like the CBI? They are scared of the very idea that without power their accountability may increase. A lot of ministers are now planning life after May 2014. Disillusionment is writ large in their attitude. Does anyone remember a single decision that the UPA government has taken in the past few months? Are Congressmen willing to seriously introspect what has gone wrong?

The problem of dynastic parties is that their strength is co-existent with and co-terminus with the potential of that generation of the dynasty which controls the party. A Pt. Nehru or Indira Gandhi could carry on the party on the strength of their personality. If the contemporary generation does not have that potential, the party collapses because of inadequate charisma of that generation of the dynasty. A structured party with a galaxy of leadership and a defined ideology still survives even in adversity. A dynastic party will sink or swim with the dynasty.

Nervousness in the Congress

Posted on 31 January 2014

As the elections appear closer, the nervousness in the Congress party has become more visible. Each one is frantically concerned about his own position rather than wanting the Congress party to get ready for a spirited fight.

Amethi was a fortress of the Congress party. It is Rahul Gandhi's constituency. It has been nourished by the family for four decades. The very idea that the Raja of Amethi, Sanjay Singh, may contest against Rahul Gandhi was enough to scare the Congress party's de facto prime ministerial candidate. The Raja of Amethi had to be accommodated in the Rajya Sabha from Assam. A firewall of sorts has to be created around Amethi to secure the constituency. Additionally, deals are being worked out with the SP and the BSP not to put up candidates from the minority community against the sitting MP. In the process, not only has the leader of the Congress party displayed his personal nervousness but the party's prospects in Assam have been considerably damaged. States in the North East and Jammu and Kashmir are particularly sensitive and want their own candidates to be elected to the Parliament. Senior leaders from Haryana, Himachal Pradesh and Chhattisgarh who should have been leading the party's campaign in this election have sought nominations for the Upper House.

The position of the allies is no different. The Trinamool Congress, the DMK and the TRS amongst the major allies have already drifted away from the UPA. Amongst the current allies the principal ones are the NCP and the National Conference. The NCP has been giving conflicting signals on a daily basis. The statements of its leaders on the 2002 Gujarat riots go contrary to the Congress party's line. The National Conference has realised that an alliance with the ruling party of New Delhi will be counterproductive to it in the Kashmir Valley. It is preparing itself for a break.

No state unit of the Congress party in recent history had the courage to defy the central leadership. Most Congressmen from Andhra Pradesh led by the chief minister have decided to defy the party line on Telangana. The next in store will be cross voting in the Rajya Sabha elections in Andhra Pradesh. All this could lead to a split in a state which provided the largest number of seats to the Congress both in 2004 and 2009.

And finally my friend, Mr P. Chidambaram, the union finance minister, appears to be planning life after the North Block. He is an extremely competent lawyer. Parliament's loss will be Supreme Court's gain. From the kind of statements he is making and the academic questions he is posing to his opponents, I suspect that he is practising to get back to column writing. I am sure his columns will make an excellent read.

Parliament Pandemonium Exposes Congress' Incompetence

Posted on 13 February 2014

We have repeatedly maintained that the UPA has lost the will to rule. Its ability to take and implement political decisions has come into severe questioning. What has happened today is on account of the UPA's inability to handle the political situation arising out of the proposal to create the state of Telangana. The Congress party itself is vertically split. Its members of Parliament from Andhra Pradesh are predominantly responsible for ensuring that Parliament is unable to function effectively. Its chief minister has ensured that administration in the state is completely paralysed.

Today's incidents in the Lok Sabha is a serious blow to India's parliamentary democracy. Dangerous and prohibited devices are used to block parliamentary proceedings. Members are unsure of what has actually happened. As against this, the BJP, including all its members from both Telangana and Seemandhra are taking a cohesive stand in support of the creation of the state of Telangana while simultaneously addressing the legitimate concerns of the people of Seemandhra. Regrettably, the UPA has completely failed in this regard. The present crisis is directly on account of this failure. It is the Congress and Congress alone which must take the responsibility for completely mishandling the situation. Today's theatre of the absurd could have been avoided only if the Congress leadership had done adequate homework and been able to control its own members.

Empty Rhetoric By the Congress Party

Posted on 8 July 2016

The Congress party has run out of ideas. It has perfected the art of scoring self-goals. The latest example is the press conference that its spokesperson held on 7 July 2016 alleging a telecom scam of Rs 46,000 crore.

Under the well-established policy of the government of India, telecom service providers pay to the government of India license fee and spectrum user charges on a revenue sharing basis. A CAG report from February 2016 has stated that the six telephone providers, between the period 2006–07 to 2009–10, have under reported their revenues to the extent of Rs 46,000 crore, thereby depleting the share of the Union government in license fee and spectrum user charges by about Rs 5000 crore. The CAG report was received by the telecom department in February this year and its supporting documents were received in June 2016 and the same are now being scrutinised so that the telecom department can take further action in the matter. As per parliamentary procedure, the CAG report is now pending before the public accounts committee.

The pertinent question is: how is this a scam of the NDA government? The under reporting by the telecom service providers relates to the period when UPA was in power. The UPA government, under its very nose, allowed this under-reporting. The Final CAG report pointed it out in February 2016 and only three weeks ago have the documents been sent by the CAG to the telecom department. Notwithstanding the fact that the issue is pending before the PAC, the telecom department, which is processing these documents, will take action. What is act of omission and commission by the present government? An impropriety took place during the UPA government for which the present government will take action.

The question, however, is the pathetic plight of the Congress party. Notwithstanding the fact that this impropriety took place during the UPA government, the Congress spokesman made an empty noise about this being an NDA telecom scam. Shrillness, non-application of the mind and a belligerent rhetoric seem to be the strategy of the Congress party. It is a pity that the party has been pushed to this desperation.

Has Prime Minister Narendra Modi Already Given to the Poor Much More Than What the Congress Promises?

Posted on 25 March 2019

No political party has betrayed India for more than seven decades other than the Congress party. It gave to the people of India many slogans and very little resources to implement them.

The Nehruvian era pushed India to the 3.5 per cent rate of growth. When the world was moving fast and opening up, we decided to regulate our economy. Indiraji understood slogans better than economics. Inflation, unemployment, corruption and erroneous policies hindered India. A large part of the economic reforms unleashed in 1991 was to undo what she did. In 1971, she gave her legendary slogan 'Garibi Hatao'. Her economics was not about increasing production and generating wealth, but only about redistribution of poverty. She supplemented her 1971 slogan while promising in election after election, the welfare of the largest number. Shri Rajiv Gandhi had a historic opportunity to remove poverty. Initially, he showed a desire to do so. But his government got caught in unsavoury controversies, preventing any significant and major changes.

In 1971, the Garibi Hatao slogan was given by Indiraji. For two-third of the last forty-eight years her party has been in power. Yet, they left behind a legacy of poverty.

The UPA government, between 2004 and 2014, conferred a large number of 'rights' without the necessary resources to implement them. The legendary bank loan waiver was announced at Rs 70,000 crore – a one-time measure. Of this only Rs 52,000 crore were actually allocated, a significant part of which went to the businessmen of New Delhi (CAG report). The MGNREGA was a rural scheme where Rs 40,000 crore used to be promised every year and the actual spent was in the nature of Rs 28,000 to Rs 30,000 crore.

Today, the Congress president has announced that those whose income is below Rs 12,000 per month, would be given a subsidy to 'attain' that income subject to Rs 6000 per month. This announcement is an admission of the fact that neither Indiraji nor her son and certainly not the UPA government controlled by her descendants, was able to remove poverty. The Congress in general and the Gandhi family in particular, since the Garibi Hatao slogan was given, has ruled India for more than two-thirds of that period. If it has failed to even address poverty during this period, why should India believe it? Even though the details of the scheme are now known, it was said that the payment will be by DBT. The Congress party's internal economist has said that there will be no additional burden on the fiscal deficit.

The loan waiver bluff

In Punjab, Madhya Pradesh, Chhattisgarh, Rajasthan and Karnataka the Congress party promised a loan waiver. In most places, the promise remains unfulfilled. The party, thus, has long legacy of slogans with no resources. It has a history of bluff announcements. Karnataka so far has spent only Rs 2600 crore, Madhya Pradesh Rs 3000 crore and Punjab Rs 5500 crore. The farmers are still waiting.

The income support

The landless and poor, amongst the villagers, get a MGNREGA payment. Minimum wages for the labour have been raised by 42 per cent. Today even most industrial workers get more than Rs 12,000 a month. The minimum starting salary in government after the Seventh Pay Commission is Rs 18,000 a month. A small and marginal farmer, besides home, road, toilet, electricity, cooking gas subsidies, crop insurance, MSP payment, will also get an income support.

The Opposition's sabotage of the pro-poor initiatives

If the Congress party and its friends have so much concern for the poor in India, why is it that its states are going slow in certifying the list of small and marginal farmers who are entitled to receiving the instalment of PM KISAN? Why are some of the states such as West Bengal, Odisha and Delhi, amongst others, not implementing Ayushman Bharat? What is the fault of their poor farmers that they want to make them pay?

How the Narendra Modi government supports the poor

In the last five years, the government headed by Prime Minister Shri Narendra Modi introduced the DBT through the banking system. Besides subsidies for food, fertiliser, kerosene, fifty-five ministries handed over subsidies to the poor through the DBT which was enabled by Aadhaar. The Congress opposed Aadhaar in Parliament and challenged it before the Supreme Court. Ironically, they now want to use the same mechanism. How much is today being given to the poor through Aadhaar, DBT or otherwise? If all other payments are also made through DBT, what will the total amount to?

Total payment from fifty-five ministries to bank accounts under different schemes	Rs 1.8 lakh crore
Add food subsidies	Rs 1.84 lakh crore
Add fertilisers subsidy	Rs 75,000 crore
Add PM KISAN payment for income support	Rs 75,000 crore
Add Ayushman Bharat subsidy hospitalisation for 50 crore people	Rs 20,000 crore
Total	**Rs 5.34 lakh crore**

The simple arithmetic is if multiple bank transfers to the five crore poor families, the existing payment to which is mostly being done. The above averages Rs 1,06,800 annually as against Rs 72,000 which is what the Congress now seeks to promise through the DBT mechanism.

Note: In addition to the above Rs 5.34 lakh crore, there are several other schemes which provide several more thousands of crores more to the poor. What is given towards Awas, cooking gas, electricity, sanitation and many other government social schemes is additional. If the Congress party's announcement is tested on simple arithmetic, Rs 72,000 for five crore families works out to be Rs 3.6 lakh crore, which is less than two-thirds of what is being given – a bluff announcement.

The Congress Manifesto 2019 – A Charter to Weaken India

Posted on 2 April 2019

Sitting in the Opposition from 2004 to 2014, I used to listen to the tall promises in the Congress Budgets. An early lesson that I gave to myself was, 'Don't go by what is said, the devil is always in the details.' In the little time available, I have read the fifty-three pages of the Congress manifesto. My worst fears have come true.

The Tukde Tukde manifesto

Point 30, p. 35, otherwise an innocuous entry which deals with review of laws, rules and regulations, repeals Section 124A of the Indian Penal Code which defines and then punishes one accused of sedition. Even for terrorists and hardcore criminals, it underlines the principle that 'bail is the rule and jail is the exception.' It seeks to dilute the provisions of the Armed Forces Special Powers Act (AFSPA). After having been spurned on various occasions to have a dialogue with the separatists who want to settle for nothing other than cessation from India, it promised to have a continuous dialogue with them. It promises to dilute the presence of the Armed Forces in the Valley.

The Congress is the principal creator of the Jammu and Kashmir problem. It created a special status; it unconstitutionally brought in Article 35A. It rigged the 1957, 1962, 1967 as also the 1988 Assembly elections. This eroded the confidence of the people of Jammu and Kashmir and now its manifesto only brings smiles on the faces of the separatists and the terrorists. A reference to 'Kashmiri Pandits' and their ethnic cleansing from the Valley is conspicuously absent in the manifesto.

The Congress has always been soft on terror. Late Shri Rajiv Gandhi introduced TADA. Later the Congress revoked it. It revoked POTA. Now it wants to go further soft on separatism and terrorism. There is only a lip sympathy in the assault required on Maoists violence, which Dr Manmohan Singh had described as the greatest threat to India. In the recent elections, as also in the case of JNU and urban Maoists, Congress and Congressmen have always flirted with the Maoists as fellow travellers.

Nyay bluff

Most economists have already rubbished the Congress party's Nyay. Between the Centre and the states, we are already giving to the poorest 20 per cent much more than what Nyay promises. As the economy expands to depleting poverty, further amounts can also be increased. To my initial query whether it will be reworking of the existing schemes or over and above the existing, the Congress

Spokesman boasted that it will be over and above. I went through the detailed paragraphs in point 9, p. 19. It contains the following statements:

- Fiscal prudence will be maintained.
- There will be pilots and testing phases.
- It will be implemented in phases.
- On how it will be funded, the Congress says that it will be funded from the future expansion of the economy.

Nyay, in the manifesto, has now become a joint scheme of central and the state governments thereby diluting the initial announcement. The state governments may well suggest that these existing subsidies are more than what Congress promises. To the vexed question of what happens to the existing subsidies, the manifesto says that 'only merit-based subsidies will continue'. So, the Centre will retain the power to say that some subsidies can be subsumed, diluted or abolished since they are non-merit based while in others the number of beneficiaries reduced since with every passing year many people are moving out of poverty.

Farm loan waivers

The Congress does not commit to the loan waiver but says that it has done so in several states. If you look at the track record of Karnataka, Punjab, Madhya Pradesh and Chhattisgarh, not even a miniscule effort has been put in. Even the PM-KISAN is on hold in Congress states.

Public health

It is extremely desirable that public health institutions be strengthened. The Congress is only giving slogans on healthcare.

Shri Narendra Modi has implemented the Ayushman Bharat where 50 crore people get free hospital treatment.

Women's reservation in legislatures

In 2010, as the leader of Opposition in the Upper House, I was instrumental in having the Constitution Amendment Bill passed in the Rajya Sabha where the Congress brought it. In the next four years, it did not press for it in the Lok Sabha. How can its track record be believed?

The GST

The manifesto repeats that the Congress will try for single rate GST. Today most food items are taxed at zero. Aam Aadmi items are taxed at 5 per cent. The 28 per cent slab is almost over. In the next round, the two standard rates of 12 per cent and 18 per cent will be merged into a mid-rate. Thus, you will have, besides the non-merit goods, goods and services, taxed at zero, 5 per cent and at about 15 per cent. The Congress says that irrespective of the product and the category of consumers using it, there will be one single rate. This effectively means that electronic goods, air-conditioners, television sets, washing machines should be taxed at the same rate as food items, chappals and coarse cloth. Rahul Gandhi got this wisdom from Singapore which does not have poverty. Both rice and Mercedes cars in Singapore are taxed at 7 per cent.

The manifesto compromises national security and has sham and bluff promises with little detailed understanding of the subjects involved. It is an irresponsible document never to be implemented, since the Congress looks a certain loser.

A Convenient Season for Being a 'Proud Hindu'

Posted on 29 April 2019

In the late 1980s and the early 1990s, the VHP would distribute stickers which became a launching pad for its slogan गर्व से कहो हम हिन्दू हैं. Barring the BJP, a few groups endorsed it, while others denounced this slogan as a symbol of communalism. I am sure those still active in the VHP from that era would have had the last laugh when the Congress leader and its candidate from Bhopal, Digvijay Singh, felt compelled to publicly announce, 'I too am a proud Hindu'. A fundamental disagreement with Nehruvian secularism, as practised in the 1950s, was that Panditji believed that Hinduism was old-fashioned, fundamentalist and obscurantist. He believed that it stood in the way of developing a scientific temperament.

This politics continued for decades. In a multi-cornered election, parties like the SP, the BSP, the RJD and, of late, even the TMC, went a step further than the Congress. They created fear in the minds of minorities and endeavoured to develop a vote combination of a specific caste or a group and that of the Muslim minority. They owed their survival to this polarisation. A significant attempt to dissent from this practice was undertaken by senior BJP leader, Shri L.K. Advani, in the 1980s and the 1990s. He strongly argued against a theocratic state, equality for minorities but his larger point was that secularism could no longer become a euphemism for majority bashing. He argued his case in modern vocabulary.

A large part of India started seeing a rationale in this. The majority community was liberal, tolerant but no longer apologetic about its own religious credentials. The Congress never understood the power of this sleeping giant. The Shah Bano legislation brought by Shri Rajiv Gandhi was a result of his inability to gauge the reaction. This mistake continued even through the UPA government where instead of treating the poor as a class, the then prime minister, Dr Manmohan Singh, announced that the minorities have a first right on the national exchequer.

Meanwhile, the socioeconomic profile of India changed in slowly consolidating and enlarging India's middle class. The middle class is aspirational. It has strong concern on national security. It is religiously inclined but not communal. At the same time, it will not accept majority bashing as the definition of secularism. The attitude of this class towards national security issues such as terrorism and a special status of Jammu and Kashmir, is extremely strong. At the same time, its reaction on both Ayodhya and Sabarimala is self-evident. This has created fear of the backlash in the minds of those who conventionally indulged in majority bashing and were compromising on issues of national security. Let us analyse some of the recent episodes.

Rahul Gandhi

Without getting into the larger issue of whether a person can inherit his grandmother's caste, the Congress has suddenly decided to proclaim its president as a Janeu-dhari Brahmin. He has now been declared a Shiv Bhakt. He does not miss an opportunity to visit temples and makes an event out of such programmes. His religious orientation was not visible in either 2004, 2009 or 2014.

Is he willing to clarify his stand on the statements that Mehbooba Mufti and Omar Abdullah are regularly making, literally supporting soft-separatism? He gets away by saying, 'I had some other views but I went by my party's views on Sabarimala,' but still not willing to spell out his stand on either Ram temple in Ayodhya or Sabarimala.

On national security, his stand has been highly questionable. He wants the sedition laws to be withdrawn. He wants the AFSPA to be removed and the army personnel in Jammu and Kashmir to be diluted. He had the audacity to visit JNU in support of those who raised the slogan 'अफजल हम शर्मिंदा हैं, तेरे कातिल जिंदा हैं' and 'भारत तेरे टुकड़े होंगे, इंशा अल्लाह इंशा अल्लाह'.

He has, to date, not explained his presence at JNU.

Digvijay Singh

The Congress candidate from Bhopal is a well-known majority basher. He claimed that the Batla House encounter during the UPA government was a fake one. He carried on a campaign in support of the terrorists and against the security forces. He even visited Azamgarh to meet the relatives of deceased or arrested terrorists. He holds the patent for manufacturing the theory of 'Hindu terror.' He took it to an illogical conclusion till the whole theory was busted. Today, realising the wrath of the electorate, he has become 'proud' of his Hindu credentials.

The AAP

The AAP has no answers. Its leaders supported those who raised the highly objectionable slogans at JNU. The party's sympathy for jihadis and separatists is apparent. Besides supporting slogans like भारत तेरे टुकड़े होंगे, इंशा अल्लाह इंशा अल्लाह, it has, for months together, held up the file at the Delhi Sachivalaya to grant sanction to the Delhi police to prosecute those who raised these slogans. Its heart is with the jihadis and separatists but it realised that the electorate in Delhi never accepts parties or candidates with credentials of this kind. The AAP has one simple question to answer: why is sanction not being given for prosecuting those who raise these anti-national slogans?

But the hypocrisy of the AAP climaxed when, in the last few days, its only lady candidate from Delhi shed her family legacy of ultra-left leaning parents, who were important interlocutors seeking a pardon for Afzal Guru, and started wearing not only her religion but her caste, her father's caste and her husband's caste on her sleeve. I was wondering why those brought up in an atheist environment start displaying their religion and caste publicly for political convenience.

India is a land of patriotic people. The contrarians are merely a fringe. The fringe can be a disgruntled lot getting a disproportionate voice on electronic and social media, one cannot belong to the fringe and win elections. This is the power of democracy. Religiosity is suddenly being discovered. Majority bashing has been replaced by a self-proclaimed title of a 'proud Hindu' or even a 'Punjabi Hindu Kshatriya'. Today, even atheists will wear their religion and caste on their sleeves. elections, after all, are a convenient season for all the neo-converts.

8

Exposed: The Limitation of Dynasty Politics

The problem with dynastic politics is that when the dynasty fails to deliver, the party itself fails. It means the party never asks the right questions and until it asks the right questions, it will not get the right answers. Instead of examining what it did wrong or how new leaders can be encouraged to grow, it merely decides that, if one member of the dynasty has failed to perform, let's look to another one. The diminishing returns of a dynasty-based party are visible. A Gandhi has not been prime minister for twenty-five years. With no effective Gandhi around, just ask yourself what Rahul Gandhi has to offer the country. The party is losing the will to fight adversity.

5 December 2013: The Congress Party Stops Trying

Posted on 5 December 2013

The voting has been concluded for the election to the five state assemblies, which went to the polls. The results are anxiously awaited. The exit polls indicated that the Congress is likely to receive a drubbing almost everywhere. The Exit Polls only indicate the likely results. They are subject to the normal margin of error. Notwithstanding this limitation of the Exit Polls they indicate a trend. The Congress appears to be completely demoralised. In the last phase of the elections, the Congress leaders almost abandoned the election campaign for Delhi Assembly. Mrs Sheila Dixit virtually fought all alone. Yesterday, the Congress spokespersons were conspicuous by their absence in the discussions on the Exit Polls. If this is the demoralisation that the Exit Polls give to the Congress party, I wonder what would happen when the actual results come in.

There is never a last day in the calendar of politics. It is an ongoing calendar. You never lose unless you stop trying. The Congress has stopped trying. This is precisely true for the Delhi elections that were abandoned by its central leadership. The mess on the economic front that the central government created, serious allegations of corruption, a policy paralysis and a non-inspirational leadership has demoralised the Congress cadres. Unless the Congress party responds to this reality, it will never find the correct answers. The relevance of charisma of a dynasty is never a long-term answer in politics. When the political parties become a crowd around a family, the strength of the party becomes synonymous with the capacity of that family. The party itself has become a dynastic party. If the dynasty cannot deliver, the party itself fails.

I am only waiting to see how the Congress party reacts to the results of the Polls on 8 December 2013. Observing this Party closely, I have no doubt that they will not ask the right questions. Unless they ask the right questions, they will not get the right answers. I will not be surprised, considering the traditional thinking of the Congress, if their solution to the problem is 'if one member of the family fails, let us try another'.

Congress Develops Cold Feet on Rahul

Posted on 17 January 2014

The Congress party has decided not to have a prime ministerial candidate. Instead their campaign will be led by Shri Rahul Gandhi. The diminishing returns of a dynasty controlling a party are now visible. In twenty-five years, a Gandhi has not been the prime minister of this country. India, indeed, is changing. The Gandhis can control a party but not the nation. It was nervousness in 2004 that kept the dynasty away. It is the prospect of defeat staring in the face, which is responsible for the reluctance to announce Rahul Gandhi as the prime ministerial candidate in 2014.

This was never the original intention. In December 2013 Sonia Gandhi had declared that the prime ministerial candidate would be announced at an appropriate time. In his recent press conference, Prime Minister Manmohan Singh gave testimonials to Shri Rahul Gandhi as a prime minister. Why did the party develop cold feet then?

The Congress is losing the will to fight an adversity. This was first visible in the Delhi Assembly elections. One poorly attended meeting of Shri Rahul Gandhi and no national leader came to address a meeting in Delhi thereafter. The nervousness is palpable now. Why puncture your only card in an adverse political environment?

There is no fire in the belly left to fight adversity. You can duck a comparison with Narendra Modi particularly when opinion polls indicate a large difference in the personal ratings of the two. Maybe it is a belated realisation of reality on part of the Congress. If there is no prospect of forming a government, why announce Shri Rahul Gandhi as a prime ministerial candidate!

The prime minister has put on a brave front. He proclaimed that victory in 2014 will be Rahul Gandhi's. Will the defeat also be debited to his account? I doubt it. The Congress party functions on the premise that the Gandhis never make a mistake. They never fail. It is the party that fails. It is the advisers who wrongly advise them. There is no accountability of the Gandhis in the party. After all, they are the party.

The Rahul Gandhi Interview

Posted on 28 January 2014

Arnab Goswami's interview with Rahul Gandhi was a lesson for the interviewer. There are advantages in letting the guest speak. By speaking, the guest may even expose his own inadequacies. After watching the interview and reading its transcript, the question that crossed my mind was: what has Rahul Gandhi to offer to this country?' or 'Is he too confused to get into the specifics and therefore goes into the generalities? I deal with some of the comments made in the interview.

Why is there no prime ministerial candidate?

The answer was clearly unconvincing. We all know that the MPs of the ruling party alone elect a leader, who is the prime minister.

We equally know that projecting shadow prime ministers is neither unconstitutional nor extra-constitutional. It happens all over the world.

On changing the system and empowerment of people

We are a parliamentary democracy. That is the system best suited for India. Which is the alternative system that Rahul Gandhi has in mind? He says he believes in democracy, in opening up the system, in RTI and giving power to the people. These are his differences with Narendra Modi. I doubt very much if these are areas of difference. Everybody in Indian politics has to believe in democracy, openness and in empowering the people. Why should he give himself a self-certification that he believes in RTI and empowerment. The fact that candidates are decided by a few people may be happening in the Congress party. In the BJP the block units and district units recommend candidates to the state units. The state units bring them to the central election committee. It is only after extensive consultation that the candidates are decided.

Even for the prime ministerial candidate we have gone through an informal process of galaxy of leaders being presented before the party and the people and the most suitable one is finally declared. The de facto prime ministerial candidate of the Congress party is decided on the basis of the family he belongs to. If Rahul Gandhi was a member of any other political party he would still be struggling to become a party office bearer. He needs to speak about the Congress party needing a change and not the whole system.

On making India a manufacturing hub

What has the UPA done in the last ten years in this regard? China's core competence is low cost manufacturing. Consumers prefer to buy goods which are cheaper. To make the manufacturing sector in India competitive, the manufacturing sector needed to be incentivised in terms of a modest interest rate regime, a world class infrastructure, competitive cost of utilities particularly power, trade facilitation, a globally competitive taxation regime, quick decision-making and labour regime flexibility. Even though the last of these is politically more challenging, has the UPA government even moved an inch with regard to the other reforms required? The answer is a clear no.

Comparison between the 1984 and the 2002 riots

In 1984 the slogan 'Khoon Ka Badla Khoon' started in the afternoon of 31 October 1984 at AIIMS where Mrs Gandhi's body lay. Congress leaders were seen leading the mobs. Sikhs were massacred at thousands of places. Nowhere did the police fire a single bullet to disperse mobs. Cases were not investigated. A Commission of Enquiry was constituted which came out with a sham report. The judge heading the commission was subsequently made a Congress party member of the Rajya Sabha. Justice evades the victims even now.

In Gujarat thousands of people were arrested. The badly over-powered police fired at several places. Almost 300 rioters were killed in police firing. Thousands of prosecutions were filed. Hundreds of people have been sentenced. The chief minister of the state government personally went through several inquiries including the Supreme Court constituted SIT and no evidence was found against him. Where did Rahul Gandhi get this idea that in 1984 there was no participation of the state?

On corruption

The Congress party has tied up with a convicted leader in Bihar. Without Lalu Prasad Yadav there is no RJD. Rahul Gandhi has looked the other way when it comes to allegations against, the chief minister of Himachal Pradesh, Shri Vir Bhadra Singh. He pays lip sympathy to probity when former chief minister of Maharashtra, Ashok Chavan, is bailed out. He chooses to keep quiet on the 2G spectrum allocation and the coal blocks allocation. He believes that some legislation will resolve the menace of corruption.

The most startling statement Rahul Gandhi makes in the interview is: 'I am absolutely against the concept of dynasty, anybody who knows me knows that and understands that.' Surely Mr Gandhi you don't expect India to believe you on that.

The Squeezing Out of the Congress Party

Posted on 23 February 2017

The 2014 general elections delivered an absolute majority for the BJP and an overwhelming majority for the NDA. This was a surprise for many. The bigger surprise, however, was that the Congress got relegated to just forty-four seats in Parliament.

Since May 2014 India has seen many state and local elections. The BJP has increased its vote in each of these elections. It has done exceedingly well in states like Maharashtra, Haryana and Assam, where it traditionally played second fiddle to regional parties. The results of the local elections in Odisha and Maharashtra have shown that the BJP is capable of winning major states on its own. The first message of these elections is that the BJP has become a pan-India party which is now fast spreading its roots even in the eastern and southern states. The forthcoming election for the Karnataka Assembly will reassert this.

But what about the Congress? In Odisha, it got squeezed out of the contest. In Maharashtra, it got pushed to third or fourth place in most cities. It is not even a major contestant in states like Tamil Nadu, West Bengal and Uttar Pradesh. It is struggling to survive by becoming the tail-ender in an alliance in these states. Many in the Samajwadi Party are wondering if it was worth leaving 103 seats for the Congress in Uttar Pradesh. Is the Congress willing to do an introspection as to why this is happening?

Having denied the Congress the position of being the ruling party, the electorate is now well on its way to deny it a role even as a principal Opposition. Once out of the power, the Congress refused to accept the reality. Its disruptive role in Parliament has projected it more as a fringe rather than a mainstream political party. It has failed to behave like a natural party of governance. It is seen as anti-reformist, anti-growth. The scandals of 2004–14 continue to tumble out.

The Congress party's stand on demonetisation of high value currency is costing it dearly. Tax evasion enables a small percentage of the population to unjustly enrich itself at the cost of the exchequer. Public resources get reduced and hence the expenditure on the vast section of population is reduced. The poor have overwhelmingly supported the demonetisation. The Congress party has lost its traditional constituency of the poor electorate to the BJP.

In any case, a party which has governed India for more than half a century cannot afford to take a stand which supports excessive use of cash and ridicules the new tools of technology which will enable digital transactions to be a substitute for cash. The Congress has lost its image as a responsible political organisation. From a natural party of governance, it has moved to the fringe. Its policies have alienated its constituency of the poor aam aadmi.

Parties which adopt dynastic succession as an alternative to merit-based leadership creation suffer from a natural disadvantage. Tall leaders do not grow in such parties. The strength of the party overlaps with the charisma of the current generation of the dynasty.

If the current representative of the dynasty lacks the ability to lead the party or the country, the party suffers. It becomes a crowd around a fading dynasty. This now seems obvious in the case of the Congress.

Refuge in Wayanad and a Refuge Away From Varanasi

Posted on 25 April 2019

Today, two major political developments have taken place. The first was the huge roadshow of the prime minister of India, Shri Narendra Modi, at Varanasi from where he is contesting the 2019 election. The roadshow culminated in the customary Ganga aarti. If the size of the support expressed at the roadshow is any indication, the prime minister is well on the way to repeating or even increasing the 2014 victory margin.

Even a casual visitor to Varanasi would tell you the difference the prime minister has made in his constituency in the last five years. The new highways, the arterial roads, the ghats, the railway station, the airport, the steamer in the Ganga and the modernisation of the electricity systems are only a few examples of the change that has happened in Varanasi. The proposed corridor connecting the Ganga ghats with the Kashi Vishwanath temple puts a new life into one of the world's oldest cities.

The second important development is the surreptitious announcement by the Congress party, fielding a political lightweight against the prime minister. The build-up of the last two weeks had been that Priyanka Gandhi would be fielded against the prime minister. She rejoiced in giving daily bytes to the media that she was ready to take on the prime minister. Her brother claimed that the party was building up the suspense for an eventual thriller.

Obviously, she quietly chickened out of the contest. I am deeply disappointed with the Congress party's decision of not fielding Priyanka Gandhi from Varanasi. The last two months that she has been in the public life have driven home the point: India has changed, dynasties don't matter.

The myths of Priyanka Gandhi stand eroded. India's conventional wisdom has been 'बंद मुट्ठी लाख की, खुल गयी तो ख़ाक की'. The myth 'Priyanka will make a difference' was worth a lakh. Today the myth has lost its value. The cards are out in the open for public scrutiny. The Gandhis must introspect on the plight of Amethi and Rae Bareli in the last forty years and compare it to what the prime minister has done in Varanasi in the past five years.

I had only hoped that Varanasi will give the new India an opportunity to decide the fate of a tried, tested and successful leader as against a new political dynast. Just repeating the same five sentences several times a day and not getting out of the obsession of 'हमारा परिवार' does not impress New India any more. I am sad that New India has been denied the opportunity to establish that it does not accept inexperienced dynasts with no other credentials. India is not a banana republic. It is the world's largest democracy.

There is one additional point that this episode established. It is only juvenile politics, where a family lives under an illusion that people will accept it irrespective of credentials, which persuades you to build a climax of Priyanka taking on the prime minister and then suffer the wrath of the anti-climax.

9

How the Nehru–Gandhi Dynasty Has Eclipsed Other Giants

Do you know the name of Sardar Patel's father? If not, it's because everyone else's contribution to building the nation has been erased by the apotheosis of the Nehru–Gandhi dynasty whose names have been pasted on to airports, streets, stadiums and universities for decades. But within political dynasties lie the seeds of their own failure. Dynastic political parties like the Congress leave no space for merit, talent, organisational structure or internal democracy. The family is all. But India is an aspirational society where such dated notions of noblesse oblige no longer find any followers.

What Was the Name of Sardar Patel's Father?

Posted on 27 November 2018

The debate whether India should be a dynastic democracy has been ignited by a self-goal of the Congress party. The prime minister's mother's age was made a subject matter of the electoral debate. His father's anonymity was commented upon as an inadequate credential of the prime minister. The argument given was that if you represent the legacy of a well-known family, it is a political point in your favour. Millions of talented political workers who come from modest family backgrounds would fail by the Congress's test of leadership. Merit, talent, ability to inspire and lead would not be a virtue. The Congress considers only a great surname as a political brand.

On hearing this rationale, I asked a few well-informed friends of mine three questions:

- What is the name of Gandhiji's father?
- What is the name of Sardar Patel's father?
- What is the name of Sardar Patel's wife?

None of my well-informed friends had a definitive answer. This is the tragedy of Congress politics and its impact on the nation. Gandhiji led the most extraordinary freedom movement of India. He created, through political awareness, Satyagraha and non-violence, an environment where the British found it impossible to continue in India. Sardar Patel's contribution was second to none. Besides being a frontline leader of the freedom movement, he, as the deputy prime minister and home minister of India, negotiated the transfer of power with the British. He negotiated the integration of India with over 550 rulers. He gave to India, within the short period of a few months, its present geography. Incidentally, Gandhiji's father was Karamchand Uttamchand Gandhi, Sardar Patel's father was

Jhaverbhai Patel and his wife's name was Diwali Ba. No photographs of his wife or details are available even after extensive research by modern-day historians.

The officially glamourised family

The reason for this is simple. Decades of Congress rule, naming colonies, localities, cities, bridges, airports, railway stations, schools, colleges, universities, stadiums after one family was intended to declare the Gandhis as India's royalty. They were officially glamourised as the blue-blooded family of India. The others did not matter. In fact, upon Sardar Patel's death in Mumbai, Prime Minister Nehru requested many of his cabinet colleagues that the best tribute to the Sardar would be to work on the day of his funeral and not go to Mumbai. The then head of state and several union ministers defied the advice. The proposal for building his statue at Vijay Chowk was rejected. The country had to be satisfied with the installation of his statue at a traffic roundabout on Parliament Street.

Many believe that Sardar Patel was a farmer leader because of his participation in Bardoli Satyagraha. On the contrary, he was one of Ahmedabad's most successful practising barristers. Panditji is passed off as a great lawyer though he never argued a single case in his entire career. He only went to court once for reasons of tokenism to sit behind senior lawyers led by Bholabhai Desai who was arguing for the three INA officers in the mutiny trial inside the Red Fort.

The danger of ignoring the great stalwarts

The dangers of officially glamourising one family at the cost of those who made a far greater contribution is dangerous both for the nation as also for the party to which they belong. The contribution of other great stalwarts like Patel and Subhash Chandra Bose is downplayed.

Members of one family are projected as being larger than life. Their aberrations become national aberrations. The party adopts them as its ideology. When Panditji promoted his daughter as his successor, he laid the foundation of India as a dynastic democracy. When the daughter, in 1975, turned dictatorial, it became the party's ideology to convert India into a 'disciplined democracy'. When the Sikh were massacred in 1984, communal polarisation against them was considered a legitimate electoral strategy. Today 'anti-BJPism' leads the Congress to a situation where it can tie up even with its political rivals and sympathise with the Maoists, separatists and disruptionists.

The country pays a price for dynastic policies as we have witnessed in several regions. Three families – two of them in Srinagar and one in New Delhi in the last seventy-one years, have played with the destiny of Jammu and Kashmir. The consequences are obvious. Following the dynastic pattern of leadership within the Congress, several other parties have followed the same principle. In such organisations there is no inner party democracy, there are no ideological principles. There is a complete flexibility to switch sides and align with your erstwhile political opponents. In Andhra Pradesh, NTR filled up the political vacuum and created an alternative to the Congress. Gradually the party went into a control of the present chief minister who is willing to switch sides in every general election. There is no second line of leadership and the option offered is of 'a coalition of rivals'.

The political parties in question also pay a price. The only leaders who have a political future are the ones which are acceptable to the leaders of the dynastic parties. You fall foul of the family, you are thrown out of the party or marginalised. Talent has no space. Merit is no virtue. Organisational structure need not exist. The charisma of the family alone is the party's votebank. The crowd around the family is the cadre.

The weakness of the dynastic parties

This model, however, has one significant weakness. Strength of the party is co-existent with the strength of the current generation of the dynasty. If he is found to be non-inspirational or inadequate in leadership, the party has to throw all its eggs in an incomplete basket. The basket may be worth only forty-four Lok Sabha seats, at times slightly less, at times slightly more. The ill-informed reactions of the leader become the new ideology. The silver lining, however, is that India is changing. It has very large middle class and very strong aspirational class aspiring to get into the middle class. This aspirational India judges parties and leaders very harshly. They don't accept whoever is imposed. They ask difficult and penetrating questions and their yardstick is very tough. They look for leaders of integrity, they look for men and women who can inspire them, who are decisive and can lead the nation. To them surnames don't matter – competence and capacity does.

The challenge of 2019

The real strength of Indian democracy would be when the charismas of some families is completely shattered and parties, through a democratic process, throw up leaders of merit and competence. This was more than adequately proved in 2014 where most dynastic parties lost miserably. India of 2019 is different from India of 1971. If the Congress party wants the 2019 elections to be between Prime Minister Modi, who is the son of lesser-known parents and someone who is known only for his parentage rather than capacity, merit and competence, the BJP would gladly accept the challenge. Let this be the agenda for 2019.

How Many Lies Need to be Peddled to Sustain a Sinking Dynasty?

Posted on 12 February 2019

Truth is both precious and sacrosanct. In mature democracies those who deliberately rely on falsehoods are banished from public life. There is no doubt that with the changing socioeconomic profile of India this will inevitably happen in India.

In modern world dynasties inherently have their limitations. Aspirational societies abhor kingdoms. They insist on accountability and performance. But the grand old party of Indian politics has sadly become a captive of a dynasty. Many of its senior leaders lack the courage and moral authority to advise the dynasts to change course. This trend started in early 1970s, climaxed during the Emergency and has continued ever since. The slave mentality of senior leaders convinces them that they must only sing the song scripted by the dynast. A contrarian opinion will cost them their political career. When the dynast speaks lies, they all join the chorus.

How many lies are necessary to be peddled to save a sinking dynasty? The contagion effect of falsehoods is fairly large. It appears to have spread to other colleagues in the mahajhootbandhan. In relation to the Rafale deal where thousands of crores of public money have been saved, a new falsehood is manufactured on a daily basis. The latest is in relation to the present CAG and his participation in the decision-making process of Rafale. In 2014–15, the present CAG was secretary (economic affairs) in the Ministry of Finance. Being seniormost at one point of time, he was also designated as the finance secretary. I say this without fear of contradiction that no file or paper relating to the Rafale transaction ever reached him nor was he in any way, directly or indirectly, associated with the decision-making on defence purchases. Expenditure to be incurred on purchases by various departments of the government needs the approval of the secretary (expenditure).

Why then is the lie in relation to the CAG having a non-existent conflict of interest being raised? The dynast knows that his 500 crore versus 1600 crore kindergarten argument was a fictional story. No one would ever buy it because facts don't support it. Even before the contents of CAG report are known, a 'Peshbandi' attack on the institution of the CAG is launched. The dynast and his friends have in the past even attacked the Supreme Court when it rejected the writ petition on Rafale. The entire pricing argument was factually wrong. The procedure argument that there was no Defence Acquisition Council, no CCS, no Contract Negotiation Committee was a blatant lie. The Rs 30,000 crore favour to a private company is non-existent. The use of sliced document by a newspaper is unprecedented in the history. The use of an incomplete document is certainly not in consonance with the spirit of free speech. The 'no integrity pact' argument is belied by the fact that even in earlier purchases through an intergovernmental agreement with Russia and the United States, such pacts were not there. Now without a shred of evidence, a fictional conflict of interest of the CAG is invented.

How many more lies will be peddled to sustain a sinking dynasty? India certainly deserves better.

Prime Minister Modi and Aspirational India Will Prevent India From Becoming a Dynastic Democracy

Posted on 15 March 2019

India is the world's largest and most populous democracy. It is a highly aspirational nation which is also the world's fastest-growing economy. Very soon we will be the fifth-largest economy in the world. After a decade, it is likely that we will be amongst the top three economies in terms of size along with the United States and China. We have witnessed an exponential growth of the middle class. The neo-middle class has emerged at a fast pace.

How does the world's largest democracy elect its governments? Should it be on the basis of leadership quality, policy, ideology, performance or should it be on the basis of dynasties and family charismas?

The Congress and the making of a dynastic democracy

After Independence, the Congress party was a political group with a galaxy of tall national leaders. Yet Pandit Nehru started grooming his daughter Indira Gandhi as his successor. He made her the Congress president ahead of many other seniors. This sowed the seeds of an effort by many others to convert India into a dynastic democracy. Indira Gandhi first encouraged her younger son Sanjay Gandhi to be groomed as a successor, but his sudden and unfortunate death prevented that. Thereafter, she groomed her elder son Rajiv Gandhi to be her successor. The Congress tried to remove itself from the shackles of dynasty for a brief period after the unfortunate assassination of Rajiv Gandhi but could not get out of its clutches for long. Sonia Gandhi then took over as the longest-serving president of the Indian National Congress and thereafter passed on the leadership baton of the party to her son Rahul Gandhi. Thus, generation after generation, the Congress party's leadership berth is reserved for a member of the preferred family. When the party is now in the doldrums, another member of the family has entered the scene.

The 1991 change

Conventionally it was only the Congress which was a party controlled by a family. Post 1991, a significant change took place in Indian politics. Most political parties which were created post 1991 converted themselves into dynastic parties. They had no organised structures, no parliamentary board and no decision-making bodies. The leader of the party was the head dynast of the family. The succession of the party was within the family. The cadres owed loyalty only to the leader. The leaders were usually charismatic. In most cases the leader amassed wealth. The party was functioned like a personal property of the family. The family took all the decisions. The party became a crowd around a family.

The demonstrative effect of family controlling political parties was that even non-dynastic parties converted their structure into a family owned party. Thus, from Jammu and Kashmir to Tamil Nadu, there are very few political parties which have a structure left. In most cases, an individual controls them. When there is no immediate family, it is either the brother or nephew being groomed. The only parties which functioned outside the family and dynastic principle are the BJP, the left parties and maybe a few smaller ones.

The dynasts believe that oligarchy helps in holding the party together, defines the line of authority and enforces discipline within the party. The ideas of the leader are their ideologies. Even his aberrations and eccentricities are accepted as the ideology. The leader's dictatorial tendencies are accepted in the larger interest of the party. Many of the leaders of such parties are highly corrupt. Charges of corruption, misdemeanour and even prosecution do not weaken their stranglehold on the party. Survival of the leader in such situations becomes the main political agenda of the party. Even when the leaders are in prison after conviction, their stranglehold on the minds of the cadres remains. When dynasts defect from one coalition to another, the cadres don't question. They call it an opportunity.

Impact on politics, policy and governance

The impact of this on politics, policy and governance is indeed adverse. Many of these parties are ill-equipped for governance. They win a reasonable number of seats and then claim their partnership share either in a state or the central government. They possess the capacity to make a difference in the arithmetic in relation to coalition politics. Since ethics in public life is a major casualty of these leaders/family owned parties, ethical standards in governance fall. These parties are indifferent to the concept of governance. They have very little interest in policy. Their political stand depends on an opportunity to better their own prospects. They prefer voicing either state issues or populist issues over sound policy. Their policy is to protect their constituency.

Inner party democracy and policy become a big casualty. Horizontal induction of talent into politics also suffers. Many well-meaning citizens get disillusioned with the politics altogether. Some compete for keeping the leader and, at times, his family members, humoured. When parties thrust on themselves or on the polity and even governance, men of inadequate stature, vision and mind, the country suffers. While many found the system of family owned parties to be convenient, others dissented against this practice and wanted a change. They were looking for men of competence, clarity and those who would make a difference. Politics, like nature, abhors vacuum. The acceptance of Shri Narendra Modi at the national level, after his tenure as a chief minister of Gujarat, was also on account of this popular desire to get rid of dynasties. Much before the BJP's parliamentary board in 2013 announced Shri Narendra Modi as prime ministerial candidate, the people of India had accepted him.

The Modi factor

Prime Minister Narendra Modi grew up in an extremely humble background. He worked in the party organisation till he was inducted into the leadership. He had to work and struggle for the positions that he got. He earned them. India was changing while the dynasts thought otherwise. If the results of 2014 elections are closely analysed, most caste-based parties suffered a blow. Most family owned parties lost. This was not because of Prime Minister Modi's popularity alone, it was also because India had changed. An aspirational India with multiple modes of communication and knowledge-gathering, realised that it is only men of merit, competence and integrity who can arouse public confidence. Mere membership of a family is no criteria. I am confident that this trend will continue in the 2019 elections. Prime Minister Modi and aspirational India will together demolish the concept of families.

Are two dynasts better than one or is it otherwise?

The key question is: will the dynastic parties learn from their 2014 drubbing and a possible defeat in 2019? Possibly not. It is here that the people of India will have to bring about a change. India is not a monarchy. Neither is it a kingdom or dynastic democracy. Dynasts disapprove persons of talent and merit. The real strength of democracy will be realised when the myth of dynasties is finally buried, and these parties are taken over by men of competence and merit. That will provide Indians with a better choice.

There is another curious feature. Most families where a single dynast created the party have moved into the next generation. In the next generation, there may be more than one heir. Both the heirs become aspirational and, therefore, the parent dynast distributes the largesse. But recent history has proved otherwise. Confucius had rightly said that just as there can be only one sun in the sky, there can be only one emperor on Earth. Where power-sharing between successor dynasts takes place, who is the ultimate emperor? Haryana, Bihar and Tamil Nadu have witnessed the battle of brothers. In Uttar Pradesh, it was father vs son. Andhra Pradesh earlier witnessed the battle of the sons-in-law. In Karnataka there is an experiment of sons sharing the state and the grandsons sharing the Centre. In Maharashtra, the initial ripples have started. The Congress has undertaken the same experiment. It believes that two owners are better than one. Will Confucius be proved right and history record that one eventually prevailed over the other or will it be otherwise. One failed. The other won't take off.

Is the Congress Party Now Paying the Cost for Its Dynastic Character?

Posted on 24 March 2019

I have consistently held the view that dynasties owning political parties is an unfortunate phenomenon which has accelerated in the last three decades. The Congress was original creator of this concept. Dynasties demolish organisational structures. They are unable to attract leaders of talent or mass following. Since the democratic structure of a dynastic party gets diminished, they become a crowd around a family. Chaudhary Charan Singh had very appropriately said that world over parties elect leaders. In India, leaders create parties. Wherever the leader goes, the party travels with him.

Dynastic parties have one major drawback. If the current generation of the party is competent, charismatic and enjoys popular confidence, the dynast can pull off major victories. There is an incentive in the party to rally behind him. However, if the current-generation dynast is lacking in charisma, understanding and popular confidence, the crowd around the family gets increasingly frustrated. Is the Congress party witnessing that?

Staring at defeat

The Congress party has been out of power for five years. Its leaders and workers are accustomed to existing with the frills of office. They stare at another possible defeat. They have to live with their leader not relying on political advisers but on some from 'non-conventional' ones who are out of sync with the Congress leaders. Since the last word on any issue belongs to the leader, there is an element of unpredictability.

For those familiar with the Congress leaders, some generic statements are frequently heard. A few illustrative ones are mentioned here:

- What can I do? He just doesn't listen.
- Wait for 24 May, our politics will begin thereafter.
- I feel like quitting.
- Our campaign planning is lagging behind. I am told Uncle Sam has come to take care of it.
- Let's prepare for 2024.

The above reflects what one generation of a dynasty can do to a dynastic party. There are three prominent non-dynastic parties in India. The BJP has elected, over the last few decades, leaders of the calibre of Shri Atal Bihari Vajpayee, Shri L.K. Advani and Shri Narendra Modi as its front rank leaders. When the new generation of the left took over, their dominant faces were men like Shri Prakash Karat and Shri Sitaram Yechury. Despite the limited impact of the left, they had decades of experience and ideological clarity. After a series of splits and mergers, the Janata Dal (United), another non-dynastic party, elected Shri Nitish Kumar who will shortly be completing his third term in his office as chief minister. It goes to his credit that he changed the governance culture of Bihar.

When leaders wrongly assess their own capacity

Dynasties impose leaders. These leaders don't become great – greatness is thrust on them. Some suffer from what psychologists now regard as the Dunning–Kruger effect. Social psychologists Dr David Dunning and Justin Kruger have given an apt description. They believe that those who suffer from this effect have a bias of illusory superiority which comes from the inability of low-ability people to recognise their lack of ability. Without the self-awareness of their limitations, such low-ability people cannot objectively evaluate their own competence or incompetence. This leads to their miscalculation in their assessment of the calibre of highly incompetent ones. They suggest that poor performers are not in a position to recognise their shortcomings and consequently are insecure and biased against the more competent ones. There is no place for men of high calibre in dynastic parties. An insecure leader is scared of the shadow of more talented people.

Is this the reason for the current mood within the Congress party? Or is it also the reason which persuades the Congress president to cross the line of decency and dignity when he refers to the prime minister?

This should suffice as a lesson for the dynastic parties. They succeed on the strength of some generations of the dynasty. They sink with the others.

Will 2019 Witness the Dynasty as a Liability?

Posted on 20 April 2019

The first two rounds of the voting for the 2019 general elections are over. What are the early trends? What are the initial lessons?

The BJP/NDA campaign is focussed. It sets the agenda. There is clarity about the leadership of Shri Narendra Modi. There appears to be a strong groundswell in his favour. The campaign focuses on major achievements of the past five years, particularly relating to strengthening the poor and the middle class, a clean government and a special emphasis on national security. The alliance is coherent, and the issues being projected are focused.

Based on fake issues, the key thrust of what the Congress was building up in the last one year has cracked up. They are now concentrating on a new scheme declared in their manifesto which is cutting no ice with people. The entire reliance on the members of the first family to deliver a sustainable campaign is proving to be a non-starter. Wherever the contest is primarily between the BJP and the Congress, the BJP is comfortably placed.

The regional parties in West Bengal and Odisha may be in for a major surprise. The left parties did badly in 2014. If at all, their parliamentary strength will weaken further. The regional parties will do well only in regions where the BJP still lacks major strength.

However, a major factor for a large part of the electorate, Prime Minister Modi appears to be the obvious choice. This is particularly true in the case of voters below thirty-five years of age. 'My vote is for Modi' is the general refrain from the ground.

The NDA is running a positive campaign. It looks at an India without poverty and which gives a much better quality of life to its people. The Congress and the regional parties concentrate on only removing one man – Narendra Modi. Where the incumbent's acceptability is at 70 per cent, they are whipping up a non-existent anti-incumbency.

The state of some caste-based and dynastic parties

The Congress is seeing some of its traditional bright faces deserting the party. Are these desertions only because of particular incident or do they reflect a larger disillusionment with the leadership? When mindsets are feudal, dynasties survive. Dynasties also survive when they are charismatic and have an ability to deliver. A lot of supporters accept subjugation because of the ability of the dynasty to put them in positions. What happens to dynasties when the feudal mindsets change and nations become more aspirational?

The socioeconomic profile of India is moving up the growth ladder. It may be difficult for a country with this socio-economic profile to accept dynasties. If the Congress's dynast has only an ability to deliver 44 seats or 60 seats in Parliament, what then is the incentive for conventional Congressmen to bear the humiliation of subjecting themselves to a dynast? Ultimately, in dynastic parties one has to accept political slavery. These Congressmen today look at a party like the BJP where men and women of talent have a huge opportunity to move up in the party, legislatures and governments. The two prime ministers which the BJP gave to India, namely, Shri Atal Bihari Vajpayee and Shri Narendra Modi, were by a mile the tallest politicians of their generation. Today, this can happen in merit-based parties, not in dynastic parties. A relevant question with this changing socioeconomic profile of India is: are dynasties an asset for a party or are they a liability? Unquestionably, the present generation of dynasts has become a liability rather than an asset for the Congress party.

A similar situation arises with regard to the caste-based parties. The INLD has cracked up. The BSP got zero in the Lok Sabha elections in 2014 and nineteen seats in the Assembly elections. The SP could only retain seats for its family members in the 2014 elections. The RJD was down to two seats. Thus, the changing socioeconomic profile of India is no longer conducive to caste-based parties perpetuating indefinitely. The sun will slowly but surely come down on that era. Another important trend visible is that wherever national parties lacked strength, the vacuum was filled up by strong regional parties.

The BJP, which was a party of the north, expanded to central and western India, and has now captured a large part of the political space in the east. To that extent, it has already consumed some of the space which was occupied by the regional parties of Bengal, Odisha, Assam and north-east. It is already lead player in the South in Karnataka. This election will witness BJP as a co-equal in Kerala. The unprecedented turnout at the prime minister's Thiruvananthapuram rally on 18 April would leave many scratching their heads for a reanalysis. The BJP has the ability to fight and occupy more political space from the regional parties is already visible. The Congress inherently lacks that instinct.

The direction of 2019

The direction of the 2019 general election is clear. The centre stage is occupied by the BJP. Both in terms of agenda-setting and leadership, the Congress is failing to make any impact. Regional parties are putting up a fight. Their agenda is mostly state-based. The national vision in their leaders is lacking. The country doesn't trust them to form a coherent, stable and long-lasting coalition. Can a federal front be trusted with an effective management of national security?

How does this election convert it into parliamentary seats?

The momentum is clearly with the BJP and Prime Minister Modi. In terms of a national leadership contest for a prime ministerial election, it is almost becoming a one-horse race. There is nobody else measuring up to Prime Minister Modi's level of capacity and acceptability.

Is history going to witness something wholly unprecedented? Are we going to witness the rejection of caste-based and dynastic parties? And will aspirational India make a harsh judgement on electing a merit-based leadership? This may well be the case.

A Dynast's Non-Existent Revenge Against the Man Who Defeated Him in 2014 – 'I Dismantled the PM's Image'

Posted on 3 May 2019

Dynasts have self-illusory opinion about themselves. They create a disproportionate image about their own abilities in their own minds and believe that the universe around them thinks alike. They tend to become megalomaniacs. Rahul Gandhi is no exception. He announced four months ago that Prime Minister Narendra Modi will lose in Varanasi and that the BJP will be reduced to only a couple of seats. He has a disproportionate impression about his oratorical skills when he challenges one of the greatest communicators of his times, Prime Minister Modi, for a public debate. He comes out with outrageous ideas about security, economy and social issues and believes that his views have found mass acceptability. With Prime Minister Modi's personal acceptability ratings today being close to 70 per cent, Rahul proclaims that he is dead sure that Modi is very unpopular. The irony of every dynast is that he buys his own propaganda even if there are not too many others willing to accept it.

Dynasts have a sense of entitlement. They believe that they were born to rule. The Gandhis suffer from this sense of entitlement. The 2014 election was an utter shock to them. Losing to a person of modest origins and being reduced to the lowest ever strength in history, became unacceptable to the dynasty. It took them more than three years to get out of the shock of the 2014 rout. The strategy devised was that Modi had to be fought and removed. He was considered a strong and a popular leader. His delivery systems were extremely clear. He enforced honesty in public life. He was a strong performer on the security front. The 'Kaamdaar' was being admired for his work.

Unacceptability of a commoner challenging the dynast and defeating him led to both envy and revenge. Rahul's statement quoted in a media organisation yesterday that 'I have dismantled Modi's image' was a giveaway. The only way a dynast with a little acceptability in the country can react to the commoner who defeated him is that 'I will damage his image'. But how do you damage the image of a person who is riding perhaps at the peak of his popularity? How do you damage the reputation of a person who is known to be incredibly honest? Can image be destroyed by a person who belongs to a family which has been tainted through generations with charges of corruption? How do you claim to have succeeded in damaging the image of a powerful personality where Prime Minister Modi's acceptability ratings are close to 70 per cent and Rahul is finding it difficult to even breach the 20 per cent mark?

It's clear that Rahul Gandhi concocts falsehoods, as in the Rafale case, starts believing his falsehoods to be true and eventually dreams that the falsehoods have destroyed his opponent. He does not gauge public opinion. He only talks but does not listen. Such people surround themselves with advisers who have also tactically learnt to only give good news to the dynast. Rahul's attitude is at complete variation with the traditional Congress way of doing things. His revenge against Prime Minister Modi may not succeed. It may well turn out to be a revenge against the Congress.

Part Four

Why the Opposition Keeps Losing

10

The Impact of the BJP's New Model of Politics on the Opposition

Is this an Opposition or a circus? With hatred of Narendra Modi their only unifying thread, the Opposition has lost its way. There is no leader, no programme, no meeting of minds. They seem to have no understanding of history, the arc of destiny, or the fact that India stands at a crossroads. Without strong leadership, political stability and focused policies, the country might falter, and it cannot afford to miss any opportunities. To do so will be to let down future generations. This is an Opposition of mavericks that is incapable of rising to the occasion, much less of leading India to the sunlit uplands.

India's Opposition Has a Lot to Learn

Posted on 3 March 2019

The Congress-led UPA government from 2004 to 2014 ran a terrible government. From 2014 to 2019, it was an even more terrible Opposition. There are occasions in history where the nation speaks in one voice. Politicians and leaders rise to the level of statesmanship. They rise above narrow partisan interest. Shri Atal Bihari Vajpayee's and the Jana Sangh's support to the government during the 1971 war is a case in point.

The terrorist attack at Pulwama on 14 February 2019 was planned and hatched across the border. Several Pakistani nationals were involved in it. Some have already been liquidated. There is enough evidence which points to this direction. It has been shared with Pakistan.

The attack generated a sense of revulsion against terrorists and its sponsors in India. The nation was determined that the blood of our martyred Jawans will continue to inspire us to eliminate terrorism.

The preemptive attack by our Air Force at Balakot across the border was intended to defend India's sovereignty. It was a perfectly executed pinpointed operation. No civilian or military installations were targeted – only terrorists were.

The retaliatory attack by Pakistan's F-16 was the most botched-up operation. In short, both the attack and our defence pointed to the valour and professionalism of our Air Force. Pakistan was globally isolated. Even the OIC refused to pay heed to it. It violated every tenet of the Geneva Convention in relation to our brave Wing Commander Abhinandan.

Not only was Pakistan globally isolated, the issue of its terrorism has reached the Security Council. So helpless was the situation that it was in no position to even admit the attack at Balakot. If it had admitted the attack and its consequences, the evidence of a terrorist camp in existence and the list of dead terrorists would have been international issue.

The whole of India was speaking in one voice. Public opinion overwhelmingly supported the government's decision and the Air Force's execution.

However, like its other friends in the Opposition, the Congress party refuses to learn. After an initial show of support for our Air Force, it tried to create a divide in India's political opinion. From the Congress and its friends, we have witnessed three recent statements.

In a meeting of the twenty-one Opposition parties, a resolution was passed, accusing the prime minister of politicising the Pulwama and Balakot incidents. The government had twice taken the leaders of Opposition parties into confidence. No evidence of politicisation was given. The statement was inappropriate. It gave a handle to the enemy.

The media in Pakistan used this statement of the twenty-one Opposition parties as a trump card. It took the statement as an endorsement of the Pakistani position that India had taken the Balakot action because of the compulsion of its domestic politics and not as a part of its policy to defend the country against terrorism.

The West Bengal chief minister went a step further. She started doubting the veracity of the incident and wanted to know the operational details. The credibility of both the government and our Air Force is being doubted. Even Congress leaders have raised similar questions.

I was most disappointed with a brief but highly objectionable statement of former Prime Minister Dr Manmohan Singh. While receiving the P.V. Narasimha Rao Award for lifetime achievement, he stated that he was disturbed with the 'mad rush of mutual self-destruction' by the two nations.

He further went on to argue that poverty, ignorance and disease were the real problems in the two countries and that saner counsel on both sides needed to think on the issue. What does this statement indicate? My analysis of the statement is as follows:

- The former prime minister elevated himself to the status of a neutral third party rather than be concerned about India's interest.
- He further developed a theory of parity and equivalence between both India and Pakistan. The perpetrator of terrorism and the victim of terrorism are both at par according to him.
- Implicitly, he doubts India's right to defend its sovereignty from those who want to damage it through terrorism.
- There is no condemnation of terrorism in that speech.
- Amongst the problems facing India that he mentions which include poverty, ignorance and disease. Violence and terrorism are of no consequence in his assessment.

Seen collectively and cumulatively, the above three statements ought not to have been made. They hurt India's national interest. Not only do they give smiles to Pakistan, they become an important instrument in Pakistan's hands to discredit India. Does the opposition want the Air Force to release operation details of the Balakot attack? The Opposition is entitled to oppose and ask questions, but then restraint and statesmanship are also an essential ingredient of public discourse. I hope, India's Opposition revisits its position and does not let down the nation.

Mahamilawat or Gathbandhan – A Race to the Bottom

Posted on 17 March 2019

India is today at the cusp of making history. Industrial revolutions bypassed us in the past. We had to fight the menace of poverty and lack of growth. A regulated economy for over four-and-a half decades had added to our woes. When we broke away from ideological shackles of the past, India witnessed a much higher rate of growth. Today we have reached a situation where we grow faster than others in the world. We are expanding the size of our economy. Our revenues are growing, and we are finally being able to transfer more resources to the poor to offer them a better quality of life. Our infrastructure – in terms of better highways, more airports, better railway systems, better urban infrastructure, surplus power, more port capacity – is growing every year. If this trend continues for the next two decades, India will evolve into a new league.

The essential prerequisite for accelerating our movement in this direction is that India must have political stability, a clear policy direction, a strong and decisive leadership. If we falter on any one of these, we will be letting down our own people and future generations. India cannot afford lost opportunities at this stage.

India's federalism

Federalism in is inherent India both geographically and constitutionally. Our Constitution defines 'India' i.e. Bharat – a Union of states. Our states must be fiscally strong. This is the essence of Indian federalism. Equally, if not more important, is the fact that for India to be a Union of states, there must be a strong Union. If there is no strong Union, both India and India's federalism will stand to suffer.

Let there be absolute clarity. India is a Union of states. It is not a Confederation of states. That is the fundamental difference between NDA and the UPA. This is also the fundamental flaw in this idea of the federal front. The framers of the Constitution had a vision. They were men of wisdom. When prominent areas like defence, sovereignty, security of India, foreign policy and eventually the war against terror were maintained as primary responsibility of the

Union government, can India be ever defended without a strong Union? There can be no federal front without a strong central party.

An analysis of the two NDA governments

The first NDA government led by Shri Atal Bihar Vajpayee had some significant features. It represented the core of India's federalism because regions were represented. But there was absolute clarity in terms of the primacy of the BJP, its size too acted an effective nucleus of the coalition. There was clarity that Atalji was the unquestioned leader of the government.

The same was true of the second NDA government led by Shri Narendra Modi. The BJP had an absolute majority of 282 seats in the 2014 general elections. Yet respecting federalism, it formed a government with its allies. The nucleus of the coalition was a large party. There was no completion for leadership. The last word belonged to the prime minister. That is how the two governments functioned. There was clarity in terms of policy and the government had the capacity to take difficult decisions and deliver on them.

The mahamilawat gathbandhan

The mahamilawat gathbandhan being envisaged is a road to disaster. It is a race to the bottom. There is a tug of war on the issue of the leader. Four people have clearly indicated their desire to be Prime Ministers – Shri Rahul Gandhi, Behan Mayawati, Mamata Didi and Shri Sharad Pawar. Each desires to expand his or her own base and reduce that of the competitor.

The BSP is trying to maximise its base in Uttar Pradesh and weaken the Congress in several states. The Trinamool Congress is trying to maximise its seats in West Bengal and it won't go with Congress in that state. It does not want Congress to win any seats in West Bengal. The Congress wants to go alone where it has some strength and is desperate to be in alliances, even with its own opponents elsewhere.

Pawar Saheb wants his ultimate dream to come true and is hoping for a hung Parliament where he has an opportunity to play his cards. Where a proxy leadership battle is visible before the elections, it will be full-fledged war post the elections.

The opportunism in this coalition is writ large. Sections of the Congress and the AAP are talking of an alliance. The AAP was formed as a reaction against the Congress's corruption. Today it is pleading with the Congress for an alliance. Shri N.T. Ramarao formed the TDP as an alternative to Congress. Today, TDP leader Shri Chandrababu Naidu is willing to be the sarthi of Rahul Gandhi.

The Congress and the left are entering into an alliance in West Bengal. Rahul Gandhi made a fake pretence of an anti-CPM speech in Kerala where they are opponents. Dr Ram Manohar Lohia was the original creator of the slogan 'Congress Hatao Desh Bachao' while Shri Sharad Yadav sits in the Congress's lap. Shri Akhilesh Yadav of Samajwadi Party appears to be more Congress than the Congress. They have buried the legacy of Dr Lohia.

Political stability and policy

The mahamilawat gathbandhan unquestionably promises only political instability. Such non-ideological alliances have only lasted for a few months. That is the unambiguous lesson of history. The governments by Chaudhary Charan Singh, Shri V.P. Singh, Shri Chandrasekhar, Shri H.D. Deve Gowda and Shri I.K. Gujral had a life of only a few months. Who would want to invest in India in an environment of political instability? Would even Indian investors prefer to go outside and look for more stable countries for investment? Where there is instability, there is corruption. People with brief political opportunities make the best of them. This is the experience of the past.

What would be the policy of a gathbandhan of this kind? Would every regional party demand a Special Status for its state? What would then happen to central funds which are meant for poverty eradication, the defence and security of India? In order to pamper certain exaggerated regional demands? Would expenditure on Armed Forces have to be cut? What will be their policy on expediting infrastructure-creation and the poverty-alleviation schemes that Prime Minister Modi has launched?

Will a war on terror be the priority of such a coalition or will it lead the battle against terror to a possible depletion of votebank politics? Will India be run with a national perspective or by a government which believes that India is a confederation of states?

What is common between the potential members of the mahamilawat gathbandhan?

There are a few commonalities between the members of the mahamilawat gathbandhan. Firstly, they have no positive programme. They ride on negativism. They just want to remove one man from office.

Secondly, most political groups comprise of dynastic parties and dynastic groups. In some cases, first generation dynast is still in control, in many others the next generation has taken over. These are parties with no inner party structures, no inner party democracy and hence no accountability. Many survive either on cost of regional feelings alone. That is their ideology.

Thirdly, most of them have serious allegations of corruption either against the top leaders or the important members who constitute the mahamilawat gathbandhan. They are rightly referred to as the Kleptocrats Club.

Fourthly, they have no ideology or philosophy in common. Pawar Saheb believes in a market economy. There are many others, including the communists, who want a more regulated economy. The Congress president proudly proclaims that he is more left than the left.

Fifthly, their track record of governance is disastrous. Temperamentally there are too many mavericks in the gathbandhan.

At the cusp of history, India and Indians have a choice to make. Are they electing a six-month government or a five-year government? Are they choosing between a tried, tested and performing leader or a chaotic crowd of non-leaders? Is India looking at a government which accelerates growth, development and poverty-alleviation or is it looking for a government made by persons who excel only at self-enrichment? I am confident that aspirational people of an evolving society will make the right choice.

A Political Circus Called 'Mahagathbandhan'

Posted on 29 March 2019

Over the last several months, India was exhausted with the talk of a mahagathbandhan. The rationale was that Prime Minister Shri Narendra Modi and the BJP were very strong and could not be challenged by individual party. The socioeconomic profile of India has changed. Indians judge politicians by their merit and capacity and no longer by any traditional loyalty.

We were promised a coalition of rivals because India had to be saved. We were promised a common minimum agenda. Each leader amongst the aspirant prime ministers wanted to become a 'sutradhar' of the alliance. He/she would periodically organise shows in his/her state and invite the entire bandwagon.

Presently when nominations for the first two phases are over and those for the third phase are about to happen, let us review the situation.

Jammu and Kashmir	The Congress – NC alliance will contest against each other on some seat.
Haryana	No alliance likely. Shri Dushyant Chautala's party has clearly announced that they are anti-Congress.
Delhi	Did the AAP ever want an alliance with the Congress? If it did align with them by sparing three seats, then eight months before the Delhi Assembly election, it would be offering its electoral base to the Congress in thirty out of seventy assembly segments. The party would be extremely courageous if it did so.
Uttar Pradesh	The Congress has been clearly told that it is unwanted. The BSP leader having fixed her own alliance, is now busy ensuring that the Congress tally is reduced not merely in Uttar Pradesh but also elsewhere.
Bihar	The hiccups in the alliance are evident. Some further partners of the NDA have bagged a share disproportionate to their strength on account of the weakness of the Congress/RJD. Some eminent former BJP men have been accepted by the Congress as a gift. We thank the Congress. Our problem is now theirs. Good luck.
Jharkhand	The RJD has walked out of the alliance.
Assam	A desperate Congress is trying to tie up with Badruddin Ajmal's party. Having antagonised the majority community, it has now found a votebank common with its new ally. The journey of Congress in Assam has been from 'Who is Badruddin Ajmal?' to 'Let us walk together'.
West Bengal	It has become a four-cornered contest. It will polarise a contest between Trinamool and the BJP. The Congress and the left fight has broken out. The three biggest noise-makers of the mahagathbandhan gave collective television bytes but are now at each other's throats. The Congress is fighting for the fourth position.

Odisha	With no ally, the Congress is fighting for the third position.
Andhra Pradesh	If the alliance between TDP and the Congress in Telangana was a marriage of convenience, Andhra has witnessed a tactical divorce between the two members of the promise mahagathbandhan. They are contesting separately. The TDP presently considers as 'untouchable' in Andhra Pradesh.
Kerala	They embrace each other at mahagathbandhan meetings but the Congress and the left are pitted against each other in Kerala.

The above states account for almost half of the total parliamentary constituencies. In the other half, stretching from Maharashtra to Punjab, which includes Himachal Pradesh, Uttarakhand, Haryana, Madhya Pradesh, Chhattisgarh, Rajasthan and Gujarat, the political winds are not exactly friendly to the Congress.

The leadership tussle

Multiple candidates have already made their desire clear to take over the mantle of the leadership. Each one of them is interested to see the strength of the other party's contender depleting. Each one of them has high hopes in a chaotic and highly hung Parliament. He/she believes that only in a chaotic situation he/she has a chance. The past track record of such governments in terms of policy, longevity and growth has to be borne in mind. Their track record of corruption is equally well known.

Federalism and coalition

Federalism requires that regional aspirations and representations find place in governance. But a larger national interest requires that India must have a national party with an electoral and legislative base which can become nucleus of such a coalition. The coalition under Late Shri Atal Bihari Vajpayee was held by both the personality of the leader and the 183 MPs of the BJP. Similarly, the BJP had an absolute majority in the last Lok Sabha, but it still formed a coalition. It is only because of the size of the BJP and clarity on leadership in the last coalition that a successful government was run under Prime Minister Modi.

Today you have no gathbandhan let alone a mahagathbandhan. It is a non-bandhan. You have no leader, no programme, no meeting of minds. Stability, which is paramount, is a major casualty. The only thing in common is negative agenda – remove one man. It is a recipe for chaos.

The Hope of the Losers

Posted on 10 May 2019

Counting for the results is only thirteen days away. Traditional political rivals have started open or secret parleys. Their best hope is that the Indian voter is neither wise nor sensible and hence would give an indecisive verdict. This presumption will be strongly belied on 23 May 2019.

Rahul Gandhi has reduced the Congress to a double-digit party. Congressmen are hoping against hope if they can break the double-digit barrier. Their level of ambition is hopelessly inadequate. Mayawati is fully determined to throw her hat in the ring. Mamata Banerjee and Chandrababu Naidu believe that they are the sutradhars of the Opposition. KCR dreams of a non-BJP, non-Congress coalition of parties.

None of these hopeful leaders have been able to understand the real trend on the ground. As the results get declared, two of the contenders – Mamata Didi and Chandrababu Naidu – would have realised that they have lost a large ground in their own states. Voters want responsible governance, not political acrobatics by the leaders they trust. Election is a time when the voters respond. The others to be shaken will be the Congress which would have failed to add any significant numbers to its 2014 tally. The anarchic Aam Aadmi Party could be reduced to virtually next to nothing in the election.

The significant features, which have been noticed as the sixth phase of electioneering concludes, are evident. Where it's Congress versus BJP, the Congress is unable to give a fight. Some regional combinations are trying to make a semblance of a fight. But India has changed. The youth defy the traditional caste arithmetic. Dynasties are more ridiculed than cherished. The New India judges the performance of its leaders very harshly. It has tried and finally trusted the leadership of Prime Minister Narendra Modi.

The new generation of the Gandhis believes that national security is a non-issue. Quite to the contrary, when national security issues are raised in large public meetings, the applause for the leader is the maximum. Are the Opposition parties unable to figure out the 'Modi Modi' shouts confronting them when their leaders pass through crowded areas? Except for those who prefer to deceive themselves, media persons travelling across the country have a uniform report that there is an extremely strong pro-Modi trend visible amongst the voters.

The prime ministerial contest is almost becoming a one-horse race. Very rarely has India witnessed such powerful ratings for an incumbent prime minister to be voted to power. The model experimented between 2014–2019 of a single party majority government, with allies participating in a coalition government, has provided India a stable and a decisive regime. A coalition of rivals only lasts a few months.

The electorate is clear that it wants a five-year government and not a five month one. It is thus confronted with the choice of a Modi vs. Chaos. Obviously, the electorate's wisdom has to be trusted when he makes a choice. The Modi mandate could be larger than 2014.

The Frightening and Scary Scenario of India's Opposition

Posted on 16 May 2019

As the seventh phase of the Election approaches closure, the groundswell in favour of Prime Minister Modi is becoming stronger. Except in the last few days, not one political analyst had foreseen the velocity of this groundswell even in a state like West Bengal. The largest of the prime minister's public rallies have been in West Bengal.

The positive reasons for the prime minister's acceptability have been his decisiveness, integrity and performance, his delivery of resources to the poor, and his security doctrine which has been a game changer. The NDA's strength has been a complete absence of any confusion about leadership or programme. There is an absolute consensus.

The not-so-positive reason for the prime minister's high acceptability levels is the absence of any cogent or coherent alternative. Conventionally, it used to be referred to as the 'TINA' factor. This effectively means that 'There is no alternative'. If the Opposition is giving vague assurances of an alternative, the same is either too scary or absolutely frightening.

The Opposition could not forge an alliance in several key states. They do not call a meeting of different Opposition parties for the obvious fear that many will not attend the meeting. The common thread which brings them together is negativism – to get rid of one person. They have no agreement on either a leader or a programme.

They are a completely fractured Opposition which could not come together before or during the election. Who will believe their assurance that they can come together after the election? They are institution wreckers. They do not allow Parliament to function. They attack and intimidate judges.

Now the Election Commission is their next target. The attack on the EVMs and the Election Commission is an advance alibi for defeat on 23 May 2019. Their leaders represent temperamental mavericks, some highly corrupt and many – a governance disaster. The electorate wonders, if they can ever provide a cogent alternative. Past history belies the longevity of such opportunistic and fragile combinations.

To the electorate, they provide an absolutely frightening scenario. I have long argued that aspirational societies look for a better tomorrow. They are averse to suicidal choices. The frightening and scary scenario that the Opposition promises will be responsible for its rout. This consolidates the grounds well in favour of Modi.

11

The Opposition Parties' Futile and Manufactured Protests

Whether it's Rafale, economic data, or criticism over the so-called destruction of institutions, the opponents of the BJP government are being disingenuous. While accusing the BJP and Narendra Modi of intolerance, it is their own ideological intolerance and refusal to accept that the old dispensation and their cosy role in it that has gone and that explains their sustained vitriol. Every single act is laid at Modi's door. These are manufactured fabrications with no merit by politicians and activists who like to pose as the 'conscience' of the nation but are, in fact, so partisan that they cannot distinguish fact from fiction.

A Manufactured Revolt – Politics by Other Means

Posted on 14 October 2015

The death by lynching of a member of a minority community at Dadri was extremely unfortunate and condemnable. No right-thinking person can ever rationalise and condone such an action. Such incidents bring a bad name to the country.

Subsequent to this incident, a series of writers have returned awards conferred on them by the Sahitya Akademi. The thrust of the writers' protest appears to be that under the present central government led by Prime Minister Narendra Modi, an atmosphere of intolerance has been created in the country.

Is this protest real or a manufactured one? Is this not a case of ideological intolerance? There are a large number of writers with left or Nehruvian leanings who have been recognised by the government in the past. Some of them may have been entitled to this recognition. I am neither questioning their academic merits nor their right to have political prejudices. Many of them have spoken out against the present prime minister even when he was chief minister of Gujarat.

After the new government was sworn in in May 2014, those who had enjoyed the patronage under the earlier establishment, have obviously been uncomfortable with the present government. This discomfort has been furthered by another political reality in India. With shrinking fortunes, the Congress is showing no signs of revival. The left is being increasingly pushed to the margin. The new strategy of anti-Modi, anti-BJP sections appears to be to resort to politics by other means.

The easiest way is to manufacture a crisis and subsequently manufacture a paper rebellion against the government in the wake of the manufactured crisis.

A few months after the present government was sworn in,

media reports were carried out that there was a series of attacks against the Christian community including attacks on churches. Protest marches were organised. It was alleged that the minority communities in the country are feeling unsafe.

Each one of those 'attacks' was investigated and most of them were found to be incidents of petty crimes such as theft or throwing bottles to break a windowpane. None of the attacks in and around Delhi could be attributed to religion or politics. The accused were arrested and are being prosecuted. The principal accused in the case of raping a nun in West Bengal was found to be a person of Bangladeshi origin.

The protest at that time highlighted two factors – firstly, that this was an attack on institutions of a minority community and secondly, the prime minister was quiet about it. Once the truth of these attacks as being cases of crime was established the propaganda and propagandists have both disappeared.

For a cause against the Modi government, the protesting writers have struggled hard to find a reason. The rationalist Mr M.M. Kalburgi was shot dead in Karnataka, a Congress-ruled government. Mr N. Dabholkar, another rationalist, was shot down on 20 August 2013 in Maharashtra, at that time ruled by the Congress and the NCP.

Both incidents need to be condemned in no uncertain terms. It is the responsibility of the state government to maintain law and order and provide security to a vulnerable target of attack. Similarly, the Dadri incident took place in Uttar Pradesh, which is ruled by the Samajwadi Party. Politics by other means, now dictates an alternative strategy.

Combine the three crimes, camouflage the truth and throw all of them in the basket of the present central government. Nobody has alleged any governmental complacency in these crimes. But to manufacture a revolt, it is necessary to obfuscate the truth and create the impression that the Modi government is responsible for these crimes even if they took place in Congress- and Samajwadi- Party ruled states.

In fact, one of the protesting writers in 2015, while returning her Padma Shri, has cited the Sikh killings of 1984 as one of her reasons. It took thirty-one years for this writer's conscience to be aroused by the genocide of 1984. There is no atmosphere of intolerance in the country. The manufactured revolt is a case of an ideological intolerance towards the BJP.

A few questions to the protestors: how many of them courted arrest, protested or raised their voice against the dictatorship of Mrs Indira Gandhi during the emergency? Did the writers speak against the Sikh killings of 1984 or the Bhagalpur riots of 1989? Was their conscience not shaken by the corruption involving lakhs of crores between 2004 and 2014?

With the Congress showing no signs of revival and an insignificant left lacking legislative relevance, the recipients of past patronage are now resorting to politics by other means. The manufactured protest of the writers is one such case.

The Compulsive Contrarian and His Manufactured Logic

Posted on 17 January 2019

In the run-up to the 2014 general elections there were many who never expected Prime Minister Narendra Modi to come to power with an absolute majority.

There are some in the political system who thought that they were born to rule. There are those who had managed to penetrate into positions of influence irrespective of the government in power. Some who were part of the ideological left and the ultra-left obviously found the new government wholly unacceptable. Hence emerged a new class of compulsive contrarians.

The contrarians believed that this government could do no good. Every act of it must be opposed. They picked holes in the proposal to give 10 per cent reservation in education and public jobs to the poor, compelling me to comment in the Lok Sabha that this was the first illustration in history where the communists were obstructing a step taken to support the poor.

Steps taken against black money were described as Tax Terrorism. The virtues of cash which was a source of black money and fuelled corruption were discovered after demonetisation. Aadhaar which became an instrument for saving money to ensure that it is fruitfully spent for the poor, was questioned on the grounds of violating personal liberty. Slogans which championed the breaking up of this country into pieces were defended as free speech. The successful surgical strikes conducted by the Army were questioned either as a routine or as dubious process.

The compulsive contrarians had no qualms about manufacturing falsehoods. They could concoct arguments even if they went against the general interest of the country. They could masquerade corruption as crusade. They could adopt double standards whenever it suited them. Let me now illustrate these with specific examples.

The Justice Loya case

Every fact alleged in the public space by the compulsive contrarians was manufactured. The judge died a natural death due to a cardiac stroke. The only persons with him at the time of the stroke and in hospital were his fellow judges. No outsiders had any contact, and yet, wild insinuations were made on friendly websites, social media campaigns, fake PILs.

The cause of the death was sought to be altered into a conspiracy for murder. The campaign went on for months altogether. The compulsive contrarians included a retired judge of the Supreme Court and a former chief justice of Delhi High Court. They had no hesitation in allowing themselves to support falsehoods without factual verification. Eventually, a three-judge bench of the Supreme Court dismissed every claim made in the case.

The judgment was delivered on behalf of the bench by Justice Dhananjaya Chandrachud. He was criticised on social media. What if the same had been delivered by Chief Justice Dipak Misra? Another vicious campaign of calumny would have been launched against him by the compulsive contrarians.

The Rafale case

The purchase of the Rafale combat aircraft is yet another case of concocted falsehood by the compulsive contrarians. This is a deal where Prime Minister Modi should be credited with saving thousands of crores for the country. The Congress had compromised national security by delaying the deal for over a decade. Fake and concocted figures were put into the public domain as the purchase price of the combat aircrafts.

The differences between a plain aircraft as a flying instrument and a weaponised aircraft was sought to be obliterated. Every fact was brought before the Supreme Court. The court conclusively rejected the challenge. The need for purchase, the quality of the aircraft, the pricing, the process and the offset issues were all gone into and upheld by the court.

The contrarians were proved to be liars and yet, instead of stopping the campaign of falsehood, they started relying on an alleged dictational/typographical error to prove the judgment was wrong. Lobbyists and career nationalists joined the compulsive contrarians. Though the court verdict should have been final, the contrarians did not stop. They again raised it in Parliament. They conclusively lost the debate in the Parliament and yet the falsehood has not stopped.

The CBI issue

Anyone with even a nodding acquaintance of the state of affairs in Lutyens Delhi would know that a few individuals in our investigative agencies had, over the last few years, become a law unto themselves. Whispers of what was going on were not uncommon. It is the duty of the sovereign government to ensure the cleaning-up of each of the investigative agencies. The government was only concerned with their accountability and integrity.

The contrarians chose to side with the questionable. Autonomy is always a great sounding idea. In the absence of accountability, an investigating agency can become a monstrosity. Let any informed person honestly ask himself a question: post the two-year fixed tenure functioning following the judgment in Vineet Narain's case and the statutory amendments that followed, has the quality of the heads of the central investigative agencies improved or deteriorated? Two views may be difficult as an answer.

Today the Contrarians have launched an attack on the committee headed by the prime minister which transferred the CBI chief. The only question before the committee was whether there was any material available as a ground to transfer the CBI head? Prima facie, the CVC report did constitute adequate and relevant material. The committee is not an appellate forum against the CVC findings. If the same had to be challenged, it can only be challenged in court. The committee could not have ignored the CVC report.

The nominated judge – member of the committee – was attacked for a non-existent conflict of interest and the person who had a real conflict of interest and should have refrained from attending the meeting became the accuser. The leader of the largest single party in the Opposition, Mallikarjun Kharge, was a petitioner before the Supreme Court, claiming that the CBI chief was an honest man and had been wrongly removed for mala-fide reasons and through a faulty process.

Having been a campaigner for the ousted chief, he obviously could not have sat in judgment over his innocence or guilt in the committee. His was a textbook case of bias. Any honourable man should have recused himself. His dissent as a biased man is non-est. Yet the conflicted man accuses one of the most honourable judges of a conflict of interest.

On judges

A press conference addressed by four hon'ble judges of the Supreme Court over a year ago has done more damage to India's judicial institutions than many would have envisaged. It brought the judges into public gaze as factionalised and battling for their own turf space.

There are a set of extra-adventurist lawyers practising in the highest court, as in every other court. Their strategy is to overawe the court. They threaten to walk out of cases, they move impeachment motions in their political capacity to flex their muscles and clout, they make public comments on judges. They use media to intimidate the court. Having involved themselves in an ugly public conduct, judges find themselves unable to exercise jurisdiction to stop such conduct by others. The last chief justice was attacked by the compulsive contrarians. A precedent has now been legitimised. His successors will find it difficult to escape similar treatment. The threat to the independence of judiciary can also come from the public pressures that these contrarians exert on judges.

Collegium proceedings and conversations in the past two

years have been faithfully reported in one particular newspaper (a compulsive contrarian), thereby underscoring the nexus. If the Law Minister invokes the seniority principle as he did last year in the case of one appointment to the Supreme Court, the contrarians call it an attack on the independence of judiciary. When the contrarians raised the issue of inter-se seniority, as had happened recently, it becomes their crusade for independence of the institution. Amazing double standards.

The Reserve Bank of India debate

The RBI has served this country extremely well. It has extremely important functions to perform. There are many instances of the past where the government and the RBI have had different opinions.

The government in recent months has strongly felt that certain sectors of the economy needed credit and liquidity support. Squeezing out both would eventually hurt this sector as also hurt growth. Recent data relating to some of those sectors has supported the position taken by the government. Every stakeholder in the market was in agreement with the government's position but the contrarians deflected the credit and liquidity issue to the issue of autonomy. After all, the government was only addressing the autonomous RBI and asking it to resolve the issues which lay in its domain.

I can go on and on with these examples. Free speech and the right to dissent are critical components of a democracy but falsehood, subversion and institutional destruction are not. The right to campaign for stifling funds to the economy in the name of autonomy, justifying corruption in the name of institutional independence, attacking judges when the verdict is not favourable, manufacturing facts – as in the case of judge Loya's death – and the Rafale deal are indicative of the mindset of the compulsive contrarians.

Nations are built by those with positive mindsets and a national vigour, not by the compulsive contrarians. Didn't left-liberals find fault with the various actions that Gandhiji took during the freedom movement? Weakening a sovereign-elected government and strengthening the unelectable is only a subversion of democracy.

'Institutions Under Attack' – The Latest Fabrication

Posted on 10 February 2019

The past two months have witnessed several fake campaigns. Each one of them has failed to cut much ice. Falsehood doesn't have longevity. The compulsive contrarians continued to jump from one falsehood to another. The Rafale deal not only strengthens the combat ability of the Indian Air Force but saved thousands of crores for the exchequer. When its falsehood collapsed, a half document was produced to perpetuate the falsehood. Little did the creators of this falsehood realise that the cost of producing half a document is the loss of full credibility.

Those who organised loot on the banks between 2008 and 2014, started alleging that industrial loans had been waived. Not a single rupee was waived. On the contrary, the defaulters have been thrown out of management. The falsehood that the government and its ministers were colluding to allow the economic offenders to escape was exposed when, one after the other, the investigative agencies were succeeding in bringing back many of the key defaulters and middlemen. The campaign against the GST fizzled out since in just eighteen months of implementation it became a consumer-friendly measure reducing taxes, exempting small businesses and ending corruption/harassment by eliminating interface of the assessee and the officials. The attack has now shifted to a new ground. Institutions are under pressure – the charge comes from none other than those who have a history of having subverted institutions all their lives. Illustratively, little did the authors of the PMLA's harsh provisions realise that the provisions could haunt the authors themselves. It is, therefore, necessary to analyse this argument of institutions under attack.

Parliament

History will record that Jawaharlal Nehru's great grandson has singularly damaged India's Parliament as an institution more than anyone else. Attempts are made at 11 a.m. every morning by the Congress party to disrupt both houses. The Rajya Sabha, once known for the quality of its debates, has become non-functional. If we analyse Rahul Gandhi's two speeches on Rafale, they are based on a personal hatred for the prime minister, emanating from envy. A failed student always hates the class topper. Additionally, the context of the speeches points more to college-level lumpenisation in content. It has been left to two Opposition members, namely Bhartruhari Mahtab of the BJD and N.K. Premachandran of the RSP, to fill up the intellectual vacuum that the Congress has created.

Judiciary

One of the key points being made in regard to the judiciary is that the government referred back one of the recommendations to the Supreme Court to the collegium for reconsideration. The government, under the present constitutional procedure, is entitled to refer back a recommendation of the collegium by recording reasons in writing. If after reconsideration the collegium re-recommends the case, the government implements the recommendation. This was done in the present case. Regarding delay in implementing the recommendations, the last five years have seen more appointments each year than in any of the UPA years. The ill-advised press conference of four judges of the Supreme Court last year has more to do with intra-court affairs than with the government.

On the contrary, what is the track record of the government's opponents with regard to their attitude in relation to the judiciary? The impeachment motion filed by the Opposition on unsustainable grounds was only an attempt to intimidate the then chief justice of India and set an example for other judges – you toe our line, or we can create an embarrassing situation for you. That was the loud-and-clear message.

Lawyers opposed to the government have consistently used intimidation of judges as a courtroom tactic. Walking out of court hearings, social media campaigns against the judges were unprecedented but today a reality. Using the instrument of falsehood, they have preferred several petitions where facts have actually been found to be false, inviting severe strictures from the court. The glaring examples in this regard are the falsehood with regard to Judge Loya's death, the Rafale issue, the fake voter list scam in Madhya Pradesh and the Vyapam case. In each of the cases, the facts stated were found to be false. Notwithstanding the judgements of the court, many Opposition leaders continue to still rely on the same falsehood. Adverse judgements have led to a campaign against the court. We witnessed a social media campaign against the judgement in the Judge Loya case. After the recent Rafale judgement, one of the petitioners (a former career nationalist) announced that the Supreme Court had lowered its credibility by deciding the Rafale case.

Election Commission

The government has consistently maintained an arm's length distance from the Election Commission. There have been no significant issues between the government and the Commission. The attack on the EVM's is not merely to allay defeat, it is an attack on the Election Commission. The EVMs were introduced into the election process when the BJP was nowhere close to power. Multiple parties have won and lost elections held through the EVMs. Without producing a shred of evidence, the EVMs are being attacked. The campaign became farcical when a fraudulent press conference was held via video by an invisible man in London claiming to have knowledge of the alleged 2014 rigging.

Armed Forces

The government and the BJP have consistently stood by our Armed Forces whether we were in the government or the Opposition. It is the Opposition which questioned first the existence of the surgical strike and then played it down as a routine action which has also taken place in the past. The Army Chief was described as a 'sadak ka gunda'. Serious doubts have been raised on the Air-Force-led choice of the combat aircraft Rafale and its negotiation process. In the face of all this, their allegation that institutions are under attack by the government would be a mockery.

Reserve Bank of India

Congress governments in the past have been liberal in asking governors of the RBI to quit. Pt. Nehru, Mrs Indira Gandhi and subsequently Mr Yashwant Sinha had asked governors to quit. During the UPA government, two governors were barely on speaking terms with the finance minister. Nothing of this kind has happened in the recent past. The government legitimately flags issues relating to liquidity and credit availability with the RBI. They were raised at the highest level of the government and through all processes – statutory and consultative. The issues were legitimate. The government is the principal manager of the nation's economy. How can raising legitimate issues relating to credit and liquidity availability be an interference with the RBI. The government consistently maintained communications with the RBI governors during its tenure.

The CBI

The government does not interfere in any investigative function of the CBI or any other investigative agency. Once the government received the recommendation of the Central Vigilance Commission with regard to transferring two squabbling officers of the CBI asking them to go on leave, the government, in the larger interest of restoring the credibility of the CBI, acted. The government's stand has been vindicated with regard to the cleansing of a key investigative agency when based on the CVC's report, the three-member high powered committee decided to recommend the transfer of the CBI director. Restoring the credibility of an investigative agency is strengthening the institution and not assaulting it. In fact, it is the Opposition which has maintained a two-way approach to the CBI – on a daily basis the CBI should be attacked when it investigates corruption but if the government takes action to restore the credibility of the CBI, the government should be put in the dock.

There are two critical features of these new emerging breed of institution protectors. They criticise the government the maximum and simultaneously argue that the free speech is in danger. They shed crocodile tears for democracy and make every effort to convert the world's largest democracy into a dynastic one. The number of BJP–RSS workers killed in left-ruled Kerala and TMC-ruled West Bengal should shock the conscience of a nation. In West Bengal, democracy is seriously under peril. BJP leaders can't land, public meetings are being prevented and the Rath Yatra was disallowed.

The Congress party's stand on multiple issues is self-contradictory. It slaughters a cow before the cameras in Kerala, and invokes the National Security Act against cow killers in Madhya Pradesh. More than any institution it is the country whose interest is paramount. These institution protectors support the legitimising of illegal infiltrators into India. They readily jump to the support of those who want to dismember India. The Congress aligned with the Maoists in the recent Chhattisgarh elections. Rahul Gandhi stood shoulder to shoulder with the Tukde Tukde gang at JNU. The Congress was at the forefront, defending the urban Naxals in court. And yet it claims to be friend of both, the idea of India and its institutions. It is about time that India and its institutions are protected from these institution wreckers.

A Campaign of Fake Issues Never Works

Posted on 16 March 2019

The real strength of India's democracy is the inherent wisdom of the voters. They know what is in their best interest. They make harsh but correct judgements. They punish non-performers and vote back those who deliver. Pollsters, political pandits and commentators can go wrong. Many catch the trend but never its intensity. It is only on the day of results that analysts discover a wave.

Why do waves occur in an election?

Like-minded people with a sense of fair judgement vote in the same direction. Unlike many western democracies, a sizeable section of India's population is not permanently politically affiliated. They have preferences. Their vote preference varies from election to election. They make a judgement on merits and then vote. When similarly situated people with same preferences vote in a direction, it constitutes a wave. Similarly hung assemblies and Parliaments are predicted only in opinion polls. The voter is far more decisive. He endeavours to elect a government with a clear mandate. The front-runner gets more seats than predicted.

It is this sense of fairness of the Indian electorate that enables it to decide on issues. The voter has a huge potential to distinguish between truth and falsehood. Truth holds. Falsehood falls apart. Political leaders are overconfident about their wisdom. Little do they realise that the electorate is wiser than them. It is capable of punishing those who resort to falsehood.

It is a recognition of the performance of Prime Minister Narendra Modi's government that the Opposition, after five years, has no real issue against the government. The government is contesting on a pro-incumbency performance platform. It is a government with a leader with whom the comfort level of the voter is high. The Opposition is in a state of panic. Its single point programme is a negative one – remove one man. The level of ambition is limited. In the absence of any real issue against the government, Rahul Gandhi has led not only his party but the entire Opposition to rely on fake and manufactured issues. They raise fake issues, create an echo effect and then believe their falsehood to be true. My purpose today is to analyse each one of these issues.

Rafale

The Opposition's fake issue of Rafale is that a costlier combat aircraft has been purchased by the present government. Favours have been shown to a domestic industrialist and procedural violations have taken place.

Truth:
Both the Supreme Court and the CAG have cleared the deal. They rejected all the above contentions. The government has saved thousands of crores in the Rafale deal as compared to the prices quoted in 2007. All procedures have been followed and not one rupee favour has been shown by the government to any domestic industrialist. Rafale is not to be manufactured in India at all. The Supreme Court has already examined and cleared this aspect.

Judge Loya's death

The sessions judge of Mumbai, Judge Loya, was hearing a criminal case in which the BJP president had been falsely made an accused. While attending a wedding in Nagpur, he suddenly died. The Opposition claimed that this was an unnatural death and the Supreme Court must appoint an enquiry into this.

Truth:
The Supreme Court heard the petition in a bench of three judges, examined each fact and found that he died of a heart attack. There were two district judges with him when he suffered the heart attack at his guest house. It was these two district judges, along with a registrar of the Nagpur bench of the High Court, who took him to the hospital where he was declared dead. A number of High Court judges reached the hospital. There was nobody there except judges

or doctors. Justice D.Y. Chandrachud, speaking for the bench, dismissed each allegation as false in nature. Strictures were passed against the petitioners.

Bank loan waiver

It was alleged by the Opposition that loans worth Rs 2,50,000 crore of fifteen industrialists have been waived off by this government.

Truth:
Not one rupee of loan has been waived. Indiscriminate loans were given during 2008–14 by public sector banks. They became NPAs. The present government enacted The Insolvency and Bankruptcy Code, removed the defaulting managements and has, in the last two years, recovered almost Rs 3 lakh crore worth of NPAs.

The EVM issue

The fake issue is that EVM machines are being tampered with.

Truth:
India's Election Commission is an extremely fair and independent institution. Millions of staff are involved in the process of manufacturing machines and conducting the elections. The electronic voting machines were introduced when the Congress party was in power. In the last two-and-a-half decades, dozens of elections have been held where parties have either won or lost. This is nothing wrong with the machines. There is a problem with the political losers. It is the same machine with which the Congress party won the recent Assembly elections.

Freedom of Speech is being crushed at JNU

It was alleged that by prosecuting those raising seditious slogans on breaking India into pieces at JNU, the government is threatening free speech.

Truth:
There is no free speech provision under the Indian Constitution which permits an individual to argue that the country can be broken into pieces. Sovereignty and national security are constitutionally provided restrictions to free speech under Article 19(2) of the Constitution.

The GST

The GST has been a disaster, alleges India's Opposition.

Truth:
All Opposition parties have supported the GST Constitutional Amendment and the legislations under it. It was a part of their manifesto. They failed to implement it when they were in power. Finance ministers belonging to governments run by Opposition parties are a signatory to every decision on tariffs. All GST Council decisions are unanimously taken. The GST has simplified India's complex taxation structure. There is one tax. There are no barriers; there are no inspectors. Small businesses up to rupees forty lakhs are tax exempted. Those with a turnover of rupees one and a half crore can compound their tax by paying at 1 per cent. Collections have gone up and the rate of taxes are brought down in favour of the citizen at almost every meeting.

Demonetisation was a failure

The Opposition alleges that demonetisation was a failure which caused tremendous hardship to the poor people.

Truth:
Demonetisation caused hard sleep only to the holders of black money. Demonetisation helped in formalising the economy. It compelled anonymous owners of cash to deposit the money in the bank, account for the same and pay taxes. It helped in formalising India's economy, increasing India's tax base. It hastened the digitisation of the Indian economy. India today collects more taxes at lower rates and uses them for the benefit of the poor.

Nirav Modi

The Opposition alleges that Nirav Modi was helped by this government.

Truth:
Nirav Modi started defrauding the banks in 2011 when the UPA was in power. His crime was detected in 2018 by the present government and its agencies. All his assets have been frozen, criminal cases filed for prosecution and extradition proceedings launched against him. Some assets are being auctioned. It is only a matter of time before India gets him to face the consequences in India. Nobody who frauds India can escape.

Vijay Mallya

The Opposition alleged that the government helped Vijay Mallya.

Truth:
Vijay Mallya and his company were given loans when the UPA was in power. In fact, banks were directed in 2010 to give a second restructuring of the NPAs of Vijay Mallya. There is documentary evidence which confirms this. It was on the strength of this restructuring that he got his account regularised and eventually did not pay the bankers. He escaped. No steps against him were taken by the UPA. The NDA has filed civil and criminal litigation against him and succeeded in the extradition proceedings. An appeal against the extradition order is now being heard in the United Kingdom.

Pulwama and Balakot

The Opposition alleges that the government is politicising the terrorist strike at Pulwama and the Indian Air Force strikes at Balakot in Pakistan wherein the JeM camps were liquidated. These are being used for a political advantage. The Opposition demands that evidence of what happened at Balakot should be placed in the public domain.

Truth:
Our security forces have liquidated innumerable terrorists in recent months. The terrorists, however, managed to strike at Pulwama. Our security forces liquidated the terrorists within days. On receiving information that a very large terrorist camp was being operated at Balakot in Pakistan, the prime minister directed the Indian Air Force to strike at the camp. The Indian Air Force did a commendable job. It was a perfect exercise. They liquidated the terrorists and the camps. They resisted the Pakistani Air Force's counter-attack on the following day by bringing down an F-16. The Air Force chief has confirmed this. Independent satellite data quoted by various Indian media

organisations conclusively establish the damage done by the strikes. The Indian Armed Forces are extremely professional. They consider it not in the interest of national security and military discipline that the details of military operations be placed in public domain.

The Special Status for Andhra Pradesh

The Opposition, particularly TDP, alleges that the government has denied a special status to Andhra Pradesh as promised.

Truth:

The Fourteenth Finance Commission recategorised the states. Such a recategorisation does not permit a special status. The Finance Commission report, which has been accepted, has a constitutional mandate. The government, therefore, found a way out by which an amount equivalent to what would have been paid under the special status would be given to the state of Andhra Pradesh as a special package. The Andhra Pradesh government thanked the central government and welcomed the proposal. Thereafter, it reversed its stand for political reasons. Shri Chandrababu Naidu and the TDP need to answer as to why they accepted the special package in lieu of special status, thanked the central government for it and then reversed their stand?

Institutions

The Opposition alleges that institutions are under threat from the central government.

Truth:

The real facts are absolutely to the contrary. It is the Opposition which has been indulging in a mass-intimidation of the judiciary.

They even brought an impeachment motion against the erstwhile Chief Justice of India. They put pressure on judges by threatening to walk out of courts along with their allies and lawyer fellow travellers. They intimidate judges who are not willing to decide in their favour. While the government and the ruling party have fully respected the Election Commission, it is the Opposition which raised allegations against them. They question the dates on which polling is to be held. They induce communalism on the dates fixed for campaign by invoking the Ramzan argument. They intimidate those media organisations and channels who do not toe their line. Recently, the RJD leader Tejashwi Yadav wrote a letter to Rahul Gandhi suggesting that till elections Opposition parties must boycott electronic media channels.

The Economy

The Opposition alleges that the Indian economy is in a disastrous situation and jobs are not being created.

Truth:
India is the fastest-growing economy in the world. The average rate of GDP growth in the past five years has been about 7.3 per cent. This is the highest ever five-year rate of growth in India. Certainly, the fastest-growing economy in the world cannot be in a mess. Our macro-economic data is the most prudent ever. Our fiscal deficit and current account deficit are under control. Our foreign exchange reserves are extremely high. Our revenues have grown exponentially. Inflation is under control.

If over a period of five years an economy grows at a rapid pace, its multiplier effect on jobs is very large. The recently released report of the Confederation of Indian Industry (CII) and the data of the Employees Provident Fund Organisation (EPFO) clearly indicates the number of jobs being added, both in the formal and informal sectors. The sixteen crore Mudra loans have helped the informal sector to grow significantly. There is no social unrest in the country. A high growth and job loss can occur only if productivity levels improve significantly. That does not appear to be the case.

Each one of the above is a fake issue. If fake issues are taken out of Rahul Gandhi's speech, nothing will perhaps be left. The Opposition is in a pathetic state. It has to manufacture fake issues against the government since the real ones don't exist. The Opposition underestimates the wisdom of the electorate. I am confident that the electorate will respond to India's Opposition parties and show them their place.

Three Fake Campaigns Busted in a Single Day

Posted on 21 March 2019

I have repeatedly maintained that a fundamental difference between truth and falsehood is that truth holds together and falsehood falls apart. To each fake campaign of the compulsive contrarians over a period of time, ultimately the truth has prevailed. Either it is the electoral mandate or the judicial process which gives the final verdict.

The vicious theory of 'Hindu terror'

The vicious theory of Hindu terror was coined during the UPA government by important UPA ministers and leaders. The compulsive contrarians adopted it. It was an effort to distract attention from Jihadi terror. It was a conspiracy to give a bad name to the otherwise liberal majority community in India. On terrorism, Hindus were drawn into equivalence. Terror is alien to Hindu culture. In fact, it's alien to India's legacy. We are amongst the few successful nations in the world which have managed to overcome terror and insurgency in several parts of the country. Not a single Indian has ever been arrested or killed while attempting a blast or a terrorist activity across the border.

In a series of incidents across the country during UPA-1, an effort was made to invent Hindu terror. In one case, the actual terrorists were arrested. Upon rethinking by the government, a charge-sheet was filed against a set of individuals belonging to the Hindu community and completely contradicting the earlier investigation. In the Samjhauta Express blast, the US state Department and the United Nations kept indicating a certain Jihadi organisation and individuals responsible for the 2007 blasts at Panipat. However, it was considered Hindu conspiracy by the then government. Yesterday's verdict by the court has judicially put the last nail in the coffin of the so-called Hindu terror theory.

The Godhra train fire of 2002

The burning of the Sabarmati Express in Godhra in 2002 was an attempt to instigate social and communal tension in the state. The accused in the case were identified. There was voluminous evidence available. The accused were arrested at different points of time, charge sheeted, their bail applications were rejected right up to the Supreme Court. Many of the accused were convicted earlier and an accused arrested subsequently has been convicted by the trial court yesterday.

Many compulsive contrarians, who had made a career out of creating social tensions in Gujarat started contending that the burning was self-engineered either by the state or the Kar Sevaks. In the most irresponsible act of the UPA government, the Ministry of Railways under Shri Lalu Prasad Yadav selected, without consultation of the Chief Justice of India, a retired Supreme Court justice, Mr U.N. Banerjee, as a commissioner for railway enquiry. The judge, willing to oblige the government and its political interest, submitted a report that there was no burning by the mob and that the fire had taken place from inside the compartment where the Hindu pilgrims were. I regard this subversion of evidence in order to cover up the heinous crime as the worst stigma on the UPA government and its prime minister. Such a report had no evidential value. Yesterday, the trial court, after perusing all the evidence, convicted one more accused.

Nirav Modi's arrest

Nirav Modi started cheating the public sector banks in 2011. It was a continuing crime. His crime was detected in 2018 by the banks and investigating agencies under the present government. His assets have been frozen are being auctioned, criminal prosecution against him has been filed, recovery actions for the dues owed to the banks and creditors are being pursued. He is alleged to have escaped from one jurisdiction to another. It goes to the credit of our investigating agencies that they were pursuing him. On our request, he has now been arrested and denied bail. There is a strong unanswerable case against him and hopefully India will get him back. Whoever cheats India and its institutions cannot get away. He will be found out. This also busts the fake campaign that the present government had anything to do with him.

There is an inherent danger in relying only on fake issues. They crack up and collapse as three of them did yesterday. I hope the manufacturers of fake campaigns learn their lesson. They don't seem to be considering their brazen attitude.

India's Opposition Is on a 'Rent a Cause' Campaign

Posted on 13 April 2019

The first phase of voting is over. The 'Modi' factor was writ large across the country. Amit Shah's challenge to the BJP workers to prepare for a 50 per cent voting target in the BJP-stronghold states even where there are Opposition alliances seems to be coming through.

The Opposition is in disarray in many states, alliances having not worked out. Multi-cornered contest obviously favours the BJP. Verbal battles between the left, Trinamool and the Congress and now AAP and the Congress are increasingly visible. On the leadership issue, the situation looks gloomier than what I had thought. BSP leader and Mayawati, Trinamool leader, Mamata Banerjee, leave no stone unturned in running down the Congress president.

To oust a popular government and an extremely popular prime minister, you need some real issues, not fictional issues. The Opposition wasted the past two years in a run-up to the polls manufacturing issues which didn't exist. The false campaign on Rafale didn't carry much weight. Loan waivers to industrialists was a lie, the EVMs as an instrument of rigging was a bigger lie. Now that they are in the midst of the campaign for over a month what is the issue which they are able to focus on?

Signature campaign propaganda

One important tactic is to get some critics of the government in different sections to sign memorandums against the BJP. Even in the 2014 campaign such desperate memorandums were signed. You will always find enough people on either side of the political divide in various disciplines who are willing to sign the memorandum one way or the other. These groups include academics, economists, artistes, ex-civil servants and now even some former soldiers – many of those whose signatures appear have not consented to their signatures being put there.

The BJP and its allies are speaking directly to the people. They speak through mass rallies, media and social media. Crores of campaigners are carrying the message of the party and the government to the people. Not having built up a single major issue against the government in the past five years, the strategy is to pick up an issue for a daily tweet or a press briefing. This is the plight of the Opposition's campaign.

A new cause on a daily basis

One day Pulwama was questioned as self-engineered. The next day Balakot was questioned as a non-existent operation. The anti-satellite missile was passed off as a Nehruvian contribution even though Panditji's correspondence with Dr Homi Bhabha established the contrary. One day BJP is accused of whipping up war hysteria, the other day it is dubbed as being pro-Pakistan.

One day the focus would be on the BJP candidate's educational qualification, fully forgetting that a public audit of Rahul Gandhi's academic credentials may leave a lot to be answered. After all, he got an MPhil without a master's degree! There is no running thread in the campaign which connects what is being said today with what has been said over the last several months.

There is no leader, no gathbandhan, no common minimum programme and no real issue. Not surprisingly there are not many takers for a failed campaign. It is a rent-a-cause campaign.

12

Rafale and the Congress Party's Desperate Lies

Of all the fake issues the Congress party has conjured up, Rafale is the most egregious lie. Narendra Modi has led a clean and scam-free government from day one and, in response, the Congress has flailed around and come up with the manufactured 'scandal' of Rafale that is based on a series of falsehoods, principally that the government paid a higher price for the deal than the UPA would have done, proper procedures were not followed, and a certain industrialist was favoured. Each is a lie peddled by Rahul Gandhi who is desperate to make a mark but succeeds only in exposing his own ignorance and bad faith.

The Congress Party and the Fake Issue of Rafale

Posted on 24 July 2018

The Congress party has a history of creating fake issues. In 1989, there was an outrage in the whole country against the Congress party and its leadership on the Bofors issue. The Congress party's strategists invented a counter strategy of diversion by creating a fake issue. A bank account in St. Kitts was created in the name of Shri V.P. Singh's son so that the Congress could now have a face-saving argument – if we are corrupt, so are you. In 1999, when the NDA led by Shri Atal Bihari Vajpayee, in the backdrop of the Kargil conflict, was likely to sweep the poll, and the Congress party was faced with a massive defeat, it manufactured an issue of sugar export to Pakistan. Some two dozen press conferences on the issue were organised to question the government's commitment to nationalism. The truth of the allegation was that a mid-level unknown Chandni Chowk trader had been exporting an OGL item – sugar to Pakistan. Needless to say that the Congress lost the election badly. Falsehoods fell apart.

The present political situation

- The Congress party realises that there is a danger of the next election becoming a referendum on Prime Minister Narendra Modi's performance. The popularity gap between the prime minister and his competitors is very wide.
- The Congress party is either non-existent or a poor third or fourth in states like Uttar Pradesh, Bihar, West Bengal, Tripura, parts of North-East, Odisha, Andhra Pradesh, Telangana, Delhi and Tamil Nadu. These states account for 50 per cent of the Lok Sabha seats. Of the balance seats, if it enters into some form of alliance, it may have to concede seats in several states to its allies. It is,

therefore, faced with the prospect of effectively contesting only about 225 seats where it will face a direct clash with the BJP.

- If the first part of the Congress Mukt Bharat was scripted by the BJP, the federal front is more than eager to script the part-2 of the same. Its message to the Congress is clear – 'you will have to support us; the other way is not possible.' For the Congress the best-case scenario is to become a tail-ender of the federal front and concede to it a large political space.
- Many in the Congress realise that 2019 is not their election. They should try and improve but concentrate as a priority on 2024. However, mid-level leaders of the Congress in the age group of sixty-five to seventy-four are unwilling to wait for 2024. They know that 2019 is their last chance and they will probably be time-barred by 2024. They are quite willing for a tail-ender's role.
- Its attack on the economy are failing since India, under the Modi regime, continues to be the fastest-growing major economy in the world. The Congress party's strategy of consolidating arithmetic against Prime Minister Modi's chemistry is a double-edged weapon for the Congress. It can push the Congress to the margins with the federal front occupying the Opposition's space.

The Congress strategy

- What does the party do if its leader has inherent and inbuilt limitations? It had been stigmatised by corruption and in contra-distinction Prime Minister Modi has led a scam-free government. Its strategy, therefore, is one of distortion. If you have no issue, manufacture one. Hence the Rafale's fake controversy.
- The Congress's strategy is, therefore, two-fold. It has manufactured the issue of the Rafale deal. The issue is failing to cut much ice. It's a government to government agreement with no private group involved. It involves national security and it is the armed

forces which have preferred this aircraft for its improved combat ability. The UPA ministers also never disclosed the cost break-up of the weaponry because that is not in larger national interest. The supplier/OEM manufacturers of defence equipment appoint their own offset manufacturers. The government has nothing to do with it. The truth always holds together. It is falsehood that falls apart. So, when Rahul Gandhi's statement that President Macron told him that there is no secrecy pact got smashed into pieces, the next day the Congress party shifted the Rafale issue to other extraneous grounds.

- The second strategy of the Congress party is directed against the federal front. By attacking the BJP on certain issues, it is engaged in an implied battle with the federal front in order to reclaim the minority vote. Comparison of Hindus with 'Taliban' and phrases such as 'Hindu Pakistan' are intended to help it against the federal front to reclaim the minority vote. This strategy also is likely to backfire. As equal participants in the Indian electoral process, the minorities have a constitutional right of a vote. But so does the majority. By redefining secularism as a euphemism for majority-bashing, the Congress party is antagonising the majority against itself. This will always happen in an election where you have an inadequate leader and no real issue.

Five Questions that Expose the Congress Party's Falsehood on Rafale

Posted on 29 August 2018

Considering the security environment around India, the highest standards of defence preparedness are required. After the Kargil experience, the Armed Forces and the Raksha Mantralaya were of the opinion that combat ability of the Indian Air Force to strike at targets needs to be radically improved. This need was first recorded by the Raksha Mantralaya in the year 2001.

Considerations of national security demanded that the IAF have the best available aircraft with the appropriate weaponry loaded on it. In principle approval for acceptance of necessity of procurement of 126 replacement aircrafts was recorded by the Raksha Mantri way back on 1 June 2001. After the UPA government came into power, the Defence Acquisition Council (DAC) approved the Acceptance of Necessity (AoN) for procurement of 126 medium multi-role combat aircrafts. An aircraft without weaponry is of little use in a war. It is only a flying instrument. It adds to the combat strength of the forces only when it is loaded with the requisite weaponry, which enables it to strike targets. The UPA government issued a request for proposal on 28 August 2007 and found two vendors – M/s Dassault Aviation and M/s EADS – to be compliant to the RFP requirements. It took the UPA five more years to commence the negotiations and in January 2012 the Contract Negotiation Committee (CNC) determined Dassault Aviation to be L1.

For reasons best known to the UPA government, on 27 June 2012, the deal was directed to be re-examined, which effectively meant that the entire eleven-year exercise was abandoned and the process was to be undertaken afresh. India's squadron strength was depleting because of age. This slow and casual approach of the UPA government seriously compromised national security requirements.

The NDA approach

On 10 April 2015, the government of India and the French government issued a joint statement where India decided to procure thirty-six Rafale aircrafts from the French government on terms better than the ones conveyed by Dassault in the L1 bid of 2007.

The same was approved by the DAC on 13 May 2015 and finally the agreement, after a detailed procedure, was signed on 23 September 2016.

The false campaign

A false campaign based on untruth has been launched by the Congress party casting a cloud on the Inter-governmental agreement. The principal arguments of this campaign are

- The NDA government paid a higher price than what the UPA would have paid if the deal had been completed on the basis of the 2007 offer of Dassault.
- Proper procedures such as negotiations by the CNC and approval of the Cabinet Committee on Security (CCS) were not obtained.
- A private industrialist in India was favoured and the interest of public sector undertaking was compromised.

Each one of the above issues raised is based on complete falsehood. It is expected from national political parties and its responsible leaders to keep themselves informed of the basic facts before they enter a public discourse on defence transactions. The Congress party and its leader, Shri Rahul Gandhi, are guilty on three counts:

- The UPA delayed the deal by over a decade and seriously compromised national security.
- Every fact that Shri Rahul Gandhi and the Congress party has spoken on pricing and procedure are completely false.
- Its effort of raising these issues is to further delay a defence procurement so that India's defence preparedness further suffers.

The questions

I have, therefore, decided to ask the following questions to the Congress party and its president. Needless to say, if replies are received in the public space or even if there is an issue diversion and no reply is received, I would be constrained to come out with further specific facts which establish truth as a victim of Shri Rahul Gandhi and his party merely peddling his falsehoods. Needless to say, I am constrained by the secrecy clause, which exists in the contract and whatever I ask or respond to would be constrained by that limitation. My questions to Shri Rahul Gandhi and his party are as follows:

On delay

- The UPA was a government which suffered from a decision-making paralysis. Do you agree that the delay of over one decade was only on account of the incompetence and indecisiveness of the UPA government?
- Did this delay seriously compromise national security? Is not the medium multi-role combat aircraft required by our forces to identify and strike at targets particularly when two of our neighbours have already enhanced their strength in this area?
- Was this delay and eventual abatement of the purchase by the UPA based on collateral considerations as had been witnessed in earlier transactions such as the purchase of the 155 mm Bofors gun?

Unsure of facts

- How is it that Shri Rahul Gandhi quoted a price of Rs 700 crore per aircraft in Delhi and Karnataka in April and May this year? In Parliament, he reduced it to Rs 520 crore per aircraft, in Raipur he increased it to Rs 540 crore; in Jaipur he used the two figures – Rs 520 crore and Rs 540 crore in the same speech. In Hyderabad, he invented a new price of Rs 526 crore. Truth has only one version, falsehood has many. Are these allegations being made without any familiarity with the facts of the Rafale purchase?

- Are Mr Gandhi or the Congress party aware of price comparison? Is Mr Gandhi aware of the aircraft's price, which was quoted in 2007 in the L1 bid? Is he aware that there was an escalation clause, which by 2015 when the NDA struck the price deal, would have further escalated the price? Would not the escalation clause have continued to escalate the price till each of the aircraft was supplied? Have the significant exchange-rate variations between the Rupee and the Euro during the same period been considered?
- Is he aware of the fact that if the basic aircraft price on which the UPA was to purchase the aircraft along with the escalation clause is compared at the price with the better terms on which the NDA government signed the deal? The basic aircraft price itself is 9 per cent cheaper under the NDA than it was under the UPA.
- Can Shri Rahul Gandhi deny that when the add-ons such as India-specific adaptations, weaponry, etc. are installed on the basic aircraft, the UPA price, which was mentioned in the 2007 L1 offer, would be at least 20 per cent costlier than the more favourable price negotiated by the NDA?
- Can Shri Rahul Gandhi and the Congress party deny if the total contract cost, that is, basic aircraft plus add-ons, including weaponry, etc., Indian adaptations plus future supplies and maintenance are all added, the NDA terms become far more favourable than the 2007 L1 offer?

Role of private industries

- Can Shri Rahul Gandhi and the Congress deny that the government of India has no contract whatsoever with any private industry in relation with the Rafale aircraft supplies? In fact, thirty-six of the Rafale aircraft with their Indian adaptations are going to be sent to India and there is no manufacturing of these thirty-six aircrafts in India.
- Any Original Equipment Manufacturer (OEM) under the offset policy of the UPA can select any number of Indian partners, both from the private sector and the public sector, for offset supplies? This has nothing to do with the government of India and, therefore, any private industry having benefitted from the government of India is a complete lie. Can Shri Gandhi and his party deny this?

On procedure

- Are Shri Gandhi and his party aware of the fact that there are two ways of acquiring a defence equipment, i.e., either by competitive bidding or by an inter-governmental agreement?
- Can Mr Gandhi and his party deny that the UPA government in 2007 itself had shortlisted the Rafale as technically acceptable and L1 in price competition?
- Can Shri Gandhi and his party deny that considering the urgency of the defence requirement, the government of India and the French government agreed to execute the supply of thirty-six Rafale aircrafts at terms better than the 2007 offer of the UPA?
- Can it be denied that both the Price Negotiation Committee and the Contract Negotiation Committee negotiated for fourteen months before concluding the deal?
- Can it be denied that before the deal was executed, the Cabinet Committee on Security approved the transaction?

I am asking the above questions and I hope Shri Rahul Gandhi and the Congress party would respond immediately.

Rafale – Lies, Short-Lived Lies and Now Further Lies

Posted on 16 December 2018

All the lies spoken on the Rafale deal have been exposed. The Supreme Court judgement is clear. Every word said against the government has proved to be false. Every 'fact' stated by the vested interests against the deal has proved to be manufactured. Truth has once again established its primacy. The creators of falsehood will still persist with falsehood even at the cost of their own credibility. Only their captive constituencies will clap.

The credentials of the disruptors

Rafale is a combat aircraft with its weaponry required to improve the strike ability of the Indian Air Force. India is geographically located in a sensitive region. It needs to protect itself. The need for such a weapon cannot be overstated. When such defence equipment is purchased obviously some suppliers lose out. The suppliers are clever people. They understand who the 'vulnerables' in India are.

As a political opponent Rahul Gandhi's opposition to the deal was a desperate attempt. It was the UPA government which had shortlisted the Rafale as it was technically the best and the cheapest. PM Modi in an Inter-governmental agreement struck a deal with the French government to further improve the terms and conditions including the prices on which the UPA had agreed.

Rahul's opposition was obviously for three reasons

Firstly, he could not tolerate the fact that PM Modi has run the cleanest government in recent Indian history. It is a scam-free government where middlemen and scamsters have had to take refuge outside the country.

Secondly, Rahul Gandhi has the burden of a stigmatised legacy which was tainted by Bofors. He was desperate trying to bring an 'immoral equivalence' between Rafale and Bofors. But Rafale did not have middlemen, no kickbacks and obviously no Ottavio Quattrocchi.

Thirdly, with international cooperation and governmental cooperation, scamsters of the UPA government are now being extradited into India. There is obviously a scare of who will talk how much.

Rahul Gandhi got instant support from the career nationalists of Lutyens Delhi. The permanent PIL petitioners have always preferred disruptions over concerns of national security. They are willing to cooperate with anyone who hurts India. A new job creation has taken place in Delhi with the 'loud mouths on hire' and 'subject experts' notwithstanding their conflict of interest. The disruptionists' alliance was, therefore, quite wide.

The lies that were spoken

The fundamental truth that Rafale was a choice both for quality and price by the UPA was forgotten.

The first lie was that only one man – the prime minister decided the transaction and that no discussion with the Air Force, Defence Ministry or the Defence Acquisition Council was held. It was alleged that there was no Price Negotiation Committee, no Contract Negotiation Committee and no approval of the Cabinet Committee on Security. Every fact was false. There were dozens of meetings of the Contract Negotiation Committee and the Price Negotiation Committee. The bulk of the negotiations were done by the experts of the Air Force and the transaction was cleared by both the Defence Acquisition Council and the Cabinet Committee on Security.

The judgement of the Supreme Court notes with satisfaction that procedural compliances have been done and the charges on the same are misconceived.

The second major lie was that as against €500 million negotiated by the UPA, the NDA paid €1600 million per aircraft. This accusation was 'fiction writing' and a poor one at that. The government submitted a sealed cover before the Supreme Court giving details in a comparative chart of the UPA era pricing and the present pricing. It showed that for the first aircraft, government negotiated a 9 per cent cheaper deal for a bare aircraft and 20 per cent cheaper for a weaponised aircraft compared to the UPA. Since the UPA had negotiated the supply of 18 aircrafts, this gain of 9 per cent and 20 per cent would have further expanded with the supply of aircrafts after the first one since a more favourable escalation clause negotiated by the NDA government would have further widened the price gap. The court looked into the prices and never commented adversely on the same.

The third major lie that the judgement of the court expressed was that the government of India favoured a particular business house. The court noticed that the government has nothing to do with the choice of the offset suppliers which was entirely done by Dassault.

After the court judgement, this debate should have come to an end. But neither lobbyists nor political opponents will ever give up their brief.

The misconceived demand for a Joint Parliamentary Committee (JPC)

The opponents of Rafale had a choice of their forum to put their facts, they chose Supreme Court as their forum.

The court conducts a judicial review, it is a non-partisan, independent and a fair Constitutional authority. The court's verdict is final. It can't be reviewed by anyone except by the court itself. How can a parliamentary committee go into the correctness or otherwise of what the court has said? Is a committee of politicians both legally and in terms of human resources capable of reviewing issues already decided by the Supreme Court? On areas such as procedure, offset suppliers and pricing, can a parliamentary committee take a different view of what the court has said? Can the contract be breached, the nation's security be compromised, and the pricing data be made available to the Parliament or its committee so that national interest is severely compromised? This would be putting the price details of the weaponry in public domain. What was the experience of Joint Parliamentary Committee (JPC) on the only occasion when they investigated a defence transaction?

The B. Shankaranand Committee in 1987–88 went into the Bofors transaction. Since parliamentarians are always split on party lines, it came out with a finding that no kickbacks were paid, and the monies paid to the middlemen were 'winding up' charges. At that time only Win Chaddha appeared to be a middleman. But then others including Ottavio Quattrocchi, whose bank accounts got detected subsequently, were not entitled to any winding up charges. The reports/documents published by Chitra Subramanium and N. Ram in *The Hindu* and all subsequent facts which came to light conclusively established each fact mentioned in the JPC to be factually false. It became a cover up exercise. After the Supreme

Court has spoken the last word, it gets legitimacy. A political body can never come to a finding contrary to what the court has said.

The CAG ambiguity

Defence transactions go to the CAG for an audit review. CAG recommendations go to Parliament and are referred to the Public Accounts Committee (PAC) whose reports are then placed before the Parliament. This was factually and accurately stated by the government before the court. The audit review of Rafale is pending before the CAG. All facts are shared with it. When its report is out, it will go to the PAC. Notwithstanding this factually correct statement made, if an ambiguity has emerged in the court order, the correct course is for anyone to apply/mention before the court and have it corrected. The past practice is that if in a factual narration anything needs to be corrected, any litigant can move to the court for the same. This has been done. It must now be left to the wisdom of the court to state at which stage the CAG review is pending. The CAG review is not relevant to the final findings on procedure, pricing and offset suppliers. But bad losers never accept the truth. Having failed in multiple lies they have now started an innuendo about the Judgement. Having failed in their initial falsehood, the Congress is now manufacturing further lies about the Judgement.

I am certain that the Congress party will prefer disruptions over discussion on Rafale during the current session of Parliament. On facts it lied. The judgement of the Supreme Court conclusively establishes the Congress party's vulnerabilities in a discussion on defence transactions. It will be a great opportunity to remind the nation of the legacy of the Congress party and its defence acquisitions – a great opportunity indeed for some of us to speak.

13

India Needs a Better Opposition than the Congress

Despite all its attacks, the Opposition is simply off the mark. It never hits a bulls-eye because it fails to appreciate that so many of the government's schemes such as the Mudra Yojana loans for the self-employed or the creation of more IITs and IIMs have proved popular. There is no coherence to the denunciations of the Modi government. They are motivated by blind anti-Modism and characterised by the absence of any alternative. The Congress by definition as a party ruled by a dynasty has no ideology, therefore it cherry picks issues randomly, jumping from sneering at pakora making as a job one day to expressing doubts about the effectiveness of the Balakot attacks. No unifying thread binds its criticism. Opportunism is no substitute for ideology.

Is Congress Becoming Ideology-less? Is Anti-Modism its only ideology?

Posted on 13 June 2018

A few weeks ago, P. Chidambaram, finance minister in the UPA government, claimed that frying pakodas is not job creation. Being cleverer than the rest of his colleagues, he was perhaps trying to neutralise the success story of the Mudra Yojana where 12.9 crore loans have been given for self-employment to various weaker sections. The total of these loans has touched Rs 6 lakh crore. This has obviously led to millions of hands generating new work for themselves and those they employ.

Two days ago, while addressing a gathering of what they claimed were their OBC supporters, Rahul Gandhi spoke on the entrepreneurial skills of shikanjiwalas, dhabawalas and mechanics. Though factually what he stated was incorrect, the larger point is that he saw virtues in these professions which can act as a launch pad for many start-ups. The great grandson of the man who authored *The Discovery of India* could with his customary inaccuracies one day give to this country his monumental work on 'The Rediscovery of Coca Cola'.

It is the NDA government under Prime Minister Modi which realised the importance of millions of such self-employment opportunities for which in the year 2015 Mudra Yojana was launched. Most of the beneficiaries took small loans, were prompt in their repayment, set up small enterprises and gave themselves, and perhaps one or two people more, employment. The UPA never did so. I repeat that it was the UPA which, during 2008–14, indiscriminately lent money through banks to these fifteen big defaulters. The Congress president prefers the Goebbelsian traditions to say the exact opposite. What he claimed before the audience is precisely what we have successfully implemented.

Why does he believe that 2.5 lakh crore bank loans have been waived? Is it because of his inability to understand that where a performing asset is not serviced by the debtor, after ninety days it becomes a non-performing asset. Its chances of recovery, as per RBI guidelines, decline. There is a shift in the column that takes place and the bank has to make provisioning on the basis that the possibility of recovery declines. But the debtor liability remains. There is no waiver. When, either through the IBC or legal processes, the debt is recovered back, the entry is reversed. For he President of a national party not to understand this basic procedure of bank functioning should be a matter of concern to the entire party as well as the country. In dynastic parties, political positions are heritable. Unfortunately, wisdom is not heritable. It has to be acquired through learning.

Why this sudden love for the other backward classes?

The OBCs deserted the Congress party in the early 1990s. The Congress was always anti-OBC. Late Shri Rajiv Gandhi made strong speech in Parliament against the Mandal Commission. Recently, the Congress party opposed the grant of constitutional status to the National Commission for Backward Classes. They voted against the constitutional amendment in Parliament. It opportunistically supported reservation for the non-backwards. It impliedly wants to reduce the quota for the OBCs knowing fully well that the judiciary will not allow 50 per cent on reservations to be waived and the new claimants would eat into the OBC quota.

Rahul's other gems

- Interacting with his interviewer in Singapore a few weeks ago, Rahul Gandhi left his audience stunned by suggesting that if MRI machines in India were connected, this would lead to a medical revolution. How? Except for breaching a patient's privacy by sharing his details with other hospitals what would this achieve?
- He told an audience in Karnataka that his party believes that there should be only one GST rate, as it is in Singapore. Singapore charges 7 per cent GST on all food items, cheap clothing and footwear, medical and education spends as on luxury items – BMW cars, alcohol and five-star hotels. India has exempted most food items. Should we have the same rate for food items, hawai chappals and BMW cars? Singapore, unlike India, has no BPL or lower-income groups.
- On education he believes we must have 200 IITs. The UPA never did so. It is the NDA which is now creating a network of IITs, IIMs and AIIMS all over the country.

In all the above statements, there is no ideological pattern. Ignorance with anti-Modism is a common thread

Dynastic political parties are family and personality dominated. Ideology takes a back seat. You can oppose the OBC when it suits you. You can shed crocodile tears for them when the opportunism so requires. You can run down jobs created by frying pakodas. You can quantify on the virtues of running a dhaba. The leader's ill-informed instincts become the ideology. This can only happen to a party which becomes ideology-less, pushes itself to the fringe, is willing to act as a tail-ender to regional parties. All this because its only obsession is a person called Narendra Modi.

India's Opposition Has a Lot to Learn

Posted on 3 March 2019

The Congress-led UPA government, from 2004 to 2014, ran a terrible government. From 2014 to 2019, it was an even more terrible Opposition. There are occasions in history where the nation speaks in one voice. Politicians and leaders rise to the level of statesmanship. They rise above narrow partisan interest. Shri Atal Bihari Vajpayee's and the Jana Sangh's support to the government during the 1971 war is a case in point.

The terrorists attack at Pulwama on 14 February 2019 was planned and hatched across the border. Several Pakistani nationals were involved in it. Some have already been liquidated. There is enough evidence which points to this direction. It has been shared with Pakistan.

The attack generated a sense of revulsion against terrorists and its sponsors in India. The nation was determined that the blood of our martyred Jawans will continue to inspire us to eliminate terrorism.

The pre-emptive attack by our Air Force at Balakot across the border was intended to defend India's sovereignty. It was a perfectly executed, pinpointed operation. No civilian or military installations were targeted – only terrorists were.

The retaliatory attack by Pakistan's F-16 was the most botched-up operation. In short, both the attack and our defence pointed to the valour and professionalism of our Air Force. Pakistan was globally isolated. Even the OIC refused to pay heed to it. It violated every tenet of the Geneva Convention in relation to our brave Wing Commander Abhinandan. Not only was Pakistan globally isolated, the issue of its terrorism has reached the Security Council. So helpless was the situation that it was in no position to even admit the attack at Balakot. If it had admitted the attack and its consequences, the evidence of a terrorist camp in existence and the list of dead terrorists would have been international issue.

The whole of India was speaking in one voice. Public opinion overwhelmingly supported the government's decision and the Air Force's execution.

However, like its other friends in the Opposition, the Congress party refuses to learn. After initial show of support for our Air Force, it tried to create a divide in India's political opinion. From the Congress and its friends, we have witnessed three recent statements.

In a meeting of the 21 Opposition parties, a resolution was passed, accusing the prime minister of politicising the Pulwama and Balakot incidents. The government had twice taken the Leaders of Opposition parties into confidence. No evidence of politicisation was given. The statement was inappropriate. It gave a handle to the enemy. The media in Pakistan used this statement of 21 Opposition parties as a trump card. It took the statement as an endorsement of the Pakistani position that India had taken the Balakot action because of the compulsion of its domestic politics and not as a part of its policy to defend the country against terrorism.

The West Bengal chief minister went a step further. She started doubting the veracity of the incident and wanted to know the operational details. The credibility of both the government and our Air Force is being doubted. Even Congress leaders have raised similar questions.

I was most disappointed with a brief but a highly objectionable statement of the former Prime Minister Dr Manmohan Singh. While receiving the P.V. Narasimha Rao Award for the lifetime achievement, he stated that he was disturbed with the 'Mad rush of mutual self-destruction' by the two nations. He further went on to argue that poverty, ignorance and disease were the real problems in the two countries and that saner counsel on both sides needed to think on the issue. What does this statement indicate? My analysis of the statement is as follows:

- The former prime minister elevated himself to the status of a neutral third party rather than be concerned about India's interest.
- He further developed a theory of parity and equivalence between both India and Pakistan. The perpetrator of terrorism and the victim of terrorism are both at par according to him.
- Implicitly, he doubts India's right to defend its sovereignty from those who want to damage it through terrorism.
- There is no condemnation of terrorism in that speech.
- Amongst the problems facing India that he mentions which include poverty, ignorance and disease. Violence and terrorism are of no consequence in his assessment.

Seen collectively and cumulatively, the above three statements ought not to have been made. They hurt India's national interest. Not only do they give smiles to Pakistan, they become an important instrument in Pakistan's hands to discredit India. Does the opposition want the Air Force to release operation details of the Balakot attack? The Opposition is entitled to oppose and ask questions, but then restrain and statesmanship are also an essential ingredient of public discourse. I hope, India's Opposition revisits its position and does not let down the nation.

Part Five

The Emergency

14

The Emergency and How Indira Gandhi Exceeded Hitler

Jaitley recounts the key moments of the Emergency, an event he says 'changed the future course' of his life. Indira Gandhi's reasons for imposing the Emergency and the manner in which she did it offer a striking parallel with events in Nazi Germany when Hitler used the pretext of the Reichstag fire to justify the emergency powers which he assumed. However, the restrictions of Mrs Gandhi's Emergency were more draconian and far-reaching than those of Hitler. It was in fighting the Emergency, along with others, that Jaitley cut his political teeth and emerged as a young leader of integrity and principle.

Forty-Two Years Ago: The Emergency

Posted on 1 July 2017

It has become customary for the critics of any government in India to casually use an expression 'Undeclared Emergency'. Those making these exaggerated comments need to introspect their own roles during the Emergency. Most of them were either supporting the Emergency or were absent in any protest against the Emergency.

The Emergency was an assault on all democratic institutions. It not only established the dictatorship of an individual, it created an environment of tyranny and fear in society. Most institutions collapsed on their own. The Emergency was declared on the midnight of 25–26 June 1975. The ostensible and the official reason was a threat to public order but obviously this was a phoney reason. The real reason was that Mrs Indira Gandhi had been unseated in an election petition by the Allahabad High Court and the Supreme Court had granted only a conditional stay of the High Court order. She wanted to continue in power and resorted to imposition of the Emergency to enable this to happen. It would be in the fitness of things to remind those who loosely use a phrase 'Undeclared Emergency' with what happened during that period.

The first Act after the imposition of the Emergency was the detention of the political opposition under the preventive detention law. District magistrates and collectors were handed over blank detention forms to enable them to detain thousands of leaders and workers of the political opposition. Just the name, father's name and address of each detainee was filled in hand. No grounds of detention existed in any case. Police stations were advised to register identical FIRs arresting ordinary political workers under the Defence of India rules after alleging that they were either members of banned organisation or were threatening to overthrow the government.

Nine High Courts in the country held that the detention order was justiciable and in the absence of the grounds of detention the same could be quashed. The Supreme Court decided otherwise.

In preparation for the Emergency, the Supreme Court had already been packed with pliable judges. Three senior-most judges of the Supreme Court were superseded and those believing in the social philosophy of the government were in control of the court. The Supreme Court held that an illegally detained detainee had no judicial recourse during the Emergency. Justice H.R. Khanna was the only dissenting judge. Pre-censorship was imposed on the entire news media. Not a word could be published in the newspaper without going through the censor. An officer of the censor stayed in the premises of every major newspaper. The entire activities of the opposition were blacked out and the media contained only governmental propaganda. Many of those who now complain of an 'Undeclared Emergency' were either active or reluctant supporters of the Emergency regime.

Both the Constitution of India and the provisions of the Representation of the People Act were retrospectively amended so that each ground on which Mrs Indira Gandhi's election had been set aside could be statutorily reversed. The pliable Supreme Court upheld the retrospective amendments to the provision of the Representation of the People Act by upholding the power of Parliament to amend any law retrospectively. The opposition members of both the Houses of Parliament stood detained. The numerical strength of Parliament was reduced. This gave the government an opportunity to amend the Constitution through a procured two-thirds majority in Parliament. A Parliament elected for a period of five years extended its own life beyond five years by amending the Constitution.

Opposition governments in some states were dismissed and India witnessed virtually a single individual rule. All the ingredients of an absolute dictatorship existed. There was no personal liberty, no press freedom, Parliament became a farce, the highest court became subservient to the dictatorship and there was no room for dissent. This now was an ideal opportunity for the dictator to perpetuate her family and, therefore, the younger son of the prime minister, Mr Sanjay Gandhi, was proclaimed as the de facto successor. The country witnessed forced sterilisation, mass scale uprooting of the poor including the minorities from their homes, and misuse of the mass media.

An era of sycophancy always suffers from a dichotomy. A dictatorial regime is often misled by its own propaganda. It becomes a consumer of its own propaganda with nobody else believing it. It misled itself to believe that the people were in support of the dictatorship. It, therefore, committed the ultimate error of ordering an election which witnessed a rebellion against the Emergency regime.

Today I wonder if those who routinely use the expression 'Undeclared Emergency' introspect and ask themselves a question 'where was I during those nineteen months and what was my publicly declared stand at that time?'

The Emergency Revisited – Part 1: The Circumstances Leading to the Imposition of Emergency

Posted on 24 June 2018

The years 1971 and 1972 were high points in the political career of Indira Gandhi. She challenged the senior leaders of her own party and a grand alliance of Opposition parties. She won the 1971 general elections convincingly. She was the key centre of political power for the next five years. There was no challenge to her within her own party.

The year 1971 also witnessed a civil revolt in East Pakistan where in a general election the Awami League led by Sheikh Mujibur Rahman had won a clear majority in the Pakistan Parliament. Zulfikar Ali Bhutto's party had fewer seats than the Awami League. How could Pakistan allow its government to be dominated by East Pakistan? It refused to accept the mandate leading to revolt in East Pakistan. It snowballed into a major crisis with the Mukti Bahini battling the Pakistani army.

Ultimately a war with India started on 3 December 1971. By 16 December the Indian forces had taken control of East Pakistan and made substantial headway in West Pakistan. The Pakistani forces in East Pakistan surrendered to India and were taken as prisoners of war. For India and Mrs Indira Gandhi the break-up of Pakistan was a major political development which led to the creation of a new nation – Bangladesh.

Mismanagement of the economy, slogans versus policy

The stage was now set for Mrs Indira Gandhi to rule India, deliver to it the promise of Garibi Hatao and bring substantial economic growth in India. At this point her popularity was very high. During the 1960s and 1970s, the average growth rate of GDP had only been 3.5 per cent. Most countries in the world were now trying to get out of a regulated economy which was proving to be counter-productive. Even communist nations were either on the brink of break up or rejecting state regulation. By keeping one party rule intact, China decided to move ahead with the liberalised economy.

The tragedy of Mrs Indira Gandhi's politics was that she preferred popular slogans over sound and sustainable policies. The government, with a huge electoral mandate at the Centre and in the states, continued in the same economic direction which she had experimented with in the late 1960s.

She believed that India's slow growth was on account of smuggling and economic offences. She enacted a preventive detention law, COFEPOSA, to deal with smuggling. She believed that confiscation of smugglers' assets could bring to India a large resource and hence SAFEMA was enacted. She believed that large enterprises with economies of scale had to be stopped and the MRTP Act was made more stringent. She believed that land regulations in terms of size, ownership must also apply to urban areas and hence the urban land ceiling law was enacted.

This led to residential construction and apartment development not taking off as large chunks of urban land got frozen. Only state development authorities were allowed to develop land. She believed that outsourcing of business was harmful and the Contract Labour Abolition Act was brought in. She nationalised insurance and the coal mine business. She botched up the nationalisation of wheat trade (subsequently reversed) to tackle the unmanageable inflation. It led to greater inflation. This led to social and trade union unrest in which a large number of man-days were lost.

The first oil shock had already had an adverse impact. Due to its tilt towards Pakistan, the United States suspended a lot of aid to India. Inflation in 1974 touched a staggering 20.2 per cent and reached 25.2 per cent in 1975. Labour laws were made more stringent and these led to a near economic collapse. There was large-scale unemployment and unprecedented price rise. Investment in the economy had taken a back seat. To make matters worse, FERA was enacted. The foreign exchange resources in 1975 and 1976 were a mere 1.3 billion dollars.

On 28 February 1974, Shri Y.B. Chavan, the finance minister, presented the Budget in which he said, 'As the House is aware the government has been deeply concerned about the acute inflationary pressure that has prevailed in the economy during the last two years, it is a matter of deep regret that despite these measures, prices continue to rise, the steep fall of 9.5 per cent in agricultural output in 1972–73 was bound to upset the balance in demand and supply, the available indications suggest that there was hardly any increase in the rate of growth of industrial production in 1972.'

In the Budget speech of 1975–76, Finance Minister C. Subramaniam used similar words: 'Inflation has been spreading and its devastating impact across national boundaries continues to impose on developing countries such as India burdens and hardships which we have been ill-equipped to withstand. The impact on the living standard of our people and on the pattern of real incomes within the country has been serious enough.'

The loss of political goodwill

By 1973 it became apparent that the government had no intention of changing a disastrous economy path on which it had embarked. Its political strategy was instrumental in the government losing the sympathy of the intelligentsia. It was engaged in a battle with the Supreme Court in order to ensure that the Golaknath judgement was reversed.

This effort failed as majority of Judges decided against the government in the Kesavananda Bharati case. The three senior judges of the Supreme Court – Justice Shelat, Justice Grover and Justice Hegde – were superseded and Justice A.N. Ray was appointed Chief Justice of India. The superseded judges resigned. The court was now packed with government-preferred judges. A dangerous thesis was propagated by Law Minister H.R. Gokhale and Steel and Mines Minister Mohan Kumaramangalam that the judiciary must follow the social philosophy of the government and judges must be appointed on the basis of their social philosophy.

The press was not spared either. One way of controlling the media was to pinch the pocket of the media. The government, therefore, passed an order putting restrictions on the number of advertisements that a newspaper could carry. It was challenged before the Supreme Court by the leading newspapers. Fortunately, the Constitution bench, by majority of four against one, struck down the government action. Justice K.K. Mathew, a pro-government judge in the Kesavananda Bharati case, was the dissenting judge who favoured media restrictions.

Two freak events

There were two freak events which were occurring in parallel in 1973. On account of the unprecedented price rise in the hostel, the mess charges of the L.D. Engineering College in Ahmedabad were increased. The second event related to the maverick socialist leader Raj Narain who had lost the 1971 elections to Mrs Indira Gandhi and had filed an election petition challenging the validity of her election before the Allahabad High Court. Political observers had initially believed these events as of little consequence to the government and Mrs Gandhi.

The low key agitation arising from the hostel price rise engulfed the whole city of Gujarat and it became impossible for Chief Minister Chimanbhai Patel to manage the social unrest. It became an unmanageable mass movement. The entire civil society was on the streets. The students of Gujarat led the movement. The veteran leader Morarji Desai sat on a fast unto death, till the Assembly was dissolved and fresh elections were held. The government had to give in, leading to the dissolution of the State Assembly and the holding of fresh elections in June 1975.

Developments in Gujarat triggered similar sentiments in other parts of the country. The immediate impact was in Bihar where, frustrated with corruption, unemployment and inflation, the Chhatra Sangharsh Samiti launched a mass movement. Shri J.P.

Narayan (JP) who had retired from active public life, jumped into the movement. He inspired the students not only in Bihar but all over the country to organise similar protests.

In 1974 as president of the Delhi University Students' Union, I convened student leaders from all over the country for a two-day coordination committee meeting with JP. I requested JP to address a mass rally on the university campus in Delhi which witnessed an unprecedented turnout. JP toured several parts of India. Student organisations and political parties, particularly the Jana Sangh, Congress (O) Swatantra Party, and the socialists all joined the movement. Gandhian and Sarvodaya leaders became active in the movement. The Akali Dal got out from gurudwara politics. Led by Sardar Prakash Singh Badal, it joined JP in a big way. So did the veterans Biju Patnaik and Acharya Kriplani.

12 June 1975 turned out to be one of the most disappointing days for Mrs Indira Gandhi. She had been unable to manage the economy. She was increasingly seen as dictatorial and vindictive. The opposition had joined ranks against her. The day began with the sad news of the demise of one of her closest advisers, Shri D.P. Dhar. By the afternoon the result of the Gujarat Assembly election had come and the Congress party lost Gujarat for the first time and Shri Morarji Desai's blessed Opposition alliance led by Shri Babubhai Desai won an absolute majority.

Then came the stunning news that Justice Jag Mohan Lal Sinha of the Allahabad High Court had unseated Mrs Indira Gandhi as a member of Parliament and declared her election as null and void. She was accused of spending more money on the elections than permissible and having secured the services of Yashpal Kapoor, a public servant, to further her election process. She was held guilty of corrupt practices.

Are individuals indispensable in a democracy?

By the evening of 12 June large demonstrations were organised outside the prime minister's residence that the judgement of Allahabad High Court should not be accepted. The rule of law was sought to be replaced by a politically dangerous principle that Indira Gandhi was indispensable. A situation was created for the party to rally behind her. An appeal to the Supreme Court was immediately prepared and filed. She succeeded in getting Nani Palkhivala to appear for her. It was the month of June and the vacation judge Justice V.R. Krishna Iyer was to hear this appeal and the possible grant of an interim order against the High Court judgement.

Before the hearing, the Law Minister Gokhale wanted to meet Justice Krishna Iyer and discuss the case with him. The judge asked Gokhale the purpose of the meeting which Gokhale told him honestly. The judge politely declined the meeting. This was disclosed by the judge in his memoirs. The judge heard Palkhivala for Indira Gandhi and Shanti Bhushan for Raj Narain and passed the usual order which is passed in election appeals. The appeal was admitted. Palkhivala's request for a stay on the judgement of the Allahabad High Court was rejected. Indira Gandhi could attend Parliament but could not speak as a member of Parliament. She could speak only as the prime minister.

The Supreme Court's order intensified the demand for her resignation. On 24 June the Opposition leader met JP at the Gandhi Peace Foundation. As the convener of youth and student organisations, I sat in the back row observing the then national leaders chalking out the strategy. A nationwide Satyagraha was to be launched from 29 June. 25 June witnessed a big rally at Ramlila Maidan. The pressure for resignation was building up.

The midnight of 25 June

Since the war with Pakistan in 1971, India was already in a declared state of Emergency under Article 352 of the Constitution. This Emergency was on account of external aggression. There was no need to declare a second Emergency. But it was Siddhartha Shankar Ray who advised her that a second proclamation of emergency was required. It was necessary, he argued, to proclaim an emergency on account of internal disturbances.

Accordingly on the midnight of 25–26 June a fresh proclamation was signed by the president on a state of internal emergency. Simultaneously with the proclamation under Article 352, another proclamation under Article 359 was issued suspending the fundamental rights under Articles 14, 19, 21 and 22 of the Constitution. Every Indian was now devoid of this fundamental right. It was a phony emergency on account of a proclaimed policy that Indira Gandhi was indispensable to India and all contrarian voices had to be crushed. The constitutional provisions were used to turn democracy into a constitutional dictatorship.

The morning of 26 June

On the midnight of 25–26 June political leaders across the country were arrested by the police. All those who were opposed to Mrs Indira Gandhi were a special target. I was one of those whose house was encircled by the police in the early hours of 26th morning. My father, a lawyer, asked for the documents for my detention, which the police did not have. They took him to the police station and then sent him back, saying that I must report to the police.

In the meanwhile, I escaped from my house and spent the night with a friend in the neighbourhood. On coming to know what was happening I started to prepare for organising a protest on the morning of 26 June. In the early morning I was trying to find out what was happening in other parts of the country. Most of the leaders had been arrested and were taken to jail.

The electricity connection at Bahadurshah Zafar Marg – Delhi's Press Street – was cut off to ensure that no newspapers were published. By 10 a.m., censorship had been imposed on the newspapers and an official of the Censor was sitting in the office of every newspaper. I led a protest of Delhi University students where we burnt an effigy of the Emergency and I delivered a speech against what was happening. The police had arrived in large numbers. I was arrested only to be served a detention order under the Maintenance of Internal Security Act.

I was taken to Delhi's Tihar Jail for the purpose of detention. I thus got the privilege for organising the only protest on the morning of 26 June 1975 and became the first Satyagrahi against the Emergency. Little did I realise that at a young age of twenty-two years, I was participating in events which were going to be a part of history. For me this event changed the future course of my life. By late afternoon, I was lodged in Tihar Jail as a MISA detenu.

The Emergency Revisited – Part 2: The Tyranny of Emergency

Posted on 25 June 2018

Having imposed the Emergency on 26 June 1975, Mrs Indira Gandhi had issued a proclamation under Article 359 suspending fundamental rights. As a result of this, the right to free speech and personal liberty was gone. Only censored news was available. On 29 June, in order to deflect attention from the suspension of democracy in India, she announced a Twenty Point Programme for the revival of the Indian economy. In fact, a large number of these twenty points were also retrograde economic measures which had to be reversed in the post 1991 economic reforms. Thousands of political detenues, journalists and academics were detained all over the country.

The jails were overcrowded. The jail conditions were horrible. I was lodged in Delhi's Tihar Jail for a week. Thereafter, along with twenty other detenues I was shifted to the Ambala Central Jail. Under the conditions of detention rules, we were allowed a daily ration in which we had to manage all the meals. The budget available per detenue for the daily food was three rupees. Thus, if there were twenty detenues in a ward, from morning tea, breakfast, lunch, evening tea and dinner, they had to manage food for twenty people within Rs 60. After months of agitation, this amount was enhanced to five rupees per detenue.

For the initial few months, no meetings with family members were allowed. After a few months, your family members could meet for a few minutes once every month, which was subsequently increased to once every week. I was, at that stage, a student of the law faculty with my final year to clear. A number of detenues filed petitions for quashing their detention. I also filed a similar petition.

Subsequently, I moved court on several occasions for permission to write my final-year law exams from jail but Delhi University was asked to change the rules to the effect that a personal presence in the examination centre is essential to write the exam. My plea that I should be taken to the centre under police custody to write my exam was rejected by the government on the grounds that my presence in the examination centre was a threat to public order. During the nineteen months of detention, I lost one academic year and was in danger of losing the second. Due to this litigation, I managed to get transferred back to Tihar Jail from Ambala.

An atmosphere of fear and terror prevailed in the country outside. Political activity had come to a grinding halt. The dissenters were mainly political workers of the Opposition party and the RSS. They kept repeatedly organising Satyagrahas where a number of people courted arrest. It goes to the credit of the Shiromani Akali Dal that it offered its cadres for Satyagraha every day throughout the Emergency outside the Golden Temple and courted arrest. This earned the Akali Dal great respect in the entire country. The RSS, which was unfairly banned, also provided a large cadre for Satyagraha.

The press was completely terrorised. Most editors and journalists surrendered and reconciled themselves to the idea of living under a dictatorship. The Congress party newspaper *National Herald* editorially commented that the time had come for India to evolve into a single party democracy. Mrs Gandhi herself called for the graduation of India from democracy to a disciplined democracy. To give it credibility at the cost of losing his own, Acharya Vinoba Bhave called the Emergency 'Anushasan Parva'. There were, however, dissenters in the media. The *Indian Express* and the *Statesman* played a legendary role in letting know their dissent against the Emergency. Ram Nath Goenka, C.R. Irani and editor Kuldeep Nayar became the symbols of press freedom during the Emergency.

Was the script of the Emergency prepared in advance?

Journalist Coomi Kapoor's book on the Emergency published in 2015 contains handwritten documents in the writing of Siddhartha Shankar Ray where he requests Mrs Gandhi to have lists of persons proposed to be arrested and outlines various other steps which were required to be taken. The document is dated 8 January 1975.

Curiously, around the same time in January 1975, *Motherland*, a daily newspaper edited by K.R. Malkani, had a front page article based on the astrological prediction by Dr Vasanth Kumar Pandit, a Jana Sangh MP and astrologer, of the proclamation of the

Emergency, the arrest of the entire Opposition, media censorship and India becoming an autocratic state. When published, I found it difficult to believe this astrological prediction.

During the Emergency, one of my co-detenues in prison was K.R. Malkani himself. Malkani told me that when arrested on the midnight of 26 June while others were straightaway taken to Rohtak Jail, he was, for three days, kept in a guest house in Haryana and taken to the jail after three days. During those three days, he was grilled by the intelligence agencies about his source of information on the basis of which that article predicting the Emergency had been enforced.

The agencies thought this was a major leak in the government and were investigating the matter.

Malkani, however, consistently maintained that this was only an astrological prediction. Cumulatively, it was these facts that persuaded me to believe that the script for the Emergency was prepared sometime in January 1975. The immediate trigger would have been the Allahabad High Court judgement and the insecurity caused by it to Mrs Gandhi's position.

Was this script inspired by what happened in Nazi Germany in 1933?

Hitler became the Chancellor of Germany on 30 January 1933. He did not have an absolute majority in Parliament. On 28 February, he got his president to invoke Article 48 of the Constitution which gave emergency powers for the 'protection of the people in the state'. The decree giving emergency powers put restrictions on personal liberty, free speech, right of assembly, association, violation of privacy, and home searches and promoted restrictions on property and all other rights.

The pretext for the imposition of this Emergency was that on 27

February, the German Parliament House, known as Reichstag, had been set on fire. Hitler claimed that it was a communist conspiracy to burn government buildings and museums. Thirteen years later, in the Nuremberg trials, it was established that the Reichstag fire was the handiwork of Nazis, and Goebbels had conceived it. Hitler continued to maintain that his actions were within the four corners of the Constitution.

Mrs Gandhi imposed the Emergency under Article 352, suspended fundamental rights under Article 359 and claimed that 'disorder was planned by the opposition in the country'. The security forces were being asked to disobey illegal orders and, therefore, in the larger interest of the nation, India had to become a disciplined democracy.

Both Hitler and Mrs Gandhi never abrogated the Constitution. They used a republican Constitution to transform democracy into dictatorship. Hitler arrested most of the opposition Members of Parliament and, therefore, converted his minority government in Parliament into a government which had a two-thirds majority of members present and voting. He therefore, brought detailed Constitution amendments vesting all power to one person.

Mrs Indira Gandhi arrested most Opposition Members of Parliament and, therefore, procured, through their absence, a two-thirds majority of members present and voting and enabled the passage of several obnoxious provisions through Constitution amendments. The 42nd Amendment diluted the power of High Courts to issue writ petitions, a power which Dr Ambedkar had said was the very heart and soul of India's Constitution. They also amended Article 368 so that a Constitutional amendment was beyond judicial review.

There were a few things that Hitler did not do which Mrs Gandhi did. She prohibited the publication of parliamentary proceedings in the media. The law which gave a mandate to the media for publishing parliamentary proceedings was popularly known as the Feroze Gandhi Bill because the late Shri Feroze Gandhi had singularly campaigned for her after the Haridas Mundhra scandal, which was raised by him in Parliament. Since Hitler's own election had been set aside, he had no change to make in this regard.

Mrs Gandhi amended both the Constitution and the Representation of People Act. The Constitution amendment made the election of the prime minister non-justiciable before a court. The Representation of People Act was retrospectively amended to insert those provisions so that the invalid election of Mrs Gandhi could be validated by changes in law. Unlike Hitler, Mrs Gandhi went ahead to transform India into a dynastic democracy.

Goebbels claimed that the 'German Revolution has just begun'. All Indian Ambassadors and High Commissioners were asked to propagate that what was happening in India now was nothing short of a revolution. The press censorship laws imposed in India and in Germany were almost similar. You had effectively a one party system in play.

Nazi leader Joachim Ribbentrop, who later became Hitler's External Affairs Minister, spoke of the need for a new legal system. He argued that the system needed to be replaced because 'Adolf Hitler too, like any other common mortal, could be tried under the same paragraph of penal law'. Indira Gandhi's 39th amendment to the Constitution making the election of the prime minister non-challengeable and a prime minister non-prosecutable actually implemented this suggestion. The Swaran Singh Committee brought in several changes in the Constitution through the 42nd Constitution Amendment.

The most objectionable change was to extend the life of Parliament by two years. The Indian Lok Sabha is elected under the Constitution for a maximum period of five years. It is the grantee of a limited jurisdiction by the sovereign – the people. It cannot perpetuate its existence, but it was done. In fact, from 1971 to 1977 the Lok Sabha lasted for six years. This amendment was subsequently reversed by the Janata government.

A Nazi leader proclaimed, 'There is in Germany today only one authority and that is the authority of Fuehrer.' The AICC President, Devakanta Barua proclaimed, 'Indira is India and India is Indira.' In a letter to Mrs Gandhi from his detention, JP wrote, 'Do not equate yourself with the nation. India is immortal, you are not.'

The most startling similarity in the script was that orders were issued to the effect that the Gestapo's actions could not be made subject to judicial review. Te Gestapo was Hitler's secret police. When we detenues filed petitions in the nature of habeas corpus before the High Court, the government argued that the sole repository of the right to life and liberty was Article 21. If Article 21 was suspended, there was neither a right to life or liberty. Even if there was an illegal deprivation of life and liberty, a citizen had no remedy.

The High Courts decided in the citizens' favour. When this argument was voiced in appeal before the Supreme Court, Justice H.R. Khanna on the Bench, asked Niren De, the Attorney General, if a person is threatened with illegal killing, does he have a remedy in law during the Emergency? Niren De promptly answered: 'My reply shocks my own conscience. It will shock your conscience too. But the natural corollary of my arguments is that he had no remedy in law.'

Justice Khanna, years after his retirement, told me that when this reply came, he looked at his four other colleagues hoping that their conscience would have been shocked. But when the four others chose to look the other way, Justice Khanna realised which way they were going to write the judgement. Eventually, the unanimous verdict of all High Courts was reversed by the Supreme Court, accepting the non-sustainable argument of Niren De with Justice Khanna dissenting.

Justice Khanna became a living legend after his dissent. He had written that his dissent was a challenge to the brooding spirit of law and the intelligence of the future generations which could correct the error into which the majority had fallen. The error was legislatively corrected by the Janata government through the 44th amendment, which made Article 21 non-sustainable but the intelligence of future generations led to a current Supreme Court judge, Dhananjay Chandrachud, reversing the majority opinion and, in particular, overruling his own father's judgement in the habeas corpus case.

The election case

The election case turned out to be another judicial monstrosity. Both the Constitution and the Representation of the People Act were amended retrospectively in order to legislatively validate Mrs Gandhi's election. The indefatigable Shanti Bhushan did not give up. He argued that a free and fair election was a part of the basic structure of the Constitution and validating an invalid election would violate the basic structure of the Constitution.

But the Supreme Court created a legal jigsaw to help Mrs Gandhi. The basic structure theory could be used only to test a Constitution amendment and not an ordinary law. So they struck down the 39th Amendment to the Constitution but held that ordinary legislation could not be tested on the touchstone of basic structure. Therefore, the amended Representation of People Act would apply to Mrs Gandhi and, therefore, her election stood valid under the retrospective amendment. What the Parliament could not do by a two-thirds majority, it could do by a simple majority. Even this proposition of law was subsequently overruled.

Absolute power corrupts absolutely

Possessing absolute power, the government unleashed tyranny on every institution. The country witnessed the silence of the graveyard. The only protest came from die-hard Opposition workers. The High Court stood firm but the Supreme Court capitulated. Fourteen independent judges of the High Court were transferred to other High Courts.

Sanjay Gandhi, the younger son of Mrs Gandhi, took over the reins of the Congress party and the Youth Congress. The Youth Congress became a law into itself. Its functioning terrorized society. Hitler had announced a twenty-five-point economic programme. Mrs Gandhi had announced twenty. To cover up the gap, Sanjay announced his five point economic and social programme.

Dissent became a sin and sycophancy the rule. Film actors and singers and playback singers were asked to join Youth Congress and its allies. If they refused, the then I&B Minister, Vidya Charan Shukla would threaten them. Kishore Kumar, the noted playback singer, was blacklisted by All India Radio and his songs were never played for his refusal to sing at the Youth Congress rallies. Devanand records in his autobiography that when he and Dilip Kumar refused to join the Youth Congress rally, Vidya Charan Shukla threatened both of them.

But both of them stood firm. Gulzar's celebrated film *Aandhi* was banned. Since absolute power corrupts absolutely, a tyranny thinks it can get away with every atrocity. Large-scale demolitions of houses and business establishments were happening all over the country. Since population control was Sanjay Gandhi's slogan, forced sterilisation was taking place.

When a police jeep entered a village, the youths of the village fearing forced sterilisation would spend their nights in the farm rather than their house. The common man who did not understand the political consequence of dictatorship, understood it because of forced sterilisation. As someone aptly put:

दाद देता हूँ मैं मर्द-ए-हिंदुस्तान की, सर कटा सकते हैं लेकिन नस कटा सकते नहीं।

Little did this dictatorial regime realise that each act was alienating the people. The government had a single source feedback that they were getting very popular and that there was no opposition. If you curb free speech and allow only propaganda, you become the first victim of propaganda because you start believing that your own propaganda is the truth and the full truth.

The Emergency Revisited – Part 3: How It Ended

Posted on 26 June 2018

As the Emergency continued, there was one major pressure on Mrs Indira Gandhi. The international media and world leaders were aghast at the very suggestion that Pandit Nehru's daughter had abandoned the path of democracy and turned dictatorial. She was always at pains to explain to her international audiences that this was a temporary phase and would not last forever. The party, however, was of the opinion that since the term of Parliament had been extended by two years, elections could wait till 1978.

Her political feedback and that of the intelligence agencies was that since there was no Opposition, she should immediately call for a snap poll, give the Opposition little time to prepare and the Congress could comfortably sweep the polls. The latter view prevailed and on 18 January 1977, she addressed the nation and announced a general election to be held in the month of March. The Opposition leaders were still in prison, the Emergency was still on and would continue. It was decided that a snap poll would take the Opposition by surprise, ensure her victory and give her government the legitimacy it needed.

Since the Tihar Jail was the centre of Opposition activities, all the political detenues met immediately after the announcement. There were two clear views. George Fernandes and C.G.K. Reddy strongly argued that it would be a farcical election and hence must be boycotted. The others believed that they must use the election as a platform to campaign against the Emergency and for democracy.

This view was shared with senior leaders in other jails. JP, who had been released on account of ill health, took the first initiative and announced that he would participate and bless the coalition of the Opposition only if all the political parties in Opposition joined hands and formed a single party. The release of detenues started within a day or two. But some, like George Fernandes, Nanaji Deshmukh and those belonging to the RSS, were not released till the elections were over. Press censorship was relaxed but not removed.

I was released from detention on 25 January 1977. On 27 January, my ABVP friends, took me in a large procession to every college of the university campus. I had suspected that we would meet student audiences filled with fear and awe. But contrary to my expectations, we witnessed an aggressive participation of students wherever we went. Amongst the released political leaders of Delhi, some of us met in that evening at 7 Jantar Mantar, which eventually became the Janata Party headquarters.

On 30 January, Shri Morarji Desai and Shri Atal Bihari Vajpayee were to address a rally. Unaware of the undercurrent, we initially sought permission to hold the rally at Chandni Chowk. The police declined the request due to the dangers of a stampede and the venue of the rally had to be forcibly shifted to Ramleela Maidan. The rally turned out to be a big success. The fear was cracking up. People were willing to speak and come out. After almost nineteen months, they were all restless and waiting to hear the Vajpayee oration. When Atalji stood up to speak at the Ramleela Maidan, he was cheered for several minutes with slogans. In his customary poetic style, he started with a couplet:

बड़ी मुद्दत के बाद मिले हैं दीवाने,
कहने सुनने को हैं बहुत से अफ़साने,
आओ जल्दी से दो बातें कर लें,
ये आज़ादी कब तक रहेगी कौन जाने।

Events were happening very fast. On 2 February three Congress leaders, Babu Jagjivan Ram, Hemwati Nandan Bahuguna and Nandini Satpathy, resigned from the Congress party and formed Congress for Democracy. They decided to align with the Janata Party. On 6 February they addressed, along with other Janata leaders, a massive rally at Ramleela Maidan.

As a student leader representing the face of youth of this alliance, I was asked to be the first warm-up speaker at the rally followed by some other leaders till Bahuguna and Jagjivan Ram spoke. Unquestionably this was the largest ever audience I have ever addressed. Mrs Gandhi had accused Jagjivan Ram of betrayal. She charged him for not informing her during the Emergency about what was going wrong. A powerful and a crafty orator, Babuji responded at this rally by saying:

कैसे बता देते? बता देते तो जगजीवन कहीं होते और राम कहीं।

The size and enthusiasm of this rally sent a signal in the entire country that a Janata wave was building up. V.C. Shukla tried a petty trick. Before the rally he announced that the popular film *Bobby* would be shown on Doordarshan at the time. But so powerful was the anti-Congress mood that people preferred to attend the rally rather than watch *Bobby*. To attend this rally, the crowd had to walk a few kilometres since the bus service was also suspended.

I got my first opportunity to participate in an election campaign.

I toured north Indian states and went through the entire heartland of Uttar Pradesh spending the last one week entirely in Rae Bareli and Amethi where Mrs Gandhi and Sanjay were contesting. Campaigning through Rajasthan, I went till Mumbai and eventually Pune. Almost everywhere, we could see a mass citizen's participation in the campaign. Both Mrs Gandhi and Sanjay lost their own seats.

When the results were announced, states in north India voted en masse for the Janata Party. In the entire north India and the Hindi heartland, the Congress could win one seat in Madhya Pradesh and one seat in Rajasthan. It lost all the seats of Uttar Pradesh, Bihar, Delhi, Punjab etc. However, it managed to win some seats in the South where the atrocities of the Emergency were relatively less. The Janata Party got an absolute majority. Before resigning, Mrs Gandhi revoked the Emergency and slowly all the detenues were released from the prisons. There was an air of freedom in the entire country.

Institutional safeguards and disturbing observations

The most disturbing observation of the Emergency was that, when the central government turned dictatorial, the entire system caved in. The Supreme Court became subservient, the media became sycophantic. Post-Emergency, Advani ji told the Delhi media that 'when asked to bend, you chose to crawl'. Over two lakh false FIRs were registered and hardly any police officers stood up to protest. Thousands of detention orders were passed when there were no grounds of detention. Hardly any Collector refused to sign an illegal detention order.

Even during the campaign when the result appeared inevitable, Mrs Gandhi was unwilling to see the writing on the wall. She superseded Justice H.R. Khanna and appointed Justice Beg as the Chief Justice of India. Justice Khanna resigned. Palkhiwala commented that the post of the chief justice was now too small for Justice Khanna.

The Morarji Desai led Janata Party government undid lot of damage that the Emergency had done so that nobody would experiment with such dictatorships in future. The power under Article 352 to impose an Emergency for internal disturbances was now restricted. Article 21 was made non-suspendable. The courts were given the power of judicial review of several detention orders. The 44th Constitution Amendment reversed most of the provisions of the 42nd Amendment. This was a major institutional safeguard.

Another significant development has been the evolution of technology which has made censorship of the media impossible. You could no longer withhold information from the people.

The role of political parties

India's left parties have always been a puzzle to me. The CPI was an unashamed supporter of the Emergency. Its political line was that Emergency was a war on fascism. Though theoretically the CPI (M) was opposed to the Emergency and critical of it, it was not an active participant in the struggle against the Emergency. Only two of its MPs were arrested. Its politburo members, central committee members and students' leaders were, by and large, not put in detention.

The Congress (O), the socialist parties, the Swatantra Party, the Jana Sangh and the RSS were the main participants in the Satyagraha and protest against the Emergency. To me, the Lohia socialists and their post-Emergency evolution has shown a very curious trend. Dr Ram Manohar Lohia was the creator of the slogan in the early 1960s 'Congress Hatao Desh Bachao'. His legacy was represented by George Fernandes, Madhu Limaye and Raj Narain, who were all consistently anti-Congress.

Today that legacy has been inherited by Shri Mulayam Singh Yadav in Uttar Pradesh and substantially by Shri Nitish Kumar in Bihar. While a trace of anti-Congressism is visible in both, the party formed by Shri Mulayam Singh Yadav is always willing to do business with the Congress. I always have serious doubts whether those who represent the political DNA of Dr Lohia and Nehru can, in the long run, ever work together.

Though I believe it is impossible for anyone in India to repeat the Emergency, the famous saying goes that democracy lies in the hearts of men and women. When it dies there, no Constitution can save it and no judge can protect it.

A personal note

Union Minister Vijay Goel has today tweeted a letter that I wrote to him and Rajat Sharma during the Emergency. Thank you Vijay. Vijay Goel and Rajat Sharma were two of my closest colleagues in the days of the Emergency. They helped me organise the 26 June 1975 protest against the Emergency.

While I was being arrested, I requested both of them to disappear, go underground and participate in the Satyagraha starting from 29 June. Both of them led the Satyagraha. Their courage was exemplary. Today Vijay Goel is a valuable colleague in the party and the government. Rajat did not continue in politics. Today he is one of India's celebrated journalists and anchors. Both continue to remain close friends of mine – almost a part of my extended family.

Part Six

Anecdotes from History

15

Reflections on Individuals and My Experiences

People like Atal Bihari Vajpayee and George Fernandes were at opposite poles of the political spectrum but they shared certain personal qualities such as integrity, courage, oratorical powers and an ability to make friendships across the board. Atalji was the quintessential gentleman while George was the classic stormy petrol. Some reflections on them, on cricket, the state of our democracy and some of the individuals Jaitley worked with.

Bharat Ratna to Atal Bihari Vajpayee

Posted on 19 November 2013

Some well-meaning friends have raised the issue regarding the awarding of the Bharat Ratna to Shri Atal Bihari Vajpayeeji.

As a much younger colleague, I have had an opportunity to work with Shri Vajpayee both in the party and in the government. Unquestionably, he is one of the tallest politicians of his generation. He was a parliamentarian par excellence. He was a public speaker whom millions waited for hours to hear. People still recollect his style of oratory. As an Opposition leader, he never lost the national vision even while attacking the government. Every word he spoke reflected the statesman in him.

As a prime minister, he was a democrat to the core. The cabinet meetings he presided over discussed each issue at length. After weighing the merits of alternative viewpoints, he nodded in favour of one and the whole cabinet instantly accepted his view. His government is remembered for its emphasis on infrastructure creation, economic management of the country, its approach on issues of national security and a new look foreign policy that he advocated.

He had a spotless public life for over five decades. Even though age and health have kept him from active politics in the last few years, he is still remembered as one of the most popular prime ministers India has ever had. Can a national award or honour add anything more to his stature and credibility? His well-meaning friends and admirers would be well advised to keep him out of any awards controversy. His stature is far taller than any award.

Thoughts on Republic Day

Posted on 26 January 2014

Today India celebrates its sixty-fifth anniversary as a Republic. It is on this day that we gave ourselves a liberal Constitution. Parliamentary democracy, a federal structure, a bundle of fundamental rights and judicial review by an independent judiciary are amongst the salient features of that Constitution.

Having witnessed various challenges and having shown great resilience to overcome these challenges, I do believe that we are a strong and vibrant democracy. I have a few areas of concern which lay down an agenda for the future. Poverty continues to be the greatest curse on Indian society. Nearly 30 per cent of our population lives below the poverty line. The poor are denied the right to live with dignity. Terrorism and insurgency remain a great threat to India's sovereignty. The threat of terror is both external and from within. We cannot afford to lower our guard on this score. The quality of politics in India needs to improve. The power of politics is immense. The stature of men who man politics must be in consonance with the huge power that politicians wield.

The declining quality of politics reflects on issues of governance. India today expects governance which will deliver on problems which confront the society. If India can grow at 9 per cent on average with bad governance, what will be the growth rate if the quality of politics and governance were to improve? India needs to become a more humane and compassionate society. Our concern for women and the underprivileged must be reflected in our attitudes. Increased offences against women and the brutality of those offences is a scar on our society. It is these and many more challenges that confront us. Let us show our determination to overcome these challenges.

My Experience at Sri Ram College of Commerce

Posted on 1 March 2014

Last week I visited my old college, Shri Ram College of Commerce, where I had spent three of the best years of my life as an undergraduate student. In the early seventies when I studied there, the college was considered the principal institution for business studies. It continues to maintain the same reputation even now.

The occasion of my visit was recording of a programme called 'Political Roots'. The programme was produced and telecast by a news channel NDTV and anchored by Barkha Dutt. It was recorded in a sports gymnasium which was built by the college as a practice facility for the 2010 Commonwealth Games. An audience of a hundred students grilled me for over an hour. Needless to say, the quality of audience and students was excellent. SRCC is able to admit students who secure more than 96 per cent aggregate marks. Obviously, the audience comprised those who must have been toppers from various educational institutions. Most of them are aspiring financial consultants, management consultants and chartered accountants. They are aiming for careers in the growing financial world.

The questions which the students asked me were on political leadership, economic policy, corruption and various current affairs. They had doubts on issues which needed to be clarified. Some of them had dissected the purported fault lines in my party and wanted to question me on them. The environment for the discussion was extremely civilised and serious. If any guest had been out of his depth, it would have been extremely difficult to tackle this audience. After the recording of the programme I drove back from the college with two thoughts crossing my mind. Firstly, can the depth and the seriousness which I observed during this interaction ever reflect in our legislative bodies. Secondly, if this is the quality of the younger generation, surely India would be a much better place in future.

Looking Back at Dr Manmohan Singh

Posted on 13 May 2014

The voting for the 2014 general elections is over. The result is awaited. We have only the exit polls and our own analysis as a base to speculate upon. Dr Manmohan Singh has announced that he would be stepping down as prime minister irrespective of the result and the mantle of the Congress party leadership in Parliament would pass on to the next generation. I have had an opportunity of observing the Prime Minister Dr Manmohan Singh from close quarters for the last ten years. In the last five years as leader of Opposition I virtually have heard his every intervention in Parliament and dissected each one of his performances. I look upon him at the conclusion of his ten years' tenure.

Unquestionably Dr Manmohan Singh was a very good finance minister. He got a lot of support from his prime minister, PV Narasimha Rao, for initiating the economic reforms in 1991. For a Congress party government which had always professed the virtues of regulation, a reformist approach was creditable. Shri PV Narasimha Rao has never been given the level of credit which he truly deserved. I am sure history will reassess him. I had recently suggested to the prime minister that I personally would be interested in reading his memoirs particularly those relating to the period 1991–96. The footprints he left behind as a finance minister during this period will be remembered for a long time.

Dr Manmohan Singh became a prime minister on account of certain circumstances which compelled Sonia Gandhi to withdraw her name from the reckoning. He was literally a prime minister announced by Soniaji. He had to function within that limitation.

There were two strong qualities of the prime minister that I discovered. Firstly, whenever you discussed a serious subject with the prime minister he came out as a man of scholarship. He was what we call to as 'a syana aadmi'. His words were measured, and he would reflect before making a comment. Secondly, his personal integrity was always above board. With an element of scholarship, he was always be well read and well prepared on any subject that he dealt with.

And yet, when he addressed the country, he never came out as a leader. The reason for not coming out as a leader was clear. He never wanted to rock the boat. He knew that he was vested with limited power and on all major decisions he had to keep the party and its first family in good humour. Thus, when the reform process was blocked on account of decisions of the National Advisory Council or when Rahul Gandhi tore apart the papers of objectionable ordinance, the prime minister was perceived as a non-leader who had to accept everything without his opinion mattering significantly. It was his inability to overrule people which affected his functioning. He did not have the last word.

Had he overruled his finance minister on the retrospective tax law knowing fully well the consequences of a retrospective taxation, the prime minister would have stood out. If he had stood up and cancelled the coal blocks allocation once the fraud was revealed or cancelled the 2G licenses himself rather than wait for the court to do it, I have no doubt that history would have recorded him very differently. It was the inability to speak up within his own party that may compel the historians to take a different view of the man.

As the curtains draw to a close and a ten-year long period of providing leadership to the government of India, the prime minister goes out with dignity and grace. He will remain an elder statesman and a man of credibility to guide the nation. If only he had stood up at the right time and disagreed, he would have been regarded with still greater honour.

I wish the prime minister a very good health and many more years of public service. If he were to write his memoirs, I will always want to read the chapter which deals with the 1991–96 period.

Atalji – The Gentle Giant

Posted on 24 December 2014

Shri Atal Bihari Vajpayeeji turns ninety on 25 December 2014. I wish him all the best. The nation has honoured him and Madan Mohan Malviya ji with the Bharat Ratna.

I first heard Atalji's speech in 1967, when I was a school student. There was a political rally near my house in Delhi for the 1967 general election. He came to address that rally. He already enjoyed a formidable reputation as a great orator. He was on way to becoming an iconic political leader. Many youngsters used to repeat the sentences that they heard in his speech. They imitated his style. I became a student activist of ABVP in 1970. Atalji was a familiar face in both Parliament and political rallies. We had invited him for several speeches at Delhi University. Whenever we wanted some issues to be raised in Parliament, we rushed to brief him. My acquaintance with him started in 1973 when I was a student leader in Delhi University. Thereafter, I started interacting with him frequently. He has been a great listener. He used to occasionally react to some enthusiastic ideas, which we gave, with humour. During JP's movement in 1974, he was active in addressing rallies across the country.

When the Emergency was proclaimed in 1975, he was detained in

Bangalore along with Shri Advani and some other politicians. I was initially detained in Ambala Jail and subsequently in Delhi's Tihar Jail. We heard about Atalji having a serious health problem with his back. He was shifted to house detention at his Delhi residence. His back problem worsened for which,he spent a significant part of the Emergency period at AIIMS where he was rushed for surgery. During this period, we received a poem he had written from his hospital bed.

The context of that poem was relevant. The doctor at the AIIMS asked Atalji if he had bent a bit too much – 'Aap jyada jhuk gaye honge' to which he replied – 'Doctor Saheb, jhuk to sakte nahi, yun kahiye mur gaye honge'. He penned a poem which was very often heard in the 1977 election. The opening sentence read: 'Toot sakte hain magar hum jhuk nahi sakte'.

Thereafter, we saw him as India's external affairs minister in 1977, an opposition MP, as the Leader of Opposition in Parliament (Lok Sabha). As he was growing in years, my image of him in the early 1990s was of 'the best man', who never became the prime minister, but history vindicated him, and he went on to become one of the outstanding prime ministers of India.

Atalji is the product of a democratic system and training in parliamentary values. He realised the virtues of both consensus and harmony. His conduct of cabinet meetings was never tense. If any of us raised any point, or even contradicted a point, he encouraged discussion. The last word, of course, belonged to him.

He was liberal in his economic thinking. He realised the importance of infrastructure creation. The national highways programme and the power sector reforms are the part of his legacy. He was committed to normalising relations with our neighbouring countries. His 'bus initiative' with Pakistan was undertaken at a great political risk, since his own constituency had to be convinced of this. In 2003, he tried to normalise relationships with China and signed an agreement on settlement of the boundary dispute.

A new chapter of Indo-US relations was authored during his tenure. He was unquestionably the greatest orator India has heard, since Independence. He could play with words, but he was always measured. He was a wordsmith. He never fell into the temptation of committing an impropriety. He realised the virtues of social harmony. His ability to rise above the party for a larger national cause was significant.

Today, as we celebrate the ninetieth year of his birth as 'Good Governance Day', we wish very good health and a long life to this Gentle Giant.

The Vindication of Amit Shah

Posted on 30 December 2014

A CBI special court at Mumbai has discharged Amit Shah, the BJP President, of all charges relating to a case of his involvement in the alleged killing of Soharabuddin and Tulsi Prajapati. I have been following this case actively from the time of its investigation, filing of charges, the arrest of Amit Shah and grant of bail to him. I had written a letter on 27 September 2013 to Prime Minister Manmohan Singh, in my capacity as leader of Opposition in Rajya Sabha. The letter pertains to misuse of the CBI against BJP leadership. In the letter I had written with regard to these two cases as under:

Sohrabuddin encounter case

The encounter in which one Sohrabuddin Sheikh was killed was an operation allegedly directed by the Intelligence Bureau of the central government. It has been a practice that when the Intelligence Bureau processes and develops intelligence, it keeps vigilance on the target.

Thereafter when an opportunity arises to arrest the target the state police is associated with the operation. Sohrabuddin was a noted mafia who operated in Gujarat, Madhya Pradesh and Rajasthan and was carrying a prize on his head in Madhya Pradesh. He was an illegal weapons dealer. He had also been convicted under TADA. The search conducted by Madhya Pradesh police at his premises in village Jharnia, district Ujjain, had yielded more than forty AK-56 rifles, hundreds of AK-56 cartridges and hundreds of hand grenades. He was an absconder from the police agencies of various state governments.

After his encounter on 24/25 November 2005 his brother filed a writ petition in the Supreme Court. The filing of said petition was also sponsored by the Congress party. The then additional solicitor general of India, Shri Gopal Subramaniam, in a pre-conceived and planned move, appeared on day one before the court and agreed to take instructions from the central government. Subsequently, the attorney general appeared for the Union of India and Gopal Subramaniam designated himself as amicus curiae without any specific order of the court appointing him.

The government of India conceded that the investigations be handed over to the CBI. Though the central government should be a mere formal party, the then attorney general used to appear and oppose even motion for adjournments. Since objections were raised with regard to the fairness of the CBI, the Supreme Court ordered investigations by a team of Gujarat police officers of the state police under its supervision. The state police reconstructed the encounter, conducted scientific investigation under the supervision of the Hon'ble Supreme Court and implicated and arrested several police officers including three IPS officers. Upon hearing the arguments of the Union of India and Shri Gopal Subramaniam, the amicus curiae and others, the Supreme Court referred the matter to the CBI.

The ground on which the Supreme Court transferred the case to the CBI was that the investigation involved inter-state ramifications and the Andhra Pradesh angle of the matter had not been probed. As a matter of fact the Congress government in Andhra Pradesh did not cooperate in the investigation by Gujarat police, which is a matter of record.

The CBI investigated the case but did not investigate any of the four points, on the basis of which the case was referred to the CBI, which were the points found lacking in the Gujarat police investigation. It did not probe the Andhra Pradesh angle of the case seriously. The probable purpose of the CBI in this case was to try and implicate the political establishment of Gujarat, setting aside the pretence of federal character of India's governance. The CBI targeted Shri Amit Shah, the then home minister and also the minister of law, transport and parliamentary affairs of the state of Gujarat with the ultimate desire of implicating Narendra Modi, the chief minister of Gujarat.

Shockingly, when the Legal department of the CBI opined that there was no case against Shri Amit Shah, the same was responded to by the Supervisory Officer of CBI, putting up a 'note' by observing that the arrest of Amit Shah would enable the CBI to get some more witnesses particularly the police officers since they would then feel intimidated. He also opined that arresting Amit Shah was necessary since it was necessary to reach the eventual target of investigation of Narendra Modi. This note was approved by the Director, CBI, Shri Ashwani Kumar.

The CBI arrested Amit Shah with no prosecutable evidence against him. In order to arrest Amit Shah they relied on the false testimony of two witnesses namely, Ramanbhai Patel and Dashrathbhai Patel, noted land grabbers of Gujarat. Shri Amit Shah, as per the CBI theory in the charge sheet, is alleged to have told both of them six months after the encounter that Sohrabuddin had left no option for himself. This was incorporated as an extra judicial confession It is noteworthy that both Ramanbhai Patel and Dashrathbhai Patel have criminal antecedents and criminal cases in Gujarat. These two witnesses were felicitated for having given such a deposition against Shri Amit Shah in a function presided over by Shri Shankersingh Waghela, then president of Gujarat Congress. The testimony of these two witnesses is based upon the alleged extortion from them to help them in PASA detention.

The record of the Gujarat government shows that no detention of these persons under PASA was never in contemplation. Said two witnesses also claimed that they have paid a sum of Rs 75 lakh to Shri Amit Shah through one Ajay Patel in three different instalments with specific dates mentioned by them in their statement. They gave the specific dates of payments on which they allegedly physically handed over the alleged amount to Shri Ajay Patel. They further claimed that they were there through all the dates. This testimony is false without any further probe inter alia on the ground that on some of the dates Ajay Patel was not even in India and his passport establishes this fact.

This was a key substance of a frivolous charge sheet filed against Shri Amit Shah. Shri Amit Shah was granted bail on this charge sheet by the Gujarat High Court by a detailed speaking order inter alia holding that there is no prima facie case against Shri Amit Shah. The CBI, however, challenged the said order and upon the request of the CBI, the Supreme Court ordered Shri Amit Shah to remain out of Gujarat and all political activities. He remained outside the state of Gujarat for a period of two years. The said order of the High Court was upheld by the Supreme Court.

Tulsi Prajapati encounter

Tulsi Prajapati was a case built up by the CBI as an extension to the Sohrabuddin case. The CBI solicited the investigation of this case by making a specific prayer in the court. Their ostensible case was that Tulsi Prajapati was a witness to the arrest and disappearance of Sohrabuddin while in custody of the police officers and correspondingly he was eliminated by the Gujarat Police. The only evidence mentioned against Shri Amit Shah by the CBI in this case was that he was regularly in touch with one police officer Shri R.K. Pandian, IPS who was an accused in the case. The vast contemporaneous record shows that Shri R.K. Pandian, IPS had been regularly in telephonic contact of Shri Amit Shah much before and after the incident as a part of his official duty since he was also heading the charge of SP, IB (Intelligence) of the state police looking after political agitations and political activities. Any home minister of any state will have to necessarily remain in touch with SP, IB (Intelligence) of the state police looking after political agitations and political activities since he had to keep himself informed about the activities on a regular basis. Without a point of evidence a separate charge sheet was filed against Shri Amit Shah in the Tulsi Prajapati case.

Very importantly, though the CBI was under the direction of the Supreme Court to complete the investigation of the Tulsi Prajapati case within six months from 11 April 2011, the CBI deliberately and as a part of political conspiracy did not obey the direction and filed the charge sheet on 4 September 2012 so as to arrest Shri Amit Shah once again just few months before the Gujarat Legislative Assembly elections which were scheduled to be held before December 2012. Shri Amit Shah had to approach the Hon'ble Supreme Court. The Supreme Court vide its order date 8 April 2013 held that no separate charge sheet could be filed in this case since CBI itself had alleged that both the cases were similar and it merged the charge sheet with the Sohrabuddin case charge sheet thereby preventing the CBI arresting Shri Amit Shah once again.

Tulsi Prajapati and the arrest of Shri Gulab Chand Kataria, former home minister of Rajasthan

Shri Gulab Chand Kataria is the former home minister of Rajasthan and the present Leader of Opposition in the Rajasthan Legislative Assembly and a very important leader of Rajasthan BJP. He is a complete stranger to even the existence of such persons known as Sohrabuddin and Tulsi Prajapati. The CBI filed a supplementary charge sheet against Gulab Kataria wherein it was alleged that the motive of elimination of Tulsi Prajapati by Gulab Kataria was extorting money from marble dealers of Rajasthan namely RK Marbles. As per the CBI there were two motives; one the Gujarat Police wanted to eliminate him in order to eliminate the eye-witness in the Sohrabdun case and the home minister of Rajasthan wanted to eliminate him for extorting money from marble dealers.

What a coincidence. It was alleged by the CBI that Shri Gulab Chand Kataria allegedly met one Shri D. G. Vanjara, IPS of Gujarat Police allegedly between 26 December 2005 and 28 December 2005 at the Circuit House at Udaipur. The CBI evidence of his presence was that the PS of Shri Gulab Chand Kataria was staying in the same Circuit House during that period and Shri D.G. Vanzara, IPS also stayed in the said Circuit House. However, records of the Rajasthan government conclusively establish that Shri Gulab Chand Kataria along with his wife had flown on 25 December 2005 to Mumbai and stayed there till 2 January 2006. He attended the meeting of the BJP National Executive and thereafter a meeting of the National Council and after celebrating New Year along with his wife, returned to Jaipur on 2 January 2006.

It is clear from the above that the charges were filed against Amit Shah at the behest of the then political government. There was legally no admissible evidence against him. Amit Shah's application for discharge was opposed both by the CBI and Sohrabuddin's brother. The court heard both their lawyers. The charge was without any basis. The fact that the CBI allowed itself to be misused is a cause for concern.

Since I had analysed the alleged evidence, both during investigation and after the filing of the charge sheet, I was amongst the few voices which had consistently maintained in the past three years that the prosecution of Amit Shah was a case of 'No Evidence'. Without analysing the evidence in detail, the media allowed itself to report as was briefed by CBI. Even a vital noting on the CBI file that the implication of Amit Shah was necessary so that the then Chief Minister of Gujarat Shri Narendra Modi could be implicated, was no news for them. I am relieved at the fact that we have an independent judicial system in India which has vindicated Amit Shah.

The Unveiling of Gandhi's Statue in Parliament Square, London

Posted on 14 March 2015

Mr Prime Minister, Ladies and Gentlemen,

I am extremely grateful to the prime minister and all those who made today's event possible, for inviting me to this historic and nostalgic occasion when Gandhiji's Statue is being unveiled.

Nobody embodies the deep and enduring connections between the world's oldest democracy and the world's largest democracy as well as Mohandas Karamchand Gandhi – the Mahatma – whose statue is being unveiled in Parliament Square today. Gandhiji will find himself set permanently in stone very close to the place he occupied transiently, in flesh and blood, on his first night in London more than one hundred and twenty-five years ago.

Gandhiji's struggle to break Britain's imperial hold over India and to force the world's oldest democracy to create the world's largest one is the stuff of history and legend. But even as he waged this struggle, he admired Britain, valued many of the things it stood for, and cherished his friendships with scores of Britons. During the Battle of Britain, he was moved to tears at the thought that Westminster Abbey might be bombarded. So great was his regard for British values that he would condemn many unfair and unjust practices as 'un-British'.

His closest friends, confidantes, and counsellors, in South Africa, which proved to be the training ground for his experiments with non-violent means of resisting oppression and Satyagraha (truth force) were English. One of his deepest spiritual bonds was struck with C.F. Andrews, the only person who called him by his first name 'Mohan' whereas the world referred to him more respectfully as Bapu or Gandhiji.

In short, Mohandas Gandhi became the Mahatma not just because Britain gave him the cause that would define his life but also the human and other connections that made the fight for that cause possible.

Today, India and Britain have come a long way since the parting at the 'midnight hour' of 1947. Historical legacies form the ties that bind our two countries: language, the enlightenment values of democracy, free speech, pluralism, religious freedoms, and rule of law, and institutions such as the merit-based civil service, civilian-controlled army, independent judiciary, and a raucously vibrant press. These bequests have had lasting effects on us.

Mature nations transcend bitterness and acrimony. In Parliament Square there is also a statue of Sir Winston Churchill, arguably the man who opposed Gandhi most resolutely. Some would detect an irony in the great prime minister sharing a public space with the man he once decried as a 'half-naked fakir'. May be there is irony but even Churchill would have acknowledged that the resolve, determination and even cunning he showed in standing up to a mighty military machine that threatened the very existence of a proud and free people was replicated by Gandhi in his seemingly unequal battle against the world's mightiest Empire. What will link Churchill and Gandhi together is their strength of character.

But it is a greater tribute to Britain to recognise Gandhiji's contributions and choose to place the 'seditious, half-naked fakir' next to his one-time nemesis, Churchill and, of course, next to the man Gandhiji inspired, Nelson Mandela.

For that gracious gesture, my government and all of India are deeply thankful to the tireless work of the Gandhi Statue Memorial Trust, including its Chairman, Lord Meghnad Desai, to the prodigious talent of sculptor Philip Jackson, and above all to the capacious, Gandhi-like spirit of the British government and its people.

Dalmiyaji: A Man in a League of His Own

Posted on 21 September 2015

I woke up early morning today in Hong Kong to receive the sad news of the passing away of Jagmohan Dalmiya, the BCCI president. His passing away is a great loss to the cricket administration, the BCCI, the CAB, his friends and family. To me it is a personal loss as we shared a warm personal relationship for over two decades.

I first met him in the early 1990s when he and Inderjit Bindra another veteran cricket administrator decided to take on the government of India and defend the BCCI's right to telecast its own cricket matches and support the game of cricket with the revenues generated by television broadcasting rights. The government contended that 'national security' would be threatened if uplinking was allowed to private parties. We succeeded in getting an Interim order from the Supreme Court and finally won the case. Thanks to the battle fought by the Dalmiya–Bindra duo, airwaves were freed in India and free speech on television became a reality and more meaningful.

Having economically empowered the BCCI with the TV money, Dalmiya realised the power of the 'eyeballs'. India alone accounted for more than seventy five per cent of the TV audiences, an equal amount of sponsorship money and hence India's influence in the International Cricket Council would also increase. Dalmiya became the President of the ICC and India's influence in the world of cricket has never looked back.

He attracted opposition both within the ICC and the BCCI. The left front government managed to oust him only briefly from the CAB but he made a comeback.

The BCCI 'created' charges of irregularities against him only to withdraw them and vindicate his honour. His eventual vindication came when the BCCI in crisis in 2013 requested him to lead it once again since they needed Dalmiya to restore its credibility. By then his health was already failing him. Cricket however was still his first love.

I last met him in Kolkata last month. He was hopeful of recovering. Destiny however, decided otherwise. The game of cricket has lost a great administrator who shifted the home of cricket to India. I have lost a personal friend.

Thank You, Arvind

Posted on 20 June 2018

A few days ago, Chief Economic Adviser Arvind Subramanian met me over video conference. He informed me that he would like to go back to the United States on account of pressing family commitments. His reasons were personal but extremely important for him. He left me with no option but to agree with him.

Arvind had joined us as the chief economic adviser on 16 October 2014 for a period of three years. On the expiry of the three years I had requested him to continue for some more time. Even at that stage he told me that he was torn between family commitments and his current job which he considered the best and most fulfilling he has ever done.

Arvind's interaction with the government in the Ministry of Finance, the Prime Minister's Office and with other departments was both formal and informal. His instantaneous communications with his interlocutors had increased his effectiveness. The chief economic adviser's job had many facets to it. He is not a spokesman of the government. He is an adviser who has to analyse and think several steps ahead. It is a unique responsibility with freedom to do the work that he enjoys.

Arvind functioned within these parameters and concentrated on the challenges to the economy. His early diagnosis of the twin balance-sheet had led us to adopt the macro economic strategy of higher public investment in the Budget of 2015–16. He conceptualised JAM (Jan Dhan, Aadhaar, Mobile) as a data base for availing public benefits. He contributed to the debate of federalism by conceptualising that Indian federalism has not merely to be cooperative but also competitive. He came out with new ideas and policy reforms in the sectors of clothing, fertilisers, kerosene, power and pulses. His report on the revenue neutral rate was of great use in forging a consensus which led to the constitution amendment enabling the GST. He participated in every meeting of GST, gave his independent views and was heard in rapt attention by almost every finance minister.

He elevated the quality of the analysis and the presentation of ideas for public deliberation in his four economic surveys. His documents for four years were treated by several independent critics as one of the best ever produced. The latest survey had about 15 million visitors from 117 countries. The economic survey today is a basic teaching material all over India. He thought ahead and, therefore, came out with futuristic ideas on rationalisation of removal of 'subsidies for the rich', universal basic income, climate change, from 'socialism without entry and capitalism without exit' and the four Cs that he had historically paralysed decision making.

He conducted the first online course on the Indian economy for the benefits of students and teachers across the country. He launched the government's online education platform 'Swayam', which became one of the most followed courses in India. He travelled across the country and spoke on public platforms on economic issues to elevate the quality of public discourse. He built up a strong team of both 'insiders' and 'outsiders' in the Economic Division of the Ministry.

Personally, I will miss his dynamism, energy, intellectual ability and ideas. He would walk into my room at times several times a day, addressing me as 'Minister' to give either the good news or otherwise. Needless to say, his departure will be missed by me. But I know that his heart is very much here. I am sure he will keep sending advice and analysis wherever he is.

I wish Arvind Subramanian and his family all the very best.

Thank you, Arvind.

Atalji, the Quintessential Gentleman – How He Made a Difference

Posted on 17 August 2018

Atalji's demise is referred to by many as end of an era. I, however, consider it as a continuation of the era of which he was one who laid the foundation.

The political and ideological journey

His political journey shaped his ideology. His convictions were shaped by his deep commitment to the nation from the student days association with the Quit India Movement to his joining the Rashtriya Swayamsevak Sangh and then being associated with Dr Shyama Prasad Mukherjee as one of the founders of the Bharatiya Jana Sangh. During his early days in the Jana Sangh, he was associated with the 'Kashmir Satyagraha' which wanted to lift several restrictions on Indian citizens in relation to the state. He was, along with Dr Mukherjee, a strong opponent of the Liaquat–Nehru Pact.

Once in Parliament from 1957 his speeches as a young parliamentarian on the Tibet crisis and the 1962 war debacle left their impact on all. At a young age, he became a principal face of the Jana Sangh. He travelled across the country and was being hailed as a charismatic orator. He once told us that till the mid-1980s most of his travel was either by trains or by roads. At times even by busses. During his tours he mostly stayed at the homes of political workers. This was when a young party was being built up.

Disillusionment with the Congress had started after the 1962 China war debacle. It was at this stage that Dr Lohia pioneered the idea of 'Congress Hatao Desh Bachao' and seat coordination in critical bye-elections between Dr Lohia, Deen Dayal Upadhyaya and Acharya Kripalani had begun. Deen Dayalji, alongwith his political team, mostly young leaders in their 30s, was busy creating an organisational structure of the party. It bore results in 1967 when the Jana Sangh emerged with a large contingent of MPs in Parliament, got the absolute majority in National Capital Territory of Delhi and made a sizeable presence in Uttar Pradesh, Bihar, Madhya Pradesh, Rajasthan and Punjab.

After Deen Dayalji's sudden demise, the mantle of Jana Sangh leadership fell on Atalji. Not compromising the party's core beliefs, he started coordinating with other political parties and became a nationally respected and acceptable face of the Jana Sangh. He had an ability to rise above partisan interests which he displayed by strongly standing behind the government during the 1971 war. In 1974, the movement led by Shri Jayaprakash Narayan witnessed the Jana Sangh under Atalji plunge into it and give it a core strength. The battle against the Emergency and for restoration of democracy was fought by Jana Sangh under his leadership. After a brief experience in the Janata government, the Jana Sangh was back to square one. The merger of the Jana Sangh and other political parties in the Janata Party had failed. It was a short-lived experiment. Thus in 1980 he revived the BJP. The inaugural session of the BJP witnessed an aspirational cadre with a self-belief chanting 'Pradhan Mantri Ki Agli Bari – Atal Bihari, Atal Bihari'.

When the BJP was formed, it suffered initial isolation. Its parliamentary presence was minimal. It faced its lowest ebb in 1984. Notwithstanding this adversity, the duo of Atalji and Shri L.K. Advaniji held on to their political space and remained determined to expand the BJP. From 89 Lok Sabha seats in 1989 to 121 seats in 1991, to 166 seats in 1996 and finally 183 seats in 1998. The isolated BJP had now become the centre-stage party of Indian politics. Atalji led the party to great victories in 1998 and 1999 and had a successful tenure as a prime minister. India has now witnessed the demolition of a single party domination in the electoral space. The BJP had expanded its geographical and social base.

Atalji's political style

The essential aspect of his political journey, true to his name 'Atal' was determination. In the world's largest democracy only the Congress party dominated in the first few decades. Atalji created an alternative, which in the last two decades became larger and bigger than the Congress. Along with Advaniji, he created a second line of leaders both in the Centre and the states. He was always open to ideas; always gave priority to national interest; was always at ease in dealing with both friends and opponents and never allowed himself to get into any petty controversy. He had no personal enemies since he spoke mostly on issues rather than individuals. He was a wordsmith. He could use the facility of language to get out of any challenging situation.

What he will be remembered for most will be his oration both in Parliament and outside. In Parliament, he was heard in pin drop silence. In his public meetings audiences waited for hours before he could arrive. His oration was always blended with humour. His ability for an instant response was unmatched. His choice of words, his turn of phrases, the poetry that he injected in his expression, gave him the ability to even explain the most complicated issue in a simple language.

His prime ministerial tenure

Besides the BJP, his coalition at different points of time had the Akali Dal, Shiv Sena, National Conference, Janata Dal (U), Trinamool Congress, BJD, TDP, DMK, AIADMK, besides individuals like Shri K.C. Pant and Shri Ramakrishna Hegde.

The Nuclear Test in 1998 was a defining moment of his government. He went out of the way to work for peace with Pakistan. But when the need arose, he inflicted a severe blow to it in Kargil. Both Pokhran and Kargil were his high points. On the economic front, he was a liberaliser. National Highway, rural roads, better infrastructure, a new telecom policy which was pragmatic, a new electricity law are evidence of this. In any intra-governmental debate, his nod inevitably was for the liberal economic view. He corrected the foreign policy imbalance in the changed global environment.

Several personal traits

As a prime minister, he was never harsh on either the bureaucrats or his ministers. In a polite but firm language he could convey more to his subordinates than what he desired. The cabinet meetings that he presided lasted for hours. He allowed a discussion on almost every subject and eventually reconciled the conflicting viewpoints depending on their merits. He loved food. Ministers in his government still occasionally speak about the quality of snacks which was served in his cabinet meetings. He even loved to experiment foods when he travelled internationally. In India, he had his own favourite places in various cities and occasionally when he got out of the trains in the morning, he would have breakfast on one of them before reaching home.

The poet in him also created a dreamer. He dreamt of his own vision. Many of those were born out of his idealism. In fact, several lines of different poems that he wrote reflected his own mood.

During the Emergency, he had a serious problem with his back. He was brought to the All India Institute of Medical Sciences while in detention for treatment. His orthopaedic doctor asked him that if he always sat straight, how could the pain occur? Kya aap jhuk gaye thhe?' The man in pain, not losing his sense of humour, replied in the context of the Emergency:

झुकना तो सीखा नहीं डॉक्टर साहब। यूँ कहिये मुड गए होंगे।

This made him pen down his famous lines against the Emergency:

टूट सकते हैं मगर हम झुक नहीं सकते।

This poem became one of the most distributed pamphlets during the Emergency.

Atalji was a democrat. His political style was liberal. He accepted criticism. He was a product of parliamentary democracy and, therefore, valued consensus. He bore no malice. He communicated even with those who disagreed. Whether in opposition or the government, his attitude never changed. He was an iconic communicator unparalleled in recent history. All this added to his charisma. His greatest asset was his credibility where he was never in any controversy. Yet in an era dominated by the Nehruvian Congress, he created a political party which was an ideological alternative to the Congress which disagreed on various issues with the Congress, which took the Congress head on, struggled for almost five decades and in the last two decades not only became an alternative to the Congress but overtook it. Atalji ran a marathon. He was a patient runner. But for him, Advaniji and their other colleagues, Indian democracy would have looked different – dominated by one party, one family with a lot of scattered smaller parties. That did not happen. Atalji and his colleagues made the difference. Atalji has left the world. But the era of which he laid the foundation will prosper even more. That is the Vajpayee legacy.

Dr Hasmukh Adhia Retires

Posted on 17 November 2018

Dr Hasmukh Adhia, the finance secretary, retires at the end of this month. He has been in the Finance Ministry for four years and held the specific responsibility of the revenue secretary for the last three years. As secretary, financial services, Dr Adhia showed his leadership in the implementation of various social security programmes of the government through banking services. His contributions in successfully accomplishing the Mudra Yojana have been laudable.

His tenure as the revenue secretary will be remembered for various initiatives where he provided the bureaucratic leadership in shaping and implementing policy. The campaign against black money both within and outside the country was the initial highlight of the revenue department. The income tax department now functions online with no physical interface between the assessee and the assessment official.

Dr Adhia's term witnessed the historic constitutional amendment on the GST being approved. After the centre-states developed a consensus on the multiple GST legislations, the drafting of rules and fixing of tariffs was achieved in a short period of time. It was his efforts supported by his team of officers from the central and state governments which made it possible to hit the deadline of 1 July 2017. Rate reductions and smoothening of the rough edges were also achieved in a record time.

Dr Adhia's tenure saw an exponential increase in the tax base and the tax realisations. He was ably supported by the two boards, CBDT and CBIC. The follow-up after demonetisation in detecting the large cash depositors and making them accountable was no mean challenge.

Dr Hasmukh Adhia executed these steps with calm and professionalism. He was unquestionably a highly competent, disciplined, no-nonsense civil servant and of course, with impeccable integrity. His only diversion from his duties was his passion for spirituality and yoga.

The government wanted to use his capability and experience in some alternative capacity. He had informed me earlier this year that he would not work for a single day after 30 November 2018. His time thereafter belongs to his favourite passion and of course his son.

I wish him all the best for his post retirement life. Thank You Dr Adhia.

George Sahib as I Knew Him

Posted on 30 January 2019

With the passing away of the veteran socialist leader George Fernandes, India has lost a political colossus. George was a politician with a difference. He had the ability to stand alone, take a position, however extreme, and sustain that position. He was a political worker, an extraordinary leader, a powerful trade unionist, a Parliamentarian that many would dread to face and above all a dissenter. In the early 1970s, when I was a student, George was one of the most charismatic speakers, much wanted to address campus audiences. My familiarity with him started at that time and I had an opportunity to work with him both in opposition and in government.

The 1967 South Bombay elections

George Sahib once narrated to me his story, the entire tale of 1967 south Bombay elections. That election would be an education for any student of psephology or electoral politics. Shri S.K. Patil was the unquestioned leader of Mumbai, then Bombay. He was a union minister and Congress party's treasurer. He had won his South Bombay seat several times by large margins. Nobody believed that Patil could ever be defeated, till a thirty-six-year-old president of the Bombay Taxi Union, George Fernandes, announced that he would challenge Patil in the elections. All the opposition parties supported George.

George's first task was to make people realise that Patil was not invincible. Posters, banners, stickers on the taxies, outside apartments were put up, all carrying one line: Patil can be defeated. Once the campaign picked up and became the talk of the town, the media asked S.K. Patil for his comments on the same. Patil inappropriately replied, 'Only God can defeat me.' Prompt came the response campaign of George. The next slogan was 'God does not vote, only you do. So, only you can defeat Patil'.

The voters dislike arrogance and defeating Patil became the flavour. With the support of the opposition and the unions, George secured a victory and entered Parliament. He quickly made a mark as a Parliamentarian, a great speaker in at least seven languages. A phenomenon very rare in India.

JP movement and the railway strike

After Mrs Indira Gandhi's sweeping victory to power in 1971, George became an active part of the JP movement (since 1974). Bihar had always been an important political constituency for both the socialists and George Fernandes. He concentrated on his trade unions and became the head of the railway unions. In 1974, he called for a railway strike for the working conditions of the railway-men. This has been one of the most tense trade union agitations ever in India. The entire country was hearing the slogan 'Rail ka chakka jaam karenge'. The events of 1974 and those which followed culminated in the imposition of Emergency.

The Emergency

The Emergency witnessed multiple reactions. Most institutions caved in. This included the judiciary, the media and the civil services. Only some outliers in these were the dissenters. Many political workers got scared and preferred inactivity, some even issued statements supporting the Emergency. The bolder political opposition workers protested and went to prisons. George Fernandes believed in militant opposition to the Emergency. Many felt that the idea of a militant opposition to the Emergency was misconceived but George was a man with his own mind. He believed that this was the only course. His opposition was shattered and, along with his colleagues, he was arrested and prosecuted.

George's idealism overtook political pragmatism when on 19 January 1977, Mrs Indira Gandhi announced the holding of the general elections. All the political prisoners in Tihar Jail had a meeting. George was in Ward 17. Some of us were in Ward 1. We were all allowed to assemble in Ward 2 for political consultations. While everybody else favoured participation in and the contesting of elections, George was a dissenter. He wanted to boycott the 1977 elections. He believed that this was going to be a make-believe farcical election through which Indira Gandhi would earn legitimacy and continue her dictatorship and hence the opposition by contesting must not give legitimacy to the elections. Though in a hopeless minority, George stood by his position.

The Janata Party was formed immediately and it decided its candidates and George was chosen to contest from Bihar. He declined to sign on the nomination papers. It finally took Morarji Desai, who came to the Tis Hazari courts (where George used to come for his trials), with a set of Nomination Papers, to get George to sign them so that he could contest from prison. George eventually yielded and signed his nomination papers. Results were declared and George won the Election by a huge margin. The Janata Party formed the government with Morarji Bhai as the prime minister. A perpetual rebel, George's first reaction was to decline to join the cabinet. He again misjudged the public mood. I remember George being gheraoed by 500 political workers at New Delhi's VP House and being compelled to yield in the face of hostile slogans to join the cabinet.

The fall of the Janata Party government was a chapter in his life that George would like to forget. He delivered in Parliament the most eloquent defence of the government, only to quit the next day under pressure from his other socialist colleagues Raj Narain and Madhu Limaye.

George spent the rest of the next decade in opposition championing the issues of the farmers, trade unions and finally Bofors. He was one of the leading campaigners against corruption in the Rajiv Gandhi era. His attacks on the government were perhaps the most aggressive ones. He had built a reputation as being both a master of facts and languages.

The defence minister and the false allegations

In the NDA government, headed by Mr Vajpayee, George as the convenor of the NDA was one of the architects of alliance formation. Even his worst critics would not attempt to level allegations of corruption against him. Yet twice as a defence minister, once during the Tehelka Tapes and second in relation to the CAG report relating to the purchase of the coffins, false allegations of corruption were levelled against him. A commission of enquiry in the Tehelka Tape issue vindicated George. The Coffingate report was an absurdity. Metallic coffins were called costlier by comparing their costs with wooden coffins. Two unequal commodities do not cost the same.

George led the most austere of lives. He washed his own clothes, cleaned his own utensils. He never owned a television till a well-wisher insisted that he needed to have one. His books and files lay scattered on the floor of his house till some friends made arrangements to get him some ordinary bookshelves. He took up causes which nobody espoused and pursued them with vigour. Ministers were scared of facing the wrath of his attack when he was in the Opposition. But eventually his health took better of him. The slowing down of his mind and various faculties could be seen towards 2003–04. He still had full comprehension but that aggression was lacking. I noticed this during a GOM in the last days of the Vajpayee government.

During 2005 Bihar elections, Advani ji on behalf of the BJP announced Nitish Kumar to be the chief ministerial candidate of the NDA. We, in the BJP, felt that this was logical and would also help us in unseating Lalu Yadav's regime. A murmur of protest came from George. When I went to meet him, I realised, because of failing health, he had not realised the full implication of his reaction. His parliamentary tenure in Lok Sabha ended in 2009. He needed an official accommodation for some more time. Nitish Kumar graciously put him up as a candidate in a bye-election for Rajya Sabha where George entered the Upper House for the first time.

His oath-taking showed his state of health. He could no longer contribute politically. He needed help and assistance at every stage. The tiger had been tamed but his escapades would be remembered for a long time. George Fernandes was a parliamentarian for several terms. He was a union minister thrice. But he will be remembered for several agitations he led, several positions he took and several causes he represented.

Epilogue

George Fernandes was the last of the veteran Lohiaites. Dr Ram Manohar Lohia, George Saheb's mentor represented the anti-Nehru, anti-Congress face of Indian politics. After the 1962 general elections and the China war debacle, Dr Lohia gave to this country the famous slogan 'Congress hatao desh bachao'. This led to an anti-Congress alliance. The first step was that Dr Lohia, Acharya Kripalani and Deendayal became the joint opposition candidates in three bye-elections to the Lok Sabha. The then Jana Sangh president, Dr Raghu Vira, lost his life in a road accident while campaigning in these elections. However, in the post-Dr Lohia era, with the emergence of the BJP as the principal pole of Indian politics, many Lohiaites shed their inhibition and started doing political business with the Congress. The left was not far behind. They called it re-polarisation. One honorable exception was George Fernandes. He was a born Lohiaite and he died as one. His anti-Congress moorings were never compromised.

16

The 2014 General Election Campaign Diary

Arun Jaitley kept a diary during the last stage of the May general election. In it he recorded his thoughts on topics ranging from the Election Commission not allowing Narendra Modi to hold a rally in Varanasi to the benefits of sitting in the Opposition, along with a prescient prediction that the Congress party will respond to defeat by setting up an A.K. Antony Committee to come out with a report.

The Duty to Vote

Posted on 1 May 2014

It is mentioned in several election speeches that even one vote can make a difference. Every eligible voter has a right to vote. He also has a duty to cast a vote. I was faced with heavy odds having been member of the Rajya Sabha, Gujarat, three times in a row. Since my vote is enrolled in the Gandhinagar parliamentary constituency, do I leave my own constituency in Amritsar to cast my vote or do I skip my vote? I started my day very early with a visit to the Golden Temple and the Durgiana Mandir. I travelled to each of the nine Assembly segments. By the time almost 50 per cent of the votes had been cast, my wife and I flew into Gandhinagar to vote. I was back in Amritsar by the evening. It was tiresome but satisfying. Those who missed the vote failed in their primary duty as a citizen.

FIR against Mr Modi: Every time senior politicians cast their vote, a large number of media persons assemble outside the polling station. They want their comments on their own vote and also on the trend of the elections. The politicians freely interact with the media. They make short comments and then leave. This is precisely what Mr Narendra Modi did. He was not expected to be rude enough and give the media no comments.

The Election Commission of India has directed that an FIR under section 126 (1)(a) and section 126 (1)(b) be registered against Mr Modi and the media organisations which have telecast his bite through the media. The substance of the allegations in the Election Commission's order is that within the 'polling area', a 'public meeting' has been held. Polling was in progress in various parts of the country. Since the comment has been telecast during the polling hours and the lotus symbol displayed, both Mr Narendra Modi and the media are liable.

From the Election Commission's order, it is not clear as to what the definition of 'polling area' is. Is it the polling station? In any event the comment was made outside the polling station. The Election Commission's order makes it appear that the entire country could be a polling area since the media comment could be seen in every part of the country.

When Constitutional institutions react in haste and even anger, they miss out the larger vision. Criminal law provisions are to be strictly construed. Their meaning can't be stretched out. A public meeting is a public meeting, the media bite is not a public meeting. If the media are to be prosecuted for displaying comments of politicians on a voting day, such a provision will fall foul of constitutional guarantee of free speech since it is not covered by the prescribed restrictions under Article 19(2).

If the whole country is a polling area, since scattered and phased elections are on in several parts of India, the political rallies and their reportage by the media when polling is going on in some other parts of the country would attract penal consequences. Professor Amartya Sen spoke to the media after his vote yesterday. He gave his reasons why he does not favour Modi. The prime minister spoke to the media after casting his vote in Assam. So did most other political leaders. I am not pleading for their prosecution. I am only illustrating that an interpretation being given by the Election Commission may fall foul.

Article 324 of the Constitution is a reservoir of residuary jurisdiction. It can't impact areas occupied by law. It cannot dilute the import and content of the right to free speech.

Why Be Scared of Being in the Opposition?

Posted on 3 May 2014

Five years as leader of Opposition in the Rajya Sabha has been a great learning experience for me. Being in Opposition is an experience by itself. You have to be vigilant and well informed. A lot of informants come to you with information. There are opportunities to put the government on the mat. Being in Opposition also gives you sufficient time to be well-informed and well-prepared. You get opportunities to improve your articulation and plan attacks on the government. There are also opportunities where you have to rise to the occasion to display statesmanship.

Opposition itself has a powerful role in Indian democracy. There is a spread of political power in a democratic system. Governments no longer are the sole repository of all powers. The Opposition, media, judiciary, bureaucracy and civil society are co-sharers in the power. The Opposition has a powerful role to safeguard public interest. Vigilance, regulation and protection of public interest are the principal objects of the Opposition.

All political parties need to be well-trained to sit in the Opposition. Why then is the Congress scared of sitting in the Opposition? It is clear that the popular mandate is not with the Congress. The Congress is likely to be a two-digit party. It cannot dream of being a part of the ruling combination. The idea of getting out of power is making the Congressmen bitter and desperate. The prime minister has become cynical. He complains to people he meets that he has been unfairly targeted. The Gandhis believe that they were God's gift to India and were meant only to rule. They frown at the very idea of a tea vendor defeating them at the polls and ruling India. Others believe that till 16 May they have unlimited power. The Shah Alams are failing to realise the limits of their jurisdiction.

The Congressmen will do well if they reconcile themselves to their seats in the Opposition. A stint in the Opposition does a lot of good to you when you introspect and plan for the future. Political positions are not permanent. If the Congressmen on the eve of their departure are laying down an agenda of confrontation with the current Opposition, they are only laying down an agenda for the future. Nobody will accept the argument that what the Congressmen are doing is justice and when the same is reciprocated, it is vindictiveness.

The BJP's Stand on Infiltrators

Posted on 6 May 2014

Election times are opportunities for raising issues of governance. However, there are many who see virtues in polarisation. Regrettably, we, in the BJP, are accused of benefiting from polarisation even if polarisation is encouraged by political opponents.

The issue of infiltration of Bangladeshis into Indian territory is one such case. A section of the Congress leadership in Assam had consciously followed the policy of encouraging infiltration since they wanted to offset the domination of the ethnic Assamese in Assam. Mass infiltration of Bangladeshis has changed the demographic character of Assam, West Bengal and some districts of Bihar. Any patriotic Indian could be seriously concerned with this infiltration. It is a pressure on economic resources. It is a pressure on land. It impacts national security. The fact that every district in Assam adjacent to the chicken's neck have witnessed a significant demographic change on account of the infiltration is a serious security concern.

It is not only the BJP's stand that infiltration must be stopped and the infiltrators be sent back. The Supreme Court described it as a silent invasion of India. It struck down the regulations which place the onus on the government rather than the infiltrator on issues of identification of citizenship. The root cause of social tension in several parts of the north-east is infiltration. Some political parties in Assam and West Bengal have regrettably made infiltration into a secular cause because infiltrators are their votebank.

Narender Modi's stance against infiltrators is justified and legitimate. We must also understand the difference between an infiltrator and a refugee. A refugee is a person who is persecuted on account of his religious beliefs or political views. An infiltrator gatecrashes only for economic opportunities. To place them at par would be naive.

Kashmir: Shri Omar Abdullah, on the Kashmiri students, is partly correct when he protests against the harassment of Kashmiri youths in NOIDA. He is wholly wrong in linking Narendra Modi to the NOIDA incident. That is on account of his political motivation.

Children from the north-east and Jammu & Kashmir must be encouraged to study and work in various parts of India. They must be welcomed in the rest of India. This will encourage an emotional integration. Any form of personal harassment is a terrible signal either in the Northeast or Jammu and Kashmir. Even occasional tales leave a terrible impact because they can be exaggerated and overstated. The cause of national integration is dearer to all of us than an occasional difference of opinion. Omar is therefore right in protesting against the NOIDA incident. He is terribly wrong in dragging Modi into it.

Disappointing Election Commission Officials

Posted on 8 May 2014

I cannot conceal my disappointment with the Election Commission. Men in constitutional offices need to be bolder. Timid men can dwarf high offices.

The Election Commission scrutinises us all the time. They are extremely vigilant in tackling the side shows in the elections. They are concerned with what adjectives are used by whom. But when it comes to preventing booth capturing which has reappeared after a decade in elections 2014, they are out of their depth.

By condoning the Returning Officer's stand on the 'No-Modi rally' in Varanasi city, the Election Commission has used the security card to prevent Narendra Modi's right to campaign in his constituency. If you can't ensure security, don't hold the polls in the country. But if you do hold the polls please provide a level playing field. You cannot deny the candidate the right to campaign. Rahul Gandhi can have a road show in Varanasi, but Narendra Modi cannot have a rally. The security card is selectively used.

The falsehoods of the Returning Officer:

- Of all the permissions given to us by the Returning Officer, two are for the landing of the helicopter. How very fair. One helicopter has been allowed to land twice – once in the rural area and once in the city.
- I withdrew all applications at 20:10 hours yesterday since it is impossible to organise a function the next day if a 'midnight' permission comes. He is allowed a prayer permission after forty-eight hours of struggle and an oral refusal earlier.
- To meet 150 eminent citizens at a hotel banquet hall he earlier said that Shri Modi cannot be allowed to drive into the city. Two hours after I withdrew all applications, he announced to

the media that he was allowing Shri Modi to meet 150 people. How very liberal. These are all the permissions with regard to the campaigning in the city. Modi's entire campaign in Varanasi city is restricted to a prayer at the Ganga ghat and meeting 150 persons in a hotel. Additionally, there are two helicopter landings.
- Can he produce any document that the BJP had agreed to an alternative site which is much smaller?

No. If the Election Commission chooses to believe such a Returning Officer and feels that this is not a denial of opportunity to campaign, my right to Satyagraha begins. The Election Commission now condones the guilt of the Returning Officer.

My advice to the Election Commission is: don't look helpless. Don't merely rely on the Returning Officer and officials of the Uttar Pradesh government. They are nominees of the people who want to prevent Modi. There is more to a campaign than a prayer and meeting of 150 people.

The Case of Narendra Modi's Caste

Posted on 9 May 2014

The fact that Narendra Modi belongs to the OBC community is a major cause of worry for the Congress party. Though Narendra Modi has never made caste his identity and his appeal cuts across castes and communities, the Congress worry is apparent. The ruling dynasty of the Congress cannot digest defeat at the hands of a commoner. It is why they made his humble origin as a tea vendor into an issue. The move backfired. Yesterday Shaktisinh Gohil, the leader of the Gujarat Congress, alleged that Narendra Modi had committed a 'paap' of including his own community into the OBC list and thus changed his stature from upper caste to OBC.

Does the Congress party believe that every time a caste is added to the OBC list it is a paap? In any case the Modh Ghanchi was added as an OBC in Gujarat on 25 July 1994 by the Congress party government headed by Chhabildas Mehta and in the Mandal Commission list by the government of India on 4 April 2000. Both these events took place much before Narendra Modi became the chief minister of Gujarat.

Do Constitutional institutions have an immunity from criticism? I do not subscribe to the view that merely because an institution is created by the Constitution, it cannot be criticised. Criticism is a way of life. To err is human. Criticism can be intended to put the institution to notice that either the current incumbent or future successors correct the error into which the institution has fallen. Courts, the Election Commission, prime ministers, council of ministers, Parliament and bodies like the CAG are all creations of the Constitution. They are manned by men either selected or elected. History is a witness to the monumental errors that some of them have committed. In England the Law Lords have held that even the judgements of courts can be criticised. Justice is not a cloistered virtue. It must continue to suffer scrutiny.

Lord Denning, the celebrated British judge, always maintained that judgements must be criticised since judges can go wrong and need to put on notice. The Indian judges have held that their decisions can be criticised but don't impute motives of doubtful integrity to the judge. When a British paper published a photograph of three English Law Lords upside down with a caption 'Those Old Fools' as a protest against their judgement, the House of Lords refused to take contempt action. One of the Law Lords later commented, 'How is it contempt? Old I am and my wisdom is a matter of opinion'.

S. Mulgaonkar and Shyam Lal, two leading editors, criticised the judges and the judgement in the habeas corpus case delivered during the Emergency. They accused the court of timidity. They were charged for contempt. The contempt notice was discharged after a hearing. The Supreme Court held that the intention of Mulgaonkar and Shyam Lal was to strengthen the institution rather than weaken it and hence there was no contempt.

In the past, I led a campaign against a member of the Election Commission on the grounds of lack of impartiality. The Chief Election Commissioner (CEC) was asked to report on a petition signed by members of Parliament. He upheld my charges. The Congress government in whose favour the bias was alleged, refused to process the recommendation of the CEC. Prime ministers, ministers, speakers of the Lok Sabha and their rulings are regularly criticised. MPs are ripped apart frequently. The CAG has not even been spared either. Where does one get the proposition that merely because you are a creation of the Constitution, there is immunity from criticism?

I have rightly criticised the Election Commission for failure to check booth capturing. I am convinced that to deny Narendra Modi the right to hold a rally in his constituency is both unfair and a denial of a right to campaign. Both the Returning Officer and the Election Commission have been rightly criticised for this blunder so that in future their successors do not fall into the same error. I do not subscribe to a vague notion of self-censorship based on an inter-institutional courtesy.

Tailpiece

My advice to the Returning Officer is that by denying the right to hold a rally he cannot restrict Modi's campaign. Yesterday's events proved that the unfairness of the Returning Officer was given a fitting reply by the people of Varanasi.

Why is Mamata Didi so Angry?

Posted on 10 May 2014

Conventional wisdom would suggest that Mamata Banerjee and her party's traditional rival in West Bengal are the left parties. The Congress party would occupy the third spot with the BJP being an also ran. Why then is the BJP the principal target of Didi's attack? Every day she crosses the Laxman Rekha and uses the choicest adjectives against Narendra Modi. Mamata Didi is an intelligent politician. There is a method in whatever she does. Good governance is never her forte. Angry and agitational politics is her strength. A large part of the vote that enabled her to rout the left in the Assembly elections were those aspirational voters who rejected the left's lack of development politics. The Bhadralok had all shifted to Didi as a reaction. It is this very vote which now wants to see Narendra Modi as the prime minister. Didi's 'Poribortan' is not good governance or development. It is anarchy, booth capturing and encouragement to illegal infiltration.

The West Bengal results for 2014 may produce a surprise. Next only to Uttar Pradesh, the BJP's vote share is expected to rise in West Bengal. Narendra Modi's rallies have attracted a mammoth response. The BJP cadres are buzzing with enthusiasm. They are all calculating as to how much this increased vote share will convert into seats. Except for a few pockets in Malda, the Congress party is marginalised.

What then is the cause of Didi's anger and worry? The Congress and the left are not likely to form a government in Delhi. Didi can never sit in the company of the left. The current problem is not New Delhi. It is West Bengal. She fears a radical shift of 15 per cent vote share that put her in power in the Assembly elections to the BJP. If that happens, she has only three votes left. Firstly, the traditional

Trinamool supporters, secondly the goons who have moved from the left to her side and thirdly the illegal infiltrators from Bangladesh.

It is the last of these votes which is Didi's mainstay. For this cause, she has to justify infiltration and abuse Modi. The more she does that, the more she alienates herself from a significant section which put her in power. How long can Didi rely on the illegally imported vote? Even if she manages to retain a large number of seats this time, the warning signals for the Assembly elections are beginning to be heard.

How Will the Congress React to Its Decimation?

Posted on 11 May 2014

As the general elections 2014 comes to a close, the logical expectation is that the Congress party will be reduced to a double digit. The question that arises is, why has this happened? How will the Congress party itself react to its lowest ever figure in history?

Electoral defeats are a part of the natural process. A party must show graciousness in defeat and be ready to learn from the causes of the defeat. It should go back to its basics, strengthen the organisation and try to throw up the most acceptable leadership. But will the Congress party ever do that?

The tragedy of the Congress party is that it has converted itself into a non-ideological crowd around a family. Its reaction to a double-digit figure can only be expected. I do not believe that it will have any role in government formation. It has the mandate to sit only in the Opposition and should gracefully accept that position. The three principal causes of the Congress party's defeat would be its mismanagement of the economy, its image of encouraging corruption, and a failure of its leadership.

Its traditional managers of the economy comprised of those with liberal attitudes. Mrs Sonia Gandhi's preference for a European socialism coupled with the domination of the NAC agenda took the party on a path of confusion. Its inability to stand up and prevent the 2G spectrum scam, the coal-block allocations, and the Commonwealth Games scam gave to it an image that it had completely compromised on probity.

Corruption along with lack of policy, stability in policy, disturbed the investment environment in the country. The mood of economic gloom that set in was predominantly because of these factors. The weakening of the institution of prime minister contributed to the disillusionment with the leadership. No country can govern itself if the office of the prime minister has diminished and its authority diluted. The consequences of a parallel extra constitutional structure in our system were obviously felt.

I have always believed that the indefinite continuation of a dynasty as a mode of leadership selection can be counter-productive for a party. The strength of a party is only as much as the acceptability of that generation of the dynasty. Rahul Gandhi's leadership failed to inspire both the nation and the Congressmen. A dynastic party will never accept that. It will at best consider that if one member of the dynasty has failed to deliver, dependence should be made on another member of the dynasty. We did see this happening during the Lok Sabha polls.

I do not expect the Congress party to change even slightly its mode of functioning if it is reduced to two digits. It will at best appoint an A.K. Antony Committee to review the failures of the party in the poll which in turn will come out with a report when everyone has forgotten about the defeat.

How Modi's Energy Dominated the Campaign

Posted on 12 May 2014

The campaign draws to a close today in what is world's largest democratic election. The strength and resilience of Indian democracy has been most visible during this campaign. Despite momentary tensions and criticisms, the elections have ended in a manner which could be a proud moment for Indian democracy.

One year ago, the expression of anti-incumbency against the UPA was visible. However, a legitimate question arose in the public mind as to whether the BJP can put its house in order and decide on who its eventual leader would be. This exercise for a democratic party is not as easy as in the case of dynastic parties. Yet, despite many hurdles, on 13 September 2013 we did manage to decide on the candidature of Narendra Modi as prime minister. I had, at that stage, expressed an opinion publicly that a Rahul versus Modi battle would be quasi presidential, and Modi would score over Rahul in the electoral contest. Anti-incumbency against the UPA was high and therefore the election will be contested on the twin basis of anti-incumbency as also a positive hope in Narendra Modi.

The high point of this election was the energy displayed by Modi. During the campaign he has not missed a single meeting. He has visited every nook and corner of India and even in areas where the BJP strength has been somewhat limited, he has managed to create a momentum in favour of the BJP.

The conventional issues which the Congress party used such as legislations like the RTI, the Food Bill and the land bill were non-issues in this election. Several populist schemes were of no avail. When the going is not so good, even populist schemes are not able to deliver. Regrettably, outgoing Prime Minister Dr Manmohan Singh was absent in the elections. Even his senior cabinet ministers were confined to addressing press conferences with the use of angry and impolite language against Narendra Modi.

Intimidation of rival political parties and capturing the environment around the polling stations and thereafter capturing the booths silently was a low point of this election. I only hope that in future the Election Commission will be better equipped to tackle this menace. The high point of this election was the return of huge rallies and a very large turnout. The campaign strategies have also expanded. Besides conventional public contact programmes, the use of media, advertisements, and social media was quite extensive. I have no doubt that in future elections multiple modes of campaigning are bound to expand.

As polling draws to a close today, exit polls will be telecast. Pollsters normally have a tendency to err on the side of caution. I have no doubt that large turnouts necessarily mean a decisive vote. A decisive vote in this election can only be a pro-Modi, pro-BJP or pro-NDA vote.

17

The Last Blog

This blog was posted on 6 August 2019, three days before Arun Jaitley was admitted to hospital.

PM Narendra Modi and HM Amit Shah Achieve the Impossible

The current session of Parliament has been the most productive where historical legislations have been passed. The Triple Talaq law, strengthening of India's anti-terror laws and the decision on Article 370 are all unprecedented. The popular belief that the promise the BJP made on Article 370 is an unachievable slogan has been proved wrong. So strong is the public mood in support of the new Kashmir policy of the government that several opposition parties had succumbed to the public opinion. For the Rajya Sabha to approve this decision by a two-thirds majority goes beyond anyone's imagination. I analyse the impact of this decision and the history of failed attempts on resolving the J&K issue.

History of the failed attempts

The Instrument of Accession was signed in October 1947. Refugees from West Pakistan had migrated to India in millions. Pandit Nehru's government did not allow them to settle in Jammu and Kashmir. Kashmir, for the last seventy-two years, has been the unfinished agenda of Pakistan. Panditji wrongly assessed the situation. He volunteered a plebiscite and allowed UN to discuss the issue. He took a decision trusting Sheikh Mohd. Abdullah to head the state. He then lost trust in Sheikh Sahib in 1953 and jailed him. The Sheikh had converted the state into a personal kingdom. At that time there was no Congress party in the state of Jammu and Kashmir. The Congressmen were National Conference members.

A Congress government in the name of National Conference was installed. It was headed by Bakshi Ghulam Mohd. The National Conference leadership formed a separate group called the Plebiscite Front. But how would the Congress disguised as National

Conference, win elections? The 1957, 1962 and 1967 elections were unquestionably rigged. One officer, Abdul Khaliq, the Collector of both Srinagar and Doda, was the Returning Officer and he prevented the nomination of any opponent in the valley. In these three elections, most Congressmen were elected unanimously. The people of the Kashmir valley lost faith in the central government.

This experiment of special status and handover of the state to Sheikh Sahib and then put Congress governments in power was a historic blunder. The history of the past seven decades shows that the journey of this separate Status has been towards separatism and not integration. It created a separatist psyche. Pakistan was more than enthusiastic in trying to exploit the situation.

Mrs Indira Gandhi then experimented with releasing Sheikh Sahib and his forming a government once again with Congress supporting the government from outside. This was in 1975. Within months of taking over, Sheikh Sahib's tone had changed and Mrs Gandhi was clear that she had been let down.

After Sheikh Sahib's demise, the leadership should have fallen in the hands of senior National Conference leaders such as Mirza Afzal Beg but Sheikh Sahib wanted to convert Kashmir into his family fiefdom. Farooq Abdullah became the chief minister as Sheikh Sahib's successor. Instead of strengthening the mainstream party, in early 1984, the Congress destabilised the government. Overnight the chief minister was changed through manipulation and jointly with a rebel group of the National Conference led by Sheikh Sahib's son-in-law Gul Mohd. Shah was made the chief minister. The new chief minister obviously could not control the situation. His subsequent statements clearly establish his sympathies with the separatists. In 1987, Shri Rajiv Gandhi again reversed the policies and jointly contested the election with Farooq Abdullah's National Conference. This election was also rigged. Some candidates, whose defeat was manipulated, subsequently turned separatists and even terrorists.

By 1989–90, the situation had gone out of control and the sentiment of separatism along with terrorism picked up. Kashmiri pundits, who are essential part of Kashmiriyat, suffered the kind of atrocities which only the Nazis had inflicted in the past. The ethnic cleansing took place and the Kashmiri pundits had to move out of the valley.

With separatism and terrorism picking up, central governments headed by various political parties made three new kinds of efforts. They tried a dialogue with the separatists which turned into a futile exercise. The dialogue with Pakistan was attempted by governments to resolve the Kashmir problem as a bilateral issue. Governments were talking to the creator of the problem in order to find a solution to the problem.

After the dialogue experiment failed, many governments at the Centre in larger national interest, decided to align with the so called mainstream parties of Jammu and Kashmir. The two national parties, at some stage, undertook the experiment of trusting the two regional parties – the PDP and the National Conference, installing them in power so that they can, with the help of the regional parties, communicate with the people. On each occasion, this experiment did not work. The regional parties spoke one language in New Delhi and another in Srinagar. The worst attempt to appease separatists thought was the 1954 decision on surreptitiously slipping Article 35A into the Constitution. It discriminated between two categories of Indian citizens and resulted in distancing Kashmir from the rest of the country. Meanwhile the Jamait started a huge campaign to convert the liberal valley from Sufism to Wahhabism.

The historic blunders of special status under Article 370 and Article 35A had cost the country both politically and financially. Today, when history is being rewritten, it has given a verdict that Dr Shyama Prasad Mukherjee's vision on Kashmir was the correct one and Panditji's dream solution has proved to be a failure.

Prime Minister Modi's Kashmir policy

In the last seven decades, after different attempts to resolve the issue proved a disaster, Prime Minister Modi decided to follow an alternative approach. A few hundred separatist leaders and armed terrorists were holding the state and country to ransom. The nation lost thousands of citizens and security personnel. Instead of spending on development, we were spending on security. The present decision makes it clear that just as the rule of law prevails in other parts of the country, it will equally prevail in the Kashmir valley.

Security steps have been strengthened. Armed terrorists have been liquidated in large numbers. Their number has been reduced substantially. The security provided to separatists was withdrawn, the income tax department and the NIA discovered the unlawful resources that these separatists and terrorists were getting. Between these two categories, only a few hundred people in the last ten months have suffered. But the remaining population of the Kashmir valley, after decades, has seen an era of peace. They were now the victims of terrorism since none other than Kashmiri Muslim lived in the valley. Many of them, out of fear, also shifted to the other states.

Enforcing law and order strictly and not sparing anyone who breached the law and making life safe for lakhs of Kashmiris and also putting pressure through all measures on the handful of separatists and terrorists – the last ten months have not seen any protest. Not even in Srinagar. The next logical step obviously is to re-examine the laws which created a separatist psyche. Total integration of the state with the country had to be done.

The argument given by the PDP and the National Conference leadership is that if Article 370 or Article 35A are diluted it will lead to Kashmir breaking away from India because it is the only conditional link between the country and Kashmir. The argument is clearly flawed. The Instrument of Accession was signed in October

1947. There were no Article 370 or Article 35A even mentioned once by anyone. Article 370 came into the Constitution in 1950.

In the Constituent Assembly, the debate lasted less than ten minutes. Leaders of the government abstained from the debate and N. Gopalaswamy Ayyangar tabled the provision with a solemn promise that this is a temporary arrangement. Only one other member spoke on the subject. This minority community member did not oppose Article 370. He demanded that it also be made applicable to the region from which he came. Today there is only one nation where every citizen is equal. Initially, Panditji did not allow even the Supreme Court and Election Commission's jurisdiction to extend to Jammu and Kashmir. Little did he realise that he was creating a sub-nation. It is only after Sheikh Sahib was removed and imprisoned that these got jurisdiction over the state of Jammu and Kashmir. The decision to reverse the situation needed clarity, vision and determination. It also needed political courage. The prime minister has created history through his absolute clarity and determination.

The negative impact of Article 370 and Article 35A

Any citizen of India could go and settle in Kashmir, make investments and create jobs for development. Today, there are no industries, hardly any private sector hospital, no credible educational institution set up by the private sector. India's most beautiful state has not even had investments from the hotel chains. Consequently, there are no new jobs for the local people, no revenue for the state. This gave rise to frustration in all regions of the state. These constitutional provisions were not cast in stone. They had to be removed/diluted through the due process of law. Article 35A was not even approved by the Parliament or State Assembly. It defied Article 368 which lays down the procedure for amending the Constitution. It was brought in through the back door by an executive notification. It permits discrimination and makes it non-justiciable.

The role of the two regional parties

The leaders of the two regional parties speak in two voices. Their statements in New Delhi are reassuring at times. But in Srinagar they speak a different language. Their stand is influenced by the separatist environment. It is a hard reality that both have lost support on the ground. Several national parties have allowed themselves to be misguided. An issue of national integration has been translated into an issue of secularism. The two have nothing in common.

The levels of popular support to this move have compelled several opposition parties to support the move. They have sensed the ground reality and do not want to face the wrath of the people. Regrettably, the Congress party legacy, which first created the problem and then added to it, fails to see reason. Just as Rahul Gandhi's support to the tukde-tudke gang at JNU was at variance with the sentiment of even the Congress workers, the same applies to this stand of the government. An overwhelming majority of Congressmen support this bill. Their private and public comments are in this direction but the national party, as a headless chicken, is further consolidating its alienation from the people of India.

The New India has changed. Only the Congress does not realise this. The Congress leadership is determined to succeed in its race to the bottom.

Index

A Note on the Author

Arun Jaitley (28 December 1952–24 August 2019) was a senior advocate of the Supreme Court and one of the most important members of the Bharatiya Janata Party. He was the Union Minister of Finance from 2014 to 2019 and the leader of the Opposition in the Rajya Sabha from 2009 to 2014. Arun Jaitley held many senior positions in government in the past, including portfolios in finance, defence, commerce and industry.

Click the QR Code with a QR scanner app or type the link into the Internet browser on your phone to download the Juggernaut app.